D1328552

THE
PERUVIAN
LABYRINTH

THE
PERUVIAN LABYRINTH

Polity, Society, Economy

Edited by

Maxwell A. Cameron

and

Philip Mauceri

With a Foreword by
Cynthia McClintock and Abraham Lowenthal

The Pennsylvania State University Press
University Park, Pennsylvania

Library of Congress Cataloging-in-Publication Data

The Peruvian labyrinth : polity, society, economy / edited by Maxwell A.
  Cameron and Philip Mauceri ; with a foreword by Cynthia McClintock and
  Abraham Lowenthal.

      p.   cm.
  Includes bibliographical references and index.
  ISBN 0-271-01660-4 (cloth : alk. paper)
  ISBN 0-271-01661-2 (paper : alk. paper)
    1. Peru—Politics and government—1968–1980. 2. Peru—Politics
and government—1980–   3. Political participation—Peru.
  4. Democracy—Peru.   5. Peru—Social policy.   6. Human rights—Peru.
  I. Cameron, Maxwell A.   II. Mauceri, Philip.
  JL3481.P47   1997
  320.985′09′045—dc20   96-42209
                                                                    CIP

CONTENTS

PART IIII
Violence and Human Rights

FOREWORD

Cynthia McClintock and Abraham Lowenthal

The Peruvian Labyrinth is the third edited volume over the span of slightly more than twenty years that seeks an in-depth, comprehensive analysis of Peru's polity, society, and economy. It follows *The Peruvian Experiment: Continuity and Change Under Military Rule*, edited by Abraham F. Lowenthal and published in 1975, and *The Peruvian Experiment Reconsidered*, edited by Cynthia McClintock and Abraham F. Lowenthal and published in 1983. All three volumes were enhanced by the dedication and editorial talent of Sanford Thatcher, who guided the publication process for the first two books at Princeton University Press and for this third volume at Penn State Press.

Few countries in Latin America have been the subject of such a trio of volumes. Indeed, relative to Peru's strategic significance, its demographic size, and its economic weight, the country has been the subject of an extraordinary amount of social-science writing, not only by scholars in the United States and Peru but elsewhere in Latin America, Western Europe, the former Soviet Union, and Japan. Why has Peru both retained the interest of those of us who were studying it in the early 1970s and attracted strong new interest in the 1980s and 1990s?

First, as the titles of the three volumes suggest, for many years Peru has been a country that perceives itself, and is perceived, as a country of unusually complex political, economic, and social problems—problems to which successive regimes have proclaimed bold new solutions. In the view of many analysts, Peru's problems began with the intensely traumatic Spanish conquest of the sophisticated Incan civilization and the country's geographical bifurcation between its coastal capital and its Andean mountain ranges, where most indigenous people lived. The problems continued with a humiliating defeat by Chile in the War of the Pacific during the late nineteenth century and were especially evident in the volatility of Peruvian politics during the twentieth century. Since 1919, no Peruvian political regime—neither constitutional nor de facto—has endured for more than twelve years.

The two regimes that have most vigorously sought to change Peru were both anomalous regimes dominated by a single individual. First, General Juan Velasco Alvarado (1969–75) led a military regime whose proclaimed goals seem fairly summarized as leftist.[1] Second, Alberto Fujimori Fujimori (1990–   ) led an elected regime whose proclaimed goals are perhaps best summarized as effective technocratic governance. In comparison with any other military government in the hemisphere (and indeed with most civilian ones), Velasco's undertook more ambitious economic reforms (nationalization of major international and domestic companies, expropriation of most large agricultural estates, the development of a worker-managed "social property" sector), more sweeping social reforms (such as requirements that all public and private Peruvian students learn the indigenous language, Quechua, and that they all wear the same school uniform), and highly unusual political initiatives (in particular, the creation of a political-mobilization agency—SINAMOS, Sistema Nacional de Movilización Social—which was supposed to move the country toward a "fully participatory social democracy").

Relative to those of other elected Latin American leaders, Fujimori's actions have been almost equally out of character. In particular, of course, he is the only elected president in recent Latin American history to rupture his country's constitutional order—ruling de facto between his 5 April 1992 *autogolpe* and his inauguration after being reelected in 1995. Throughout Latin America, the democratic credentials of many recent regimes have been questioned by scholars; the pejorative term *delegative democracy,* coined by Guillermo O'Donnell for Argentina, Brazil, Ecuador, and Bolivia, as well as for Peru, has been widely endorsed.[2] But as Maxwell Cameron and Philip Mauceri point out in their conclusion to this book, the Fujimori government has stood out for the strength of presidential power and the weakness of civilian political institutions even among these

1. The word *leftist* is vague. Here, the term is used to denote nationalistic, statist policies and efforts to reduce the power of traditional economic and political elites in the country and to increase popular political participation. By contrast, *rightest* policies are construed as policies congruent with the desires of major international powers; free-market policies without antipoverty or other measures aimed at more equal income distribution; and policies that do not seek greater popular participation in decision making.

2. See, for example, O'Donnell (1994). Delegative democracies meet traditional criteria for democracy insofar as elections are clean, but they are majoritarian. The elected president is empowered "to become, for a given number of years, the embodiment and interpreter of the high interests of the nation . . . voters/delegators are expected to become a passive but cheering audience of what the president does" (60).

Latin American nations, so that in their judgment and in ours Peru falls beyond O'Donnell's "delegative democracy" typology. At the time of Fujimori's election in 1990, Peru was reeling from economic decline and pervasive political violence, and analysts listed Peru in more critical condition than any other Latin American country except Nicaragua; Fujimori's key goal was to get the country back on its feet.

This point brings us to the central questions in our foreword: What are the similarities and differences between the Velasco and Fujimori governments? What are the similarities and differences in the problems that the two governments were trying to resolve? To what extent did the Velasco regime create conditions to which Fujimori was responding? And, finally, can we foresee the likely legacy of the Fujimori era by reflecting upon the legacy of the Velasco period?

There are striking similarities between the Velasco and Fujimori governments. As already indicated, both were executive-dominated governments that sought dramatic changes in Peru's economy, society, and polity. Although neither Velasco nor Fujimori was truly charismatic—neither was a mesmerizing orator, beloved by his followers, as was Alan García for a period—both figures were perceived as can-do leaders. The primary institutional base of both presidents was the Peruvian military. For about five years in the case of Velasco and longer in the case of Fujimori, both presidents enjoyed strong popular support. Perhaps insignificantly but perhaps not, although Velasco's roots were Peruvian and Fujimori was the son of Japanese-born parents, both were from lower-middle-class families, and both were nicknamed "El Chino."

Relative to the constitutional governments that preceded Velasco and Fujimori, the two *caudillos* were much more effective in achieving their goals and implementing their policies. (Whether or not these policies were actually the most appropriate for Peru at the time is, of course, a different question, to which answers are more subjective.) General Velasco moved Peru sharply leftward. Probably Velasco's highest priority was to eclipse the power of Peru's traditional oligarchy that had controlled much of the country's key economic and political resources. As Francisco Durand and Christine Hunefeldt indicate in their chapters, this goal was achieved; subsequently, traditional elite families were not able to regain their privileges. Also, as Carol Wise describes, the Velasco government institutionalized a much larger role for the state in the Peruvian economy.

The Velasco government's record on its social and political agendas is more mixed. The authors in *The Peruvian Experiment* and *The Peruvian Experiment Reconsidered* disagreed about the motives and sincerity of the military government's claims that it was seeking a "fully participatory social democracy."[3] The authors in *The Peruvian Labyrinth* are also divided on this point. Carol Wise writes of "hierarchical corporatist structures imposed by the Revolutionary Government of the Armed Forces," whereas Carmen Rosa Balbi believes that the government "sought to incorporate workers and sponsor the formation of new trade unions," and that the government's establishment of "nearly absolute job security" afforded workers much more power in their relationship with employers. In *The Peruvian Experiment* and *The Peruvian Experiment Reconsidered,* we underlined the ambiguities in the Velasco government's political model: the government's claim that it was enhancing political participation was contradicted by its refusal to surrender its own authority and by its rejection of national and local elections. Moreover, in the so-called no-party thesis, the government repudiated political parties, including a progovernment party, on the grounds that they tended to be clientelistic vehicles for their leaders. Commented Velasco: "[Most pre-1968 political parties] were pure blah-blah-blah."[4]

However, all of us scholars, including Carol Wise and Carmen Rosa Balbi in this volume, agree that whatever the Velasco government's political intentions were, the result was a dramatic increase in the strength of popular political organizations, in particular of the political Left. Political parties of the Marxist Left won 29 percent of the vote in Peru's 1978 Constituent Assembly election, in contrast to less than 4 percent in the 1962 and 1963 elections.[5]

For Fujimori's part, there is no doubt that Peru is off the critical list of Latin American countries. As Cameron and Mauceri indicate in their conclusion to this book, gross-domestic-product growth in Peru was Latin America's highest in 1994 and among the highest in 1995. Hyperinflation was tamed. Perhaps of even greater importance for most Peruvian citizens was the reduction in political violence; in 1994, the death toll attributed to political violence was 20 percent of 1990 levels.[6] Carlos Iván Degregori

---

3. General Velasco said that "we must build . . . a political order where the power of decisions, rather than being the monopoly of political and economic oligarchies, is widespread and rooted in social, economic and political institutions directed, with little or no mediation, by the men and women who form them." See Velasco Alvarado (1972, 271).

4. Interview with Velasco, *Caretas,* 3 February 1977, 30–33.

5. Tuesta (1987, 231, 261–63).

6. Palmer (1996, 70).

points out in his chapter that the capture of Sendero Luminoso's leader, Abimael Guzmán, by the antiterrorist police unit DINCOTE on 12 September 1992 was the pivotal event that punctured the movement's mythical aura and demoralized its militants.

As did Velasco, Fujimori claims that his authoritarian rule was a short-term measure necessary for the longer-term goal of a "true" democracy for Peru.[7] Indeed, the period of de facto rule was much shorter under Fujimori than under Velasco: Constituent Assembly elections were held within nine months of the autogolpe; the new constitution was narrowly approved in an October 1993 referendum;[8] and Fujimori was reelected in a landslide in the 1995 presidential elections.

Still, both scholars and Peruvian citizens doubt Fujimori's commitment to democratic principles—perhaps even more than they doubted Velasco's. As Cameron and Mauceri mention in the conclusion, Peruvians have dubbed Fujimori Chinochet, a play on the words *Chino* and *Pinochet*. Velasco was constrained in his decision making by the Peruvian military institution more than Fujimori has been in his decision making since the autogolpe, by either the military or his political party, Cambio 90. Although political parties were discouraged by the Velasco government, popular organizations became more numerous and more vigorous during the era; in contrast, under Fujimori, not only have political parties virtually disappeared, but, as Christine Hunefeldt and Carmen Rosa Balbi suggest in their chapters, the strength of popular organizations in both rural and urban Peru has eroded dramatically. Further, it appears that Fujimori, believing that dialogue is inefficient and an obstacle to effective governance, sought and achieved the depoliticization of Peru. As Carol Wise writes, "Civil society . . . has been largely written out of the present institutional blueprint." One of Fujimori's campaign banners in the 1995 presidential election was "Mis obras son mis palabras" (my actions are my words).[9] Comments one journalist: "*Politician* is today one of Peru's dirtiest words."[10]

---

7. On 8 April 1992, Fujimori said in a speech that "the only thing we are looking for is the restoration of true democracy. . . . Our final objective is democracy. I don't have the slightest doubt that democracy is the best system when it functions authentically as it should, but not when it is only a formality used to consecrate antidemocratic privileges." See Nathaniel Nash, "Peruvians Backing Leader's Actions," *New York Times*, 9 April 1992, 3.

8. Given the narrow margin of the "yes" relative to the "no" in his referendum (52.2 percent to 47.7 percent), and the serious irregularities in the contest, analysts doubt the validity of the official result. See McClintock (1994a, 28–29).

9. A campaign banner observed by Cynthia McClintock in Trujillo, February 1995.

10. Sally Bowen, "Pity the Politician," *Financial Times*, 7 March 1996, 4.

Both Velasco and Fujimori emphasized that authoritarian rule was necessary for a period because of the failure of the previous democratic administrations—particularly the failure of the various political parties—to implement the changes that appeared appropriate for the era. In the arguments of both leaders, reforms were seriously overdue, but the country's political parties were an obstacle rather than an impetus to the establishment of the necessary reforms. Both in 1968 and 1992, leaders' and citizens' perceptions of a need for radical change were galvanized in part by fears of guerrilla insurgencies (albeit very different kinds of insurgencies).

How valid were Velasco's and Fujimori's criticisms of Peru's political parties? Or, put somewhat differently, were both Velasco and Fujimori responding to a similar problem—the country's weak political institutions? Did both "have" to take charge?

For 1968, the scholarly consensus has been that Peru's democratic institutions were indeed fatally flawed.[11] In the prevailing constitution, illiterates were prohibited from voting—a prohibition that was likely to have skewed political representation in a more conservative direction. Still, despite the underrepresentation of this presumably reform-minded constituency, the desire for leftist reforms was intense in Peru in the early 1960s, and in the 1963 elections two reformist parties won more than 70 percent of the vote. Acción Popular's Fernando Belaúnde Terry was elected president of the country, and Haya de la Torre's Alianza Popular Revolucionaria Americana (APRA) won a plurality in the legislature. However, despite the common reform agenda of the two parties, they not only failed to become allies but were in virtually constant conflict. Reforms were not forthcoming. Both parties were putting their short-term interests above the reform preferences of the Peruvian people. In particular, APRA's behavior during this period provided little hope that, if it won the 1969 presidential election (as it was expected to), its members had the political skills to assuage the historical conflicts between the party and other sectors of the Peruvian polity, especially the military.

By contrast, most scholars have not perceived fatal flaws in Peru's 1980–92 democratic institutions that in some way "required" an autogolpe.[12] As Mauceri, Cameron, and Wise highlight in their chapters, the major traditional political parties during 1980–92 were extremely deficient in nu-

11. See McClintock (1994b, 375–77) and Jaquette (1971).
12. See Cameron in this volume; see also Mauceri (1995), Rospigliosi (1994, 35–62), and Pease (1994). However, Charles Kenney (1995) does suggest legislative obstruction of the executive.

merous respects.[13] However, given these very deficiencies—and the fact that owing to these deficiencies the parties were discredited among most Peruvians—they were not well positioned to obstruct the policies of a popular president. Indeed, despite Fujimori's party's minority position in the legislature between 1990 and 1992, most of the executive's key policy preferences were implemented.[14] As Cameron indicates in his chapter, FREDEMO and many conservative legislators were interested in an agreement with Fujimori that would have led to a stable governing majority in the legislature; indeed, representatives from the executive and legislative branches were about to propose such an agreement to the legislature two days before the autogolpe. Accordingly, most scholars believe that the key reason for the autogolpe was Fujimori's own desire for a different political model, a model in which power would be almost completely delegated to the executive by the Peruvian people, and in which the executive could run for reelection.[15]

Also extremely different, as suggested above, were the policy goals of Presidents Velasco and Fujimori. To a significant degree, the Velasco regime encouraged economic and social trends that the Fujimori government reversed. President Velasco distanced Peru from the United States; as Kenneth Roberts and Mark Peceny note in their chapter, President Fujimori returned Peru to the good graces of the international financial community, although his autogolpe complicated what had been an improving relationship with the United States. Velasco spearheaded the establishment of state ownership of key Peruvian industries, whereas Fujimori opted for the privatization of these same companies. Velasco championed agrarian reform, establishing cooperative enterprises in lieu of haciendas; Fujimori maintained the trend toward individual ownership of agricultural land that had begun in the early 1980s. As Francisco Durand discusses in his chapter, under Velasco the political power of traditional economic elites was eclipsed as the power of organized labor and other popular groups increased, whereas under Fujimori the political power of business elites expanded as that of popular groups declined.

Despite these contrasting agendas, however, both Velasco and Fujimori believed that it was necessary to demolish past Peruvian democratic institutions in order to build new ones that would work better. Both leaders' messages had a great deal of appeal among the vast numbers of citizens

---

13. See also Cotler (1995, 323–53).

14. See McClintock (1994b, 380–86).

15. See O'Donnell (1994). Scholars emphasize too that given the discrediting of Peru's 1980–92 institutions, Fujimori was confident that his promise of dramatic political reform would be supported by the Peruvian people as well as by the military.

who were suffering amid the failures of these institutions. But can a hermetic political elite, at best ambivalent and perhaps hostile to civil society, create a sustainable democracy?

Sadly, in Velasco's case the answer was no. Like most of the authors in this book, we fear that the most likely answer in Fujimori's case will also be no. The Fujimori period will probably reinforce Peru's traditional vicious political cycle: weak democratic institutions leading to failures of democratic governance leading to potential for legitimate authoritarian rule leading to weak democratic institutions. In the past, Peru's popular authoritarian leaders—Augusto Leguía (1919–30), Manuel Odría (1948–56), and Velasco—became illegitimate when the Peruvian economy faltered and their political models unraveled. In these previous cases, because political parties were marginalized from the policy-making arena, they did not adapt, mature, or effectively recruit new democratic leaders. One case in point is Peru's only long-standing institutionalized political party, APRA, which was excluded from executive power in Peru after the early 1930s, and whose dismal governing performance between 1985 and 1990 was in part a reflection of its troubled history.

We hope, however, that our prediction will prove too pessimistic and that Peru's vicious political cycle will be overcome. There are various structural changes in the country that bode well for its democratic future (or at least for its democratic future as the term *democracy* is currently defined in the United States). Whereas Peru's vigorous political Left during the 1980s put the country at odds with the rightist global trends of that period, currently the country's political spectrum is more similar to that in the rest of the Americas. Also, Peru's business sector is better organized and represented than in the past, and a significant political role for business leaders tends to be correlated with political stability.[16] Peru's citizens are less politically mobilized but at the same time are more politically sophisticated; they are more understanding of the constraints upon the Peruvian economy, and their expectations for their future living standards are lower. Also important, during the autogolpe the international community's commitment to electoral principles for Peru was made clearer than ever before. In short, our hope is that, at the threshold of the twenty-first century, Peru is overcoming its troubled history and will achieve effective governance and sustainable democracy.

---

16. As Durand indicates, the reasons are various, including the opening of greater space for businessmen hailing from middle-class families during the Velasco years, the galvanization of business unrest by García's bank-nationalization initiative, and Fujimori's eagerness to bring business leaders into his cabinet.

ACKNOWLEDGMENTS

We have incurred many debts in the process of editing *The Peruvian Labyrinth*. A number of colleagues have provided tremendous support and encouragement, above all Cynthia McClintock and Henry Dietz. Others who have helped along the way include Cindy Sanborn, Susan Stokes, Liisa North, and Christine Penzich. We are also grateful to Sandy Thatcher for his professional advice and editorial judgment.

Carlos Rosales did a superb job of translating the chapters by Carmen Rosa Balbi and Carlos Iván Degregori. Larisa Galadza carefully edited the entire manuscript, with support from the Norman Paterson School of International Affairs. Max Cameron is grateful to the Social Sciences and Humanities Research Council of Canada for a research grant that covered some of the expenses of this project. Philip Mauceri would like to acknowledge the supportive environment provided by the Instituto de Estudios Peruanos in Lima, the Center of Latin American Studies at the University of Connecticut, and the Department of Political Science at the University of Northern Iowa. None of the above individuals or institutions are responsible for the errors or deficiencies of this book.

As editors of *The Peruvian Labyrinth,* we worked in an equal partnership and our names appear in alphabetical order. Although the process of putting this book together has taken much time and work, it has been intellectually rewarding for us both. Finally, we would like to thank our wives, Fabiola Bazo and Miryam Antúnez de Mayolo, for their support, encouragement, and companionship.

INTRODUCTION

Maxwell A. Cameron and Philip Mauceri

When President Alberto Fujimori forcibly closed Congress and suspended Peru's constitution in April 1992, he was backed not only by the armed forces but also by a solid majority of Peruvians from all walks of life.[1] Although members of the closed Congress attempted to rally the populace to defend democratic institutions and procedures in the face of Fujimori's actions, there was little public support for a return to the previous constitutional status quo. Opponents of Fujimori's authoritarian measures encountered a public skeptical of traditional political parties and willing to support the *autogolpe* (or "self coup"),[2] in spite of the fact that the government had pursued painful economic adjustment policies.[3] Fujimori's authoritarianism and the public's acquiescence can best be understood in the context of the profound social, political, and economic transformations that had gripped Peru in the previous two decades.

In the 1980s and early 1990s, the Peruvian political panorama was one of the most troubling in Latin America. Economically, the country experienced staggering economic difficulties, including a bout with hyperinflation, two deep recessions, massive informalization of the workforce,[4] and a burdensome external debt. Successive governments swung from orthodox to populist and back to orthodox policies with little success in managing the macroeconomy (Pastor and Wise 1992). Peru seemed condemned to

1. Opinion polls showed that 60 to 70 percent of Peru's population supported Fujimori's actions. Polls also indicated that nearly half the country believed that Peru was still a democracy. For a further discussion of polling data, see Stokes (1996) and Conaghan (1995).

2. For our purposes, we define an *autogolpe* as "a temporary suspension of constitutional guarantees and closure of Congress by the executive, which rules by decree and uses referenda and new legislative elections to ratify a regime with broader executive powers" (Cameron 1994, 146).

3. On the impact of Fujimori's shock therapy, see González de Olarte (1993) and Wise's chapter in this volume.

4. Portes and Johns (1989, 116) define the informal sector as all economic activities lacking the following characteristics of the formal economy: (1) an explicit, written labor contract; (2) state regulation of wages and working conditions; (3) a clear separation between ownership of labor and capital. See also Portes (1985).

a Hobbesian world of poverty, polarization, and the collapse of social and political institutions. A decade of violence provoked by two major insurgent groups and the expansion of a lucrative transnational cocaine trade drew the armed forces into a dangerously high-profile role.

Unlike in other countries that underwent transitions from authoritarianism in the 1970s and 1980s, human-rights abuses in Peru were far worse during the period of civilian rule than during military rule. Social violence and instability contributed to economic uncertainty and decline, and politics was viewed by the public as a struggle for power reminiscent of Hobbes's state of nature. Brutality and misery invaded the daily lives of a growing majority of the population (Bourque and Warren 1989).

Fujimori's enduring popularity—and reelection in 1995—was in large measure due to his success in vigorously attacking the problems of economic decline and political instability. His administration brought hyperinflation under control and captured Abimael Guzmán, the leader of the Shining Path, a revolutionary organization responsible for the loss of an estimated 27,000 lives (Roberts and Peceny in this volume) and $22 billion in material damage (Boloña 1993, 5). Fujimori's success in restoring economic stability, however, came at the expense of an increase in poverty and inequality, and pacification was pursued at the expense of human rights and democracy.

The purpose of this book is to understand the complex and contradictory political trends that have manifested themselves in Peru during the 1980s and 1990s. While there have been disappointing setbacks, such as the autogolpe, the last two decades have also witnessed positive social, political, and economic changes. Our goal is to analyze and interpret these events in order to provide a guide through the labyrinth of Peruvian politics.

Themes of the Book

The authors have conducted extensive research on their subjects during the last decade. Despite the unique perspectives and interpretations that the contributors to this volume bring to bear on their topics, there are nonetheless three themes in common to each of the chapters that follow: institutional change, state-society relations, and democratization.

Institutional Change and Disintegration

The first theme is the dramatic disintegration of Peru's institutions from the 1970s through to the early 1990s (Matos Mar 1985). At the most general level, institutions are the basic rules of the game within which societal actors must interact, as well as the mechanism for their enforcement. Institutions are important because they shape social outcomes by structuring the incentives facing individuals and organizations. In other words, institutions make certain courses of action costly and others profitable. When they weaken or change, social patterns are altered in often unanticipated ways. The lack of institutional consolidation is at the heart of many of the political and economic problems facing Peru, from the growth of the informal economy to the abuse of human rights.

Violence and corruption, for example, have sources in institutional failures. The failure of the judiciary to punish terrorists contributed to human-rights abuses by the armed forces, whose policy of executing prisoners was partly a response to the perception that the courts were too intimidated to convict or sentence terrorists. Corruption and inefficiency in the judiciary undermined the rule of law. Not surprisingly, few Peruvians came to the defense of a system of justice that contributed to a climate of impunity and lawlessness.

Strong institutions provide a stable framework within which individuals and organizations can develop reasonable expectations and plan for the future. In Peru, institutional disintegration affected a wide range of organizations such as the state, parties, unions, and business groups. Macroeconomic instability and a failed effort to expropriate the banks in 1987 not only had predictably deleterious consequences for investment, they also mobilized business into political action. Exchange rates and other controls had perverse effects on the economy: businesses began to devote more effort to speculating and rent seeking than to productive investments. As tax avoidance increased, the state saw revenue decline in the late 1980s to a quarter of the levels of the previous decade.

Workers were equally affected by the crisis of institutional disintegration. Legislation on wages, working conditions, and job security became increasingly irrelevant or unenforceable under conditions of economic collapse. As unemployment soared, organized workers lost confidence in the ability of union leaders to keep up with inflation and provide job security. Oddly, as Carmen Rosa Balbi reports in her chapter in this volume, many workers supported institutional reforms that rolled back the very labor legislation from which workers ostensibly benefited. Moreover, many workers believed that trade-union activities were often irresponsible and counterproductive.

Finally, political parties were marginalized by the rise of independent candidates challenging established political elites. The weakening of political parties contributed to the concentration of executive power in the hands of the president. The ease with which Fujimori overturned the constitution of 1979 and closed the Congress and the margin of later electoral victories suggested that Peruvian political parties no longer represented credible, meaningful, or stable channels for political representation and articulation of demands.

State-Society Relations

A second issue these collected essays address is the changing nature of relations between the state and society. We define the state in Weberian terms, as a relation of domination crystallized in a set of public institutions that exercise the monopoly of legitimate force within defined territorial boundaries. The role of the state, and relations between civil society and the state, have changed dramatically since the reforms of the Velasco era (Mauceri 1996; McClintock and Lowenthal 1983; Stepan 1978; Lowenthal 1975). Societal groups have acquired greater power and new methods of resisting or influencing the initiatives of the state (Stokes 1991; Stephens 1983).

The state expanded its activities in the 1970s and early 1980s, while efforts to extend its control over civil society through corporatist mechanisms or clientelist networks failed. Traditional mechanisms of intermediation and domination—such as the power of rural bosses (or *gamonales*), and clientelistic political parties and unions—have also collapsed. The cumulative result has been a tremendous crisis of societal representation and state power.

Following the failure of populist economic policies under President Alan García Pérez (1985–90), Peru, like the rest of Latin America, has undergone a fundamental shift away from state interventionism toward a search for market-oriented solutions (see Hojman 1994). This shift led to the privatization of state-owned enterprises and peasant cooperatives, a major overhaul of the tax system, elimination of regulations on foreign investment, liberalization of trade, and a drastic reduction of social spending. Efforts to achieve improvements in equity or distribution were abandoned in favor of an overwhelming policy emphasis on macroeconomic stability, liberalization, "reinsertion" into the international financial community, and reduction of the role of the state in the economy. The chapters in this volume provide a wide range of explanations for this change: Wise focuses on the failure of previous statist models of development; Durand highlights the growing assertiveness and sophistication of the Right; Hunefeldt looks at peasants' disillusionment with the role of the state in the rural sector, while Balbi explores disillusionment among workers; and Cameron explains the effects on the political system of the informalization of the economy.

Democratization

The situation in Peru during the 1980s and 1990s created many dilemmas for the country's fragile democratic institutions (Dietz 1992; McClintock 1989; Cotler 1988). On the one hand, the twelve years between 1980 and 1992 were an extended period of uninterrupted electoral democracy, unprecedented in the previous fifty years. As well, those years were characterized by unusually widespread and open participation. On the other hand, Peru's "democracy" was highly restricted. Sixty percent of the population in the 1980s lived under a state of emergency as a result of violence. Freedom of speech and assembly, and the right of due process, were severely limited. In addition, the legitimacy of many democratic institutions was undermined by corruption, clientelism, and the authoritarian arbitrariness of governing officials.

The dilemmas of democracy become even more stark if one considers that Peru is one of the most notorious violators of human rights in Latin America and the Third World; torture and forced disappearances have been widely accepted practices among security officials. Added to these limits were institutions—political parties, the judicial system and the Congress—whose legitimacy was undermined by corruption, clientelism and authoritarianism. With democratic norms and institutions hampered by clearly undemocratic practices, it is easier to understand why many in Peru failed to rally in support of the system when Fujimori swept it away.

As is evident even from this brief sketch, there is an intimate link between the themes of institutional disintegration, state-society relations, and the dilemmas of Peruvian democracy. For example, any discussion of new social organizations and grassroots democracy must address the economic crisis that has forced the popular sectors—workers (both formal and informal), peasants, the lower middle classes—to find new and innovative institutions. It must also address the failure of existing institutions, including the state, to respond to the needs of the popular sectors. Democratization is thus linked to the changes in state-society relations and institutional disintegration. Similarly, the changing nature of state-society relations has much to do both with the increasing democratization of civil society and the disintegration of the state and intermediary institutions.

Organization of the Book

The book is divided into three sections. Part I provides the background for explaining the economic and political crises of the late 1980s and 1990s. Chapter 1, by Philip Mauceri, examines the transition to civilian rule in the 1977–80 period and suggests that while the process was highly controlled by elites and narrowly focused on finding a formula for the orderly withdrawal of the military, it also froze into place the vast socio-economic changes introduced by the Velasco military regime (1968–75), including the agrarian reform, a large state sector, and new rights for workers.

The contradictions of a transition process that was elite controlled and yet, to a large extent at the military's insistence, produced a reformist constitution, left many social and economic sectors dissatisfied. Moreover, both the "extractive" nature of the transition (O'Donnell 1992b) and the disinterest on the part of the Left with political-institution building meant that the new institutional arrangements did not reflect a broad social consensus on democratic norms and procedures.

While many of the social movements that emerged in the 1970s found a voice in a resurgent Left (which in the 1980s formed the United Left [IU] electoral coalition) and in the populism of a renovated American Popular Revolutionary Alliance (APRA, or Alianza Popular Revolucionaria Americana) party, their support for these parties was transient and fleeting, and full incorporation remained elusive. In Chapter 2, Maxwell A. Cameron examines the interplay between the informalization of the economy and the breakdown of democracy in Peru. He argues that the growth of the informal sector undermined the party system and created an opportunity for anti-system candidates. The 5 April 1992 autogolpe was the act of a renegade politician who feared that his political enemies, namely APRA's

Alan García and the Shining Path's Abimael Guzmán, could not be defeated within the straitjacket of existing political arrangements.

The origins and implications of Peru's economic crisis in the 1980s and early 1990s are explored by Carol Wise in Chapter 3. She traces the origins of the 1980s crisis as far back as the late 1950s, when Peru began an unsuccessful search for alternative development models. Each model failed to provide sustainable and equitable growth. Instead, they produced a series of economic failures characterized by intense social conflict, a burdensome foreign debt, deficits, inflation, and production imbalances. Wise emphasizes that failure had more to do with poor domestic policy choices and the unwillingness to address serious organizational deficiencies than with the drawbacks of any particular model. In doing so, she focuses on the interplay between political and economic decisions and questions the choice of some policies over others. Thus, if one is to comprehend Peru's economic failures, one must first have a clear understanding of the institutional, historical, and social context of the last decades.

Part II of this volume examines how disintegration and democratization affected three key groups in society: business, labor, and the agrarian sector. The peasantry benefited from an agrarian reform that eliminated semifeudal exploitation and stimulated a new level of political organization in the 1970s. It also suffered the consequences of underdevelopment, marginalization, state neglect, economic crisis, and terrorist violence more directly than almost any other sector. In Chapter 4, Christine Hunefeldt provides a tour d'horizon of the agrarian sector since the 1969 reform. She cautions against seeing the agrarian economy as homogeneous and explores the diverse strategies and dynamics of rural change. Hunefeldt emphasizes the manifold ways in which privatization and parcelization of land have occurred in recent years. While her analysis demonstrates multiple layers of conflict and violence in the countryside, she also demonstrates the persistence of cooperation in the rural sector.

Carmen Rosa Balbi's contribution to this volume examines how neoliberal economic reforms have affected workers in urban areas. Balbi traces the radicalization of workers to reforms in the Velasco era, especially to changes within industrial organizations and the system of labor relations. These reforms led to a more combative or "class-struggle oriented" (clasista) union leadership affiliated with the political Left. Defective labor-relations institutions contributed to the rise of clasista unions, but also defined their limits as unions and management were unable to reach compromises.

A crisis of representation in the labor movement has also occurred: union leadership has been challenged by the Shining Path on the shop floor, and the trade-union movement has been neutralized as a national political force since the 1990 election of Fujimori. Stressing the phenomenon of the temporary worker and more precarious labor relations, Balbi's chapter helps explain why Fujimori's policies challenged the power of the Left, which was rooted in the organized labor movement, yet won widespread popular support among workers.

The final chapter in this section is by Francisco Durand, who looks at the growing politicization of the country's business elite. Again, this examination begins with the traumatic impact of the policies of Velasco for the elite. He traces the elite's organizational and ideological response, which was crystallized by the García government's disastrous effort to nationalize the banks in 1987 and the mobilization of a Right-wing coalition behind the unsuccessful presidential candidacy of Mario Vargas Llosa. Durand ends by outlining the relationship between business and the Fujimori administration, which has put into place many of the neoliberal policies long defended by business organizations. His article is attentive to tensions within the business elite that cut across race and ideology; he provides a stunning illustration of how elites attempt to reconcile the need for adaptation with resistance to social change.

In Part III, the focus of the book turns to the problems of violence and human-rights abuses. The rapid expansion of the Shining Path during the 1980s confounded observers and policy makers alike. In his chapter on the Shining Path, Carlos Iván Degregori emphasizes the fundamentalist character of the Shining Path and the cult of personality surrounding its leader. An implication of Degregori's analysis is that the capture of Guzmán was a near-fatal blow for such a hierarchical terrorist organization. Guzmán's leadership will be difficult to replace. Yet the fundamentalist character of the movement also suggests that its legacy will be more profound than previous insurrectionary and guerrilla movements in Peru. The Shining Path successfully served as a conduit for the articulation of a potent political force: the rage of excluded groups in a deeply racist and impoverished society.

Massive rights abuses undermined the ability of the state to win the support of the peasantry and combat the Shining Path. Peru's armed forces have been among the worst violators of human rights in the hemisphere. Chapter 8, by Kenneth Roberts and Mark Peceny, examines the question of human rights in Peru. They begin with the observation that

Peru was a civilian, constitutional regime with formal democratic arrangement, yet it had one of the worst records of human-rights violations. They address the reasons why successive governments have been unable to devise a counterinsurgency strategy consistent with democratic accountability. The chapter ends by examining the role of human rights in the complicated relationship between Peru and the United States.

Over the last few years the North American public has increasingly become aware of how events in Peru—whether drug trafficking, debt moratoria, the 1991 cholera epidemic, violence against aid workers and technicians, or the Fujimori coup—affect people in the rest of the hemisphere. At a time when military, drug-enforcement, economic, and other forms of aid to Peru are headline news, it is crucial to be able to interpret current events in Peru in light of the historical and theoretical perspectives provided in this book. Simplistic images and interpretations can be dangerous when trying to comprehend a complex and problematic country like Peru. The common objective of all the chapters in *The Peruvian Labyrinth* is to provide a synthesis that will serve as a guide for students, researchers, policy makers, human-rights activists, and the interested public as they attempt to make their way through the complex maze of social, political, and economic changes that have taken place in Peru.

PART I

THE LEGACY OF PAST CHOICES: REGIMES, COALITIONS, POLICIES

1

THE TRANSITION TO "DEMOCRACY" AND THE FAILURES OF INSTITUTION BUILDING

Philip Mauceri

The transition to civilian rule in Peru during the 1977–80 period is similar in many respects to other recent transitions in Latin America. As were others, it was an elite-controlled process in which timetables and rules were negotiated behind closed doors by traditional party leaders and military officers. They were pushed in different directions by the struggle between hard-liners and soft-liners, moderates and radicals within their respective camps (Przeworski 1991, 62), and out of these conflicts and negotiations—the so-called game of transition—the new civilian order emerged.[1]

Despite this similarity, however, Peru's transition provides an interesting contrast with those of most of Latin America during the 1970s and 1980s. Although the transition was directed by the elite, it involved an elected Constituent Assembly charged with writing a new constitution. Moreover, at the insistence of the military, the new constitution incorporated the vast social reforms carried out during military rule, including agrarian reform, workers' rights, and guarantees for the cooperative sector of the economy, in what was one of the most socially inclusionary constitutions in the region.

Together, these conditions could have laid the basis for a more participatory transition than those found elsewhere and created broad support for institutional arrangements during the consolidation period. As we

---

1. On the dynamics involved in the transition, see O'Donnell and Schmitter (1986). They focus on the transition as a series of "political moments" involving negotiations, understandings and/or pacts between the military and party elites.

shall see, the opportunity for doing so was not grasped. Actors on the Right and Left took maximalist political strategies and were never fully committed to the political, social, and economic system embodied in the 1979 constitution.

This chapter will examine the limits, possibilities, and paradoxes that the 1977–80 transition created for democratic consolidation during the following twelve years. It will be argued that many of the weaknesses of Peru's subsequent democratic order were the result of a process that failed to create an institutional framework to which all actors felt committed. The result was an erosion in the efficacy and legitimacy of democratic institutions, a condition that ultimately facilitated the breakdown of democracy in 1992.

The early literature on Latin American democratization pointed to the conservative nature of the transition and the restrictions this imposed on political participation in the post-transition period (O'Donnell and Schmitter 1986). Recent analyses (Smith 1991; Remmer 1990) have also suggested that transitions to democracy and the democracies they create are inherently conservative (Rueschemeyer, Stephens, and Stephens 1992; Przeworski 1991). Democracy is a political system in which no single actor can impose its interests on society; support for democracy requires a willingness to accept the outcome of institutional procedures, even though they are uncertain and often unpredictable (Przeworski 1991, 12–13, 49–50). To ensure elite compliance with democratic rules, it is frequently necessary to provide the elite with guarantees against threats to their basic interests, even when this means closing off the possibilities of enacting needed social or economic reforms.

Transitions to democracy involve many powerful actors and, as Przeworski (1991, 134) notes, they may "get stuck" in collusion between politicians and the military while seeking to maintain the favorable positions acquired during the transitions. The compromises necessary to make the transition set the parameters of future political contestation and participation, often restricting the possibilities for subordinate groups to represent their interests. Thus, limited democracies resulted from the post-1958 transitions in Venezuela and Colombia; in the 1980s, Brazil was the best example of this dynamic.

The Peruvian transition to democracy was politically conservative even though civil society had become increasingly radical. A highly controlled, top-down, conservative transition process coincided with an intense mobilization of increasingly militant popular sectors. Expanding the circumscribed boundaries of democracy in the post-transition period required political institutions and norms that could address the demands and pressures of new social actors.

However, the norms and institutions inherited from both the authoritarian and pre-authoritarian periods often inhibited democratic practice in the 1980s and 1990s. While democratic ideals had widespread acceptance and legitimacy in Peru, they were not always reflected in political practices. Clientelism, corporatism, government centralization, personalist party structures, and an authoritarian political culture were all part of the historical legacy that burdened Peru as it entered the 1980s.[2] The tension between the changes in civil society and the restoration of a restrictive political democracy led to conflicts in state-society relations that culminated in the breakdown of democracy in 1992.

At the same time elite sectors, especially in the expanding financial sector, were not always pleased with the institutional framework set up in the 1979 constitution. Throughout the 1980s, as Durand notes in his chapter in this volume, the business sector was increasingly influenced by free-market ideas and organized to promote pro-business policies. The "social market" explicitly endorsed in the 1979 constitution, and embodied in the vast state sector inherited from the military government, was viewed as an obstacle to the reduction in government regulation. Constitutional guarantees of "estabilidad laboral" that prevented employers from firing workers and restrictions on landownership were seen as inhibiting the operations of the free market.

Efforts to modify these elements were thwarted during the Belaúnde administration, and the election of the populist Alan García in 1985 suggested that such changes were unlikely to be openly endorsed by the electorate. García's failed attempt to nationalize the banking system in 1987 further alienated elite sectors from the existing political system. Although opponents of this measure were able to defeat it through the legislative and judicial process, the resulting political conflicts led to the first serious rumors of coups and democratic breakdowns. An additional factor corroding the legitimacy and efficacy of Peru's nascent institutional framework was one of the most profound socioeconomic crises of twentieth-century Latin America. The massive foreign debt, unemployment, hyperinflation, and capital flight that affected all of the region's new democratic regimes in the 1980s put enormous strains on the resources of the state as well as on most social groups. Expanding the limits of democracy

2. A study of recent democratizations that places particular emphasis on these factors is Diamond et al. (1989).

that had been established during the transition proved extremely difficult under these conditions.

The effects of the crisis on the state were the same almost everywhere: the efficacy of the public sector declined dramatically as investments in infrastructure and personnel fell off (Mauceri 1996). Corruption corroded confidence in public institutions. Policy solutions to the crisis almost always involved austerity plans backed by international financial actors, and the costs fell hardest on the poor and their organizations, particularly unions.[3]

Stabilization plans also tended to give a new and critical role to technocratic elites linked with international banks within the state apparatus, marginalizing democratic institutions such as the legislature and local governments in the making of economic policy. By the early 1990s, some were coming to view those institutions themselves as fundamental obstacles in the way of needed reforms.

The case of Peru illustrates both the region-wide dynamics and some specific exceptions. The first part of this chapter examines the game as it was played out between 1978 and 1980. The negotiated transition between traditional party leaders and the military produced as much continuity as it did change. While a change of regime occurred at the end of the process, there was substantial continuity in policies and institutional norms with that of the Morales Bermúdez government (1975–80) authoritarian period. Those continuities were the source of dissatisfaction and conflict for actors across the political spectrum.

The second part of the chapter examines those continuities and how they shaped responses to the socioeconomic challenges of the 1980s. It will be argued that they represented important constraints on expanding democratic practices and actually reenforced the authoritarian biases of elite sectors.

The Breakdown of the Authoritarian Regime, 1973–1977

The regime of General Juan Velasco Alvarado (1968–75) was responsible for introducing the most radical social and economic changes in recent Peruvian history. The military's reform project developed as a result of the

---

3. On the process of neoliberal reform and its costs, see especially Smith et al. (1994), Przeworski (1991), and Nelson (1990).

"new professionalism" that refocused the military's conceptualization of national security away from external threats and toward the problem of ending internal strife. It was also the result of the inability of the civilian regime of Fernando Belaúnde (1963–68) to enact needed reforms in the face of a conservative-controlled Congress.

The first five years of the self-proclaimed Revolutionary Government of the Armed Forces (RGAF) witnessed the nationalization of the oil industry and other mineral industries, the development of an expanded state sector, and the enactment of a far-reaching agrarian reform that effectively destroyed the land-based oligarchy (see McClintock and Lowenthal 1983; Lowenthal 1975).

As the military regime introduced these vast socioeconomic changes, it also sought to completely reorganize society into corporatist structures. The purpose of such structures was to ensure control over the revolutionary process and also provide a political base for the regime among the newly mobilized lower-class sectors. Yet problems confronted the military's project from the beginning of its effort.[4]

First, unlike during the economic reforms, there was never a programmatic consensus within the military over the corporatist structures to be instituted. Differences within the military centered upon the ultimate purpose of these new organizations. Some claimed that Peru should move toward socialism, while others proposed a vague Christian or humanist agenda, and still others sought a neo-fascist model.

Second, the military's organizational efforts encountered stiff opposition from other political groups, particularly on the Left, who viewed the process suspiciously. The Left organized independently of the regime and in many instances utilized the resources of the state for their own organizational purposes. Corporate institutions, especially in the cooperative sector, were thus turned into focal points of opposition to the regime.

By 1973 these contradictions in the military's corporatist project were an increasingly evident source of conflict. Growing factional disputes within the military became public as officers searched for civilian allies to bolster their own position, and a rebellion by conservative naval officers suggested declining internal consensus over government policy. This was accompanied by rising social conflict, especially in the labor sector, which witnessed the first wave of strikes since the 1968 coup.

Such conflicts were spurred on in part by the new predominance of

---

4. Evaluations of the corporatist project are found especially in Gorman (1982), McClintock (1981), and Stepan (1978).

radical leftist—especially Maoist—unions in this period, whose primary strategy was to confront the regime with radical demands and tactics. As Balbi notes in her chapter, New Left unions developed *clasista* tactics that emphasized confrontation with employers as well as with the government. Social protests were primarily seen as ways to instill class consciousness among workers. Yet rising social conflicts were also facilitated by a significant downturn in the economic situation of the country. After a period of steady growth wages began to fall, deficits from the newly nationalized industries were felt, and the country struggled with the effects of the worldwide global slowdown that was provoked by the oil crisis of 1973–74. Added to these difficulties facing the regime was the specter of a leadership crisis provoked by General Velasco's illness, which had left him an invalid.

This uncertainty, combined with rising social conflict and the worry among key officers over the factionalization of the armed forces, led prime minister General Francisco Morales Bermúdez to carry out a bloodless coup against Velasco in August 1975. While promising revolutionary continuity in a "second phase" of the military government, it soon became apparent that the Morales Bermúdez regime would take a far different path than its predecessor. The new regime quickly dismissed most of the "progressive" officers associated with Velasco, initiated a crackdown on popular organizations, and opened a dialogue with traditionally conservative parties.

This apparent move to the Right by the new regime was reinforced by a dramatic switch in economic policy, away from the economic nationalism and state capitalist model utilized by Velasco and toward a neoliberal program. As Carol Wise points out in her chapter in this volume, this shift responded as much to the external pressures facing Peru in the mid-1970s, particularly from the International Monetary Fund (IMF), as to the internal problems of the Velasco programs.

Liberalization, 1977–1979

The movement to end the authoritarian regime began shortly after the removal of Velasco. The end of that government also ended the raison d'être of military rule. The 1968 coup had been justified on the grounds that profound social reforms were needed, and many in the military argued that by 1975 such a need had ended. Moreover, it was clear that the period of social reforms had sharply divided the military institution and created levels of economic and social disorder that the military was unable to confront. In this section, the military's extrication from power will be reviewed. I will argue that political parties and civil society responded to the military's liberalization in sharply differing ways.

While the parties and groups on the Left were more interested in continuing social reforms and limiting the power of conservative military officers, those on the Right sought political compromises with the military that would ensure their participation in the new civilian regime. In the end, the transition reflected the consensus forged by the military and conservative parties. Little attention was given by either the Left or Right to reforming political institutions to assure that the new civilian regime could consolidate its legitimacy.

Extrication and the New Order

Following the purge of the last "progressive" officers in mid-1976 (which included prime minister General Jorge Fernández Maldonado), the Morales Bermúdez government promised to hold elections for a Constituent Assembly. Over the course of the next year, the military regime signaled a new opening to conservative opposition groups. First, the regime began a series of consultations with the leaders of the traditional parties—the Partido Popular Cristiano (PPC), Acción Popular (AP), and the Alianza Popular Revolucionario Americano (APRA) party—over the timing and nature of the new elections. Second, the regime appointed civilian technocrats to the cabinet, something the Velasco regime had strenuously avoided doing. Both steps were symbolic gestures to traditional elites, locked out of the channels of influence under the Velasco government, of the new willingness to listen to their complaints.

The Constituent Assembly elections took place against the backdrop of a series of strikes, including a successful second national strike organized by the Confederación General de Trabajadores Peruanos (CGTP) and the announcement of a "package" of price rises. While the conservative PPC and APRA endorsed the electoral process, former president Belaúnde's Acción Popular decided not to participate in the election, arguing that a lack of guarantees existed for a clean election. The campaigns conducted by the Left attempted to capitalize on the regime's weakness, running on an anti-military platform.

Its attempt paid off. Although APRA received the largest share (35 percent) of votes, the five leftist parties that presented candidates (Unidad Democrático Popular [UDP]; Partido Comunista del Perú [PCP]; Partido Socialista Revolucionario [PSR]; Frente Obrero, Campesino, Estudiantil y Popular [FOCEP]; and Frente Nacional de Trabajadores y Campesinos [FNTC]) unexpectedly captured a third of the vote. One of the problems the Left faced was a high degree of factionalism, and, in order to strengthen their chances, the twenty-plus leftist parties that existed had formed a set of alliances, reducing their number to five for electoral purposes.[5]

Even so, they had little chance of receiving a significant share of the votes. With the exception of the Peruvian Communist Party (Partido Comunista del Perú, PCP), none had participated in elections previously. Yet an important factor that worked in their favor was the strength of their candidates, most of whom were leaders of lower-class organizations, had been active in politics for at least a decade, and were known as prominent opponents of the regime.

Although leftist parties lacked sophisticated "electoral machines" geared to getting potential voters to the polls, they had close links with new popular-sector organizations. In choosing their candidates, these parties picked their most visible leaders, who were also prominent members of union and peasant federations. Since the "parties" that backed them were recently formed electoral fronts composed of small factions and organizations, leftist candidates were more known as leaders of lower-class groups than as representatives of established political parties. Included among the more than thirty leftist members elected to the Assembly were the most prominent union, peasant, and shantytown leaders and advisers of the 1970s.[6] Moreover, these same figures were the most vocal and active opponents of regime policies. Many of them had organized the two national strikes against the regime or had been exiled. Of the parties that

5. The leftist parties that participated in the elections divided the share of the votes as follows: Partido Comunista del Perú (PCP), 6 percent; Union Democratica Popular (UDP), 4.5 percent; Partido Socialista Revolucionaria (PSR), 7 percent; FOCEP, 12 percent; and FNTC, 4 percent. None of the Maoist parties (Patria Roja, Bandera Roja, Sendero Luminoso) participated in the elections. A detailed analysis of the Left during this period is found in Jorge Nieto (1983) and in Tuesta (1979).

6. For example, Victor Cuadros (UDP) led the miners' federation; Hugo Blanco, Genaro Ledesma and Saturnino Paredes (FOCEP) were associated with the peasant federation CCP; Isidoro Gamarra and Luis Castillo (PCP) led the labor federation CGTP; and Leonidas Rodríguez and Antonio Meza Cuadra (PSR) were well-known Velasco-era army officers.

presented candidates in the election, only the Left had campaigned on an explicit anti-military platform and a record of anti-regime activity. A vote for the Left was therefore the clearest means of expressing opposition in these elections.

The Constituent Assembly election was planned as a first step in the transition to a civilian regime, but to opponents of the regime, and to many voters, the election was a plebiscite on regime performance. It was apparent that there was little consensus in political circles over the course and nature of the transition. With AP abstaining and the Left intent on using the new Assembly as a forum to challenge regime legitimacy, only the conservative PPC and APRA saw in the assembly a means to create a new political system. Both also had hopes of designing such a system to their own political advantage.

Almost immediately after the election, Aprista[7] leaders reached an agreement with the PPC, which had gained 24 percent of the vote, assuring joint APRA-PPC control of the Assembly. The aging leader of APRA, Víctor Raúl Haya de la Torre, was elected president of the Assembly, and the leadership of Assembly committees was distributed among both parties. APRA-PPC control neutralized the influence of the Left and laid the basis for a cooperative relationship between the military and the Assembly. The conversations that had been taking place between members of the military cabinet and APRA leaders during the previous year were now expanded to encompass the agenda of the Assembly.

Morales Bermúdez designated a secret Coordinadora composed of three high-ranking officials from each service branch, appointed by their respective commander generals, to coordinate affairs between the regime and the Assembly leadership. The Coordinadora met regularly with APRA and PPC leaders, however it never met with representatives from the Left. Aside from the semi-formal mechanism of the Coordinadora, informal weekly agenda-setting meetings were also held between Haya and the prime minister, General Molina.[8]

Both APRA leaders and military officials denied the Left's charge of a "pact," and the absence of signed agreements lent credence to Haya's characterization of these consultations as expressions of "mutual understanding." In effect, the discussions were merely a continuation of the

---

7. The term *Aprista* refers to members of the APRA party.
8. Interview with former air force representative of the Coordinadora, Lima, 16 November 1988.

cooperative relationship established between APRA and the Morales Bermúdez regime during the 1976–77 period. Both actors were interested in
a stable transition and controlling the new influence of the Left. APRA
was especially interested in the latter, given its loss of control over the
union movement. The regime found itself besieged by a growing popular
movement and an uncooperative political Left. Though both the military
and APRA shared these common goals, neither saw an advantage to explicit alliances.

The entire transition process had been initiated by the military to extricate itself from the sort of political commitments that an explicit alliance
with APRA would have meant. The position of Apristas during military
rule was to call for an immediate return to civilian rule and free elections.[9]
An open alliance with the military would have undoubtedly prolonged
the transition process and postponed those elections, while clearly linking
the party to a military regime over which it exercised little influence.

APRA-PPC control of the Assembly and the cooperative relationship
established with the regime ensured that the agenda of the Assembly
would encompass only the purpose for which it had been convoked: writing and approving a new constitution. From the start, initiatives to expand
the purpose of the Assembly were rejected. The Left's proposal to give it
executive powers and declare an end to military rule was voted down by
the majority amid reiterated reminders by the military cabinet of the purpose of that body.[10] The decree issued in October 1977, which had authorized elections, noted that the Assembly "will have as an exclusive end the
adoption of a new constitution for the State." That restriction served as a
clear warning that the military was not willing to share governmental responsibilities with the Assembly. The Assembly was to serve as an arena of
open political debate over the future of the country, but not to have any
powers over the military regime's policy.

An added restriction that the military imposed concerned the structural
reforms that Velasco had enacted. The same decree that defined the purpose of the Assembly also declared the inviolability of those reforms, stat-
ing that the new constitution would include "the regulations which institutionalize the structural transformations . . ."[11] This restriction was a clear

---

9. On APRA's policy toward the military in this period, see Pease (1981) and Valderrama
et al. (1980).

10. DESCO, *Cronologia Politica 1978* (Lima: DESCO, 1979), 3222.

11. Citations from Decreto Ley No. 21949, Article 2. During the campaign all of the
parties attacked this article, however once installed, the APRA-PPC majority did not challenge its authority. See Bernales (1980, 30).

indication that the military would not accept a constitution that rolled back the basic changes introduced, such as the agrarian reform, job security, and industrial communities. A debate on these issues would not only have effectively annulled a decade of military rule but also could have opened old wounds and disagreements within the military institution over the Velasco period and its reforms. Given the search for unity inherent in the institutionalist position of the military, such a debate would have been counterproductive. Ironically, a conservative and narrowly managed transition produced a "socialist" constitution.

The coordination established between the APRA-PPC majority and the regime helped avoid major conflicts between the Assembly and the military during the one-year period established to write the constitution.[12] The restrictions imposed by the military were tacitly accepted by the majority of members of the Constituent Assembly. An additional factor contributing to the lack of significant conflicts was the continued predominance of the institutional position within the armed forces. The commitment to extricate the military institution from direct political rule within the armed forces meant that both the military and key civilian politicians were in agreement over the end goal of the transition: a return to civilian rule.

The degree to which that position facilitated cooperation can be seen from the debate over the role of civil-military relations in the new constitution. There was a consensus among Assembly members that the constitution should incorporate mechanisms dissuading future military interventions in politics.[13] The proposals approved on the initiative of APRA included clauses declaring the armed forces "non-deliberative" institutions (Article 278), giving the population the "right to insurgency" in defense of the constitutional order (Article 82), and voiding payment of all public debts contracted by military regimes (Article 141). These articles were approved by the Assembly without comment from the military, thus indicating their tacit acceptance. Withdrawal from active involvement in "politics" was now the military's own position, and as a result there was

12. A dispute that arose early on concerned suffrage rights for illiterates. The regime favored granting such rights in the constitution, however both APRA and the PPC were reluctant to include such a clause for fear of its benefiting the Left. When it appeared, the Assembly voted the clause down, but the regime issued a decree establishing this right nonetheless (*Marka*, 14 December 1978, 9).

13. For a review of the various interventions of this theme, see the *Diario de los Debates de la Asamblea Constituyente Plenario General*, vols 1–8 (Lima: República Peruana, 1978–1979). With few exceptions, Assembly members expressed the need to include "anti-golpe" mechanisms and clauses asserting the primacy of constitutional rule.

little that the military institution could object to in the articles. But the military's position on these clauses did not mean that it was foregoing control of the transition process.

As the transfer of power in 1980 approached, members of the regime attempted to demonstrate the military's continued control of the transition agenda. Shortly after the Assembly elections, Morales Bermúdez declared that the entire process was a "transfer of government but not of power." That had followed earlier warnings that after the transition, the military would remain "present in POLITICS with capital letters."[14] The message appeared to contradict the non-deliberative clauses of the just-enacted constitution (which did not take effect until after the transfer of power). These ominous statements were meant to assert the military's understanding of the limits of this process, and to indicate their opposition to the Left's maximalist goals. For the military, the transition was to encompass a transfer to civilian rule and not the initiation of a revolutionary project.

Although these statements appeared to be a warning to the Left, by late 1978 there was little to suggest that the military would alter the transition schedule. No public suggestions were ever made by members of the regime hinting at such a possibility, and following the removal of the last hard-liners in mid-1978, there was apparently no inclination within the regime to alter that process.[15]

Popular Protest During the Transition

In contrast to the conservative character of the transition, popular protest during the late 1970s demonstrated a radicalization and mobilization of civil society. Throughout the transition period, Peru was rocked by successive national and regional strikes. There were strikes in key sectors such as mining and among state employees, especially teachers; shantytown dwellers invaded urban lands. As elsewhere in Latin America, the effects of popular protests on the transition process were indirect.

Protests tend to strengthen the cooperation between soft-liners within the military and moderate politicians, by creating a common need to control what seems to be a "popular upsurge" neither anticipated nor wanted. In the end such upsurges tend to be coopted, repressed, or ma-

14. *Cronologia Politica 1978* (Lima: DESCO, 1979), 3234.
15. General Morales Bermúdez emphatically argues that at no point after the 1978 elections was a postponement of the transition schedule considered within the regime. Interview with General Francisco Morales Bermúdez, Lima, 30 June 1988.

nipulated and neutralized (O'Donnell and Schmitter 1986, 53–56). While these solutions resolve the short-term crisis for elites, they may create the sorts of exclusionary norms and structures in the post-transition period that impair the ability of new democracies to expand and consolidate.

In the case of Peru, the combination of economic crisis and regime repression had seriously dampened social protest by the 1980 election. Street protests and strikes declined, and leftist leaders, who had received much of the protest vote in 1978, turned their attention toward forming an alliance among their fractious parties. But the shift from the streets to the ballot boxes did not necessarily mean democratic institutionalization had taken place.

Unlike the APRA-PPC majority, the leftist parties in the Constituent Assembly did not place much importance on writing the constitution and refused to sign it. The position of these parties was that the Assembly was only part of a larger political struggle and should be used to promote the demands of unions and other lower-class groups.[16] Their participation in the elections and the Assembly, according to one UDP document, was meant to "create a leftist current in the country."[17] Leftist Assembly members such as Hugo Blanco and Javier Diez Canseco often took part in street protests and rallies, in order to demonstrate their opposition to the regime and to support protesting groups.

The main goal of the Left was radical social change and not a return to civilian rule. In this, the Peruvian Left during the authoritarianism of the 1970s differed significantly from their counterparts elsewhere in Latin America. For Peru's Left, civilian rule was identified with the conservative governments of the 1940s and 1960s. By contrast it was an authoritarian regime that had introduced the sort of radical reforms the Left had long advocated. The transition to democracy, therefore, was seen as a step backward, away from reform and toward the return of conservative elites.

Participation in the Assembly and opposition to both the regime and the APRA-PPC majority helped forge a growing collaboration between the New Left,[18] velasquistas,[19] and the PCP, groups that had been political

16. See Nieto (1983, 89–90) and Moncloa (1980, 12–24). Also see the report "La Izquierda en la Constituyente," *Marka*, 9 August 1979.

17. *UDP: Balance y Tareas de la Unidad* (Lima: UDP, March 1978), 8.

18. The New Left refers to radical groups that competed with the orthodox Partido Comunista del Perú for control over a variety of unions and social movements.

19. *Velasquista* refers to a follower of General Velasco, and to the idea of a "third way" between capitalism and communism.

competitors during the Velasco period. Discussions to achieve a united
front among these parties were initiated soon after the Assembly began to
function, though until late 1979 these talks were limited to questions of
collaborating in the Assembly and not the possibility of forging a common
electoral front.[20]

The increased collaboration among the leftist parties in the Assembly
was only a reflection of the broader efforts at unity among different lower-
class organizations during this period. The successive national and regional strikes between 1977 and 1978 provided important cooperative experiences among different often antagonistic groups.[21] Labor federations,
campesino federations and new shantytown federations (CCLUB) opened
a dialogue and formed part of the organizing committees for national
strikes. In the labor movement, the CGTP consolidated its position as
Peru's dominant labor federation. The prolonged strike of the teachers
federation (SUTEP) in 1979 was indicative of the degree to which the
situation in the labor movement had changed since the Velasco period.
Unlike the strikes of the early 1970s, which underscored the split between
the New Left and the PCP, the SUTEP strike in 1979 received the support
of all leftist parties and organizations. The strike that began in June lasted
over eighty days and resulted in a series of solidarity strikes by other
unions, street protests, and a hunger strike by leftist Assembly members.[22]

By early 1979, however, the wave of protests and strikes appeared to be
weakening. The seventy-two-hour national strike declared by the CGTP in
mid-January failed to receive the significant adhesion of the two previous
strikes, while the *paro* (strike) declared in mid-July was only partially successful.[23] Similarly, throughout 1979 and early 1980, no major peasant or
regional strikes took place. The apparent difficulties of the protest movement by 1979 reflected a significant change from the pattern of lower-
class protests predominant during the previous years. With these sectors
suffering from the effects of the prolonged economic crisis and the new

20. See *Marka,* 6 June 1979, 19; 12 July 1979, 11; and 22 November 1979, 12.
21. One of the most important regional strikes outside the southern sierra in this period
was the 1978 strike in Chimbote. Begun in solidarity with striking steelworkers, the strike
lasted fifty-two days and involved the local pueblo joven committee, SUTEP, student groups,
and the powerful fishermen's union. The strike caused two deaths as well as dozens of
injuries and detentions. See the pamphlet "Chimbote: 52 Dias de Lucha" (Chimbote: n.p.,
1978); see also "Chimbote: Cronologia de una Huelga," *Marka,* 19 January 1978, 13.
22. *Marka,* 23 August 1979, 12; 13 September 1979, 15.
23. See Tovar (1982, 26). Though the number of strikes actually increased in 1979, they
tended to be shorter and involve fewer workers.

demobilization measures adopted by the regime since 1977, the organizations that had engaged in organizing the protest of these groups in the past found that their task was more difficult. Rising unemployment and greater repression raised the costs of participating in protests. Moreover, with elections less than a year away, all major political actors turned their attention away from the streets and toward the approaching elections.

With Peru's gross national product (GNP) falling sharply in this period, including negative growth rates in 1977 and 1978, the impact on the less-privileged classes was especially dramatic.[24] Wages were reduced by nearly one-half, while the cost of living quintupled between 1973 and 1979 (Tovar 1982, 15). The economic austerity measures initiated by earlier finance ministers in 1977 were continued in 1978–1980 by a new economic team led by Javier Silva Ruete and Manuel Moreyra. Silva Ruete implemented a neoliberal stabilization policy that prioritized an accord with the IMF in return for new funds, reduction of state subsidies, liberalization of import restrictions, and reduction of the balance of payments deficit. Unlike the neoliberal experiments of the Southern Cone, however, there were no major efforts to privatize state companies or reduce the state's economic regulations. By 1979 the policy had achieved most of its objectives, as the economy showed signs of recovery. Peru's GNP grew over 3 percent for the first time in four years, while exports increased over 78 percent from the previous year (Portocarrero 1980, 99). Nonetheless, for the lower-class groups that had borne the brunt of the regime's austerity measures, the cost of that timid recovery had been extremely high.

The prolonged economic crisis clearly raised the costs for the lower class of participating in protests. Organizers of the failed January 1979 national strike attributed the high cost of not working during three days, and the consequent loss of pay amid economic uncertainty, as a key reason for the failure of that effort. Aside from that crisis, however, a series of new regulations and modifications of Velasco-era reforms increased the risks of adhering to protest measures. Already by 1977, the regime had restricted the criteria governing job security and industrial communities, while declaring a new law that allowed for the dismissal of labor leaders involved in the 1977 national strike. That was accompanied by a sharp reduction in the rate of new unions recognized. While the organization of labor had flourished under Velasco, with an average of 295 new unions

---

24. A detailed analysis of this crisis is found in Portocarrero (1980), Schlydowsky and Wicht (1979), and Amat y Léon (1978). Also see the chapter in this volume by Carol Wise.

recognized per year, that effort languished during the Morales Bermúdez period, with an average of only 70 new union recognitions per year, a percentage even lower than under the Belaúnde government of the 1960s (Sulmont 1985, 213). The favorable conditions for labor mobilization opened by the state under Velasco were thus closed by Morales Bermúdez.

The crackdown on lower-class protests was not only restricted to the labor sector. The regime was also severe with the two peasant federations, withdrawing official recognition from the Confederación Nacional Agraria (CNA) and the Confederación Campesina del Perú (CCP). Even the nascent shantytown (pueblo joven) movement did not escape the regime's new demobilization initiatives.

In the late 1970s new national *centrales* were formed with the aim of creating a national movement. In addition to marches and rallies in demand of basic services such as water and electrification for their districts, these organizations played an important role in the national strikes of this period, as a focal point of street confrontations between residents and the security forces.[25]

In mid-1979 the regime issued decrees designed to limit the special role of shantytowns conceded by the Velasco regime. One decree, Decreto Legislativo No. 22612, designated that a pueblo joven lost its status as such once titles of land ownership had been granted, thereafter forming part of the municipal district in which it was located. An additional decree (Decreto Legislativo No. 22250) granted local municipalities greater control over the distribution of services such as water, a control that had been exclusively exercised by the central government up until that point.

The purpose of both decrees was to transfer greater responsibilities over shantytowns to the municipalities in an attempt to reduce the special privileges that designation as a pueblo joven under Velasco had implied. As part of a municipality, demands for services were no longer channeled directly to the Ministry of Housing, but through local district municipalities. The regime thus hoped to decentralize and disperse shantytown mobilization.[26] In a district municipality, a pueblo joven's demands had to compete with other demands, and as a relatively new and poor neighborhood, its demands would normally be at a disadvantage with those of

25. One of the largest marches of the period involved residents of Villa El Salvador. An estimated twenty thousand residents marched on the presidential palace in demand for better services.

26. See "El Gobierno no Quiere mas Pueblos Jóvenes," *Marka*, 2 August 1979, 32. Also see Calderón and Olivera (1979) and Quijano (n.d.).

more established actors. Moreover, the procedures and channels available to shantytowns would vary from district to district, making it more difficult to concentrate demands at a city-wide or national level.

The difficulties revolving around the pueblos jóvenes underscored the larger problem of the transition period, namely the lack of a broad consensus in political and civil society behind the creation of new democratic institutions. Peru's 1977–80 transition to democracy was an elite-controlled process. It represented the withdrawal of an exhausted and divided military from power and the compromise between the military and conservative political groups on basic rules for a new civilian regime. The political order that emerged from the Constituent Assembly reflected the compromise between the military and the APRA-PPC majority, with little input from other political forces in the country. Part of that exclusion, as we have seen, was voluntary. Creating liberal democratic procedures and institutions was not a high priority of most groups on the Left, which defined the political struggle in terms of the need to restore and expand a process of social reforms in the country.

At the same time, the inability of conservative sectors to alter the structural reforms of the Velasco period in the new constitution created a source of dissatisfaction. The transition period was thus characterized by a strong disjunction between political society and the state on one side and civil society on the other. This disjunction would persist throughout the 1980s. While successful as a mechanism to extricate the military from power, the new system created by the Constituent Assembly still preserved a centralized system with strong authoritarian characteristics and left both conservatives and radicals dissatisfied with the new institutional mechanisms.

Democracy with an Asterisk: 1980–1992

The results of the first presidential elections in seventeen years appeared to suggest that very little had changed in the interval. The man who had been elected president in 1963 and overthrown in 1968, Fernando Belaúnde Terry, was returned to power by a wide margin while his party, Acción Popular, which had abstained from the 1978 elections and maintained a low profile during the 1970s, gained control of the new Congress. But rather than reflecting continuity with the pre-1968 status quo, that victory demonstrated the exhaustion of the political actors that had dominated Peruvian politics during the 1970s: the military, APRA, the Left, and the popular movement. Torn by personal and ideological squabbles, each of these actors appeared to offer only more of the same to a populace weary of economic crisis. In this context, Fernando Belaúnde and his campaign slogan of "trabajar y dejar trabajar" (work and let work) appeared as a familiar and reassuring face on the political scene, someone untouched by the political conflicts of the 1970s. Behind the apparent return to pre-1968 "normality" that the election of Belaúnde represented, it quickly became clear that there were significant continuities—of institutions, norms, and policy—between the new civilian regime and its authoritarian predecessor.

The second Belaúnde administration continued to pursue the neoliberal policy agenda of the Morales Bermúdez regime. Regulations on business were relaxed, foreign investments were encouraged, and an effort to privatize state companies was implemented. At the same time, little effort was made to reach out to the popular sectors. The continued weakness of the popular sectors, however, was only partly attributable to state policy. The recessionary period of 1983–85 took an enormous toll particularly on organized labor. Real salaries in the manufacturing sector fell by 14 percent in 1983 and by over 20 percent the following year (Parodi 1986, 23). A continued reliance on primary product exports, along with foreign financing, made the economy vulnerable to international economic cycles and dependent upon international economic actors such as the IMF.

In policy terms, it was not until the administration of Alan García Pérez (1985–90) that a significant break with transition-era policies took place. García's populist economic and social agenda seemed to offer a new policy agenda for a country that had followed the same orthodox prescriptions through a decade of military and civilian rule. Yet whatever hope was held that this policy break would finally extend democratic participation or further institutional consolidation quickly faded in the normative and institutional quagmire of an administration rife with corruption, clientelism, and mismanagement.

The causes of the García administration's failures are complex, but a large share of the blame must be placed upon the leadership and norms that predominated in the government. Decision making within the García government took place in a very personalist context. García, like his predecessor, made decisions in consort with a small group of personal advisers and relied on his personal charisma to mobilize support. Even major decisions, such as the bank nationalization discussed by Durand in this volume, were adopted following this personalist pattern. The near-plebiscitarian reliance on charisma and personal popularity combined with clientelist methods aimed at favoring APRA party members and tended to freeze out opposition opinion and leave little room for compromise.

By the end of the García administration, Peru had entered its most polarized political situation in half a century. García's difficulties were compounded by a series of corruption scandals that affected various cabinet members and members of the APRA party in Congress. The president himself was accused in the media and the courts of having participated in kickback schemes, and ultimately he was forced into exile by his successor.

As mentioned earlier, institutional rules designed during the transition left many social actors increasingly dissatisfied during the 1980s. The new social movements that had emerged in the 1970s continued to use the protest methods developed in that decade; however, as Balbi and Hunefeldt note in their chapters, they were less effective in promoting social change. On the political Right, the ideological shift toward liberalism discussed by Durand created a growing frustration with a constitution that still embodied the "socialist" elements of the Peruvian revolution. García's 1987 bank nationalization furthered the growing alienation of conservatives from Peru's political system.

Moreover, the persistent personalism, clientelism, and corruption during the 1980s testified to a general lack of democratic leadership and norms among the political elite. Institutional rules created during the transition period by political elites were designed to return the country to its pre-1968 "normality," but this normality had little built-in accountability and weak balance of powers.

Part of the problem may be found in the delegation of extensive powers to the executive in the 1979 constitution, including among others the ability of Congress to delegate legislative authority to the president (Article 188) and the vaguely worded power to administer public finances (Article 211). But the extraordinary presidentialism of Peru's democracy in the 1980s goes beyond the presidentialism of the 1979 constitution. As McClintock notes (1994b, 304), presidents from Belaúnde to Fujimori have assumed "the mantle of messiah," embodying the hope for dramatic social and political change that can be easily frustrated. The inability of both leaders and followers to institutionalize executive leadership patterns was thus a serious shortcoming of Peru's 1980–92 democracy. But these problems affected other institutions as well. Three in particular merit noting: parties, the Congress, and the military.

The transition period witnessed a significant change in the party system but little in party structures. In the 1950s and 1960s, Peru's party spectrum was dominated by the Right and center-Right. In the six elections of the 1980s, as Cameron points out in this volume's chapter two, the Left demonstrated unprecedented electoral strength, especially at the municipal level, relying upon solid support from the urban popular sector and the poor departments of the highlands. Though the Left represented the new political forces that had developed under the Velasco regime, its unity was far from solid. Disputes persisted throughout the decade, ending with a final rupture of the coalition Izquierda Unida (IU) in 1989.

The divisions of the Left were symptomatic of the problems facing all of the parties. By and large the parties remained highly personalist, fragmented, and authoritarian structures. Party leaders, including many from the Left, were generally from the *criollo* elites in Lima. In this respect, the parties were virtually unchanged from what they had been in the pre-1968 period. Each was dominated by a party boss—in the case of AP and the PPC by their founders, and in the case of the Left and APRA by cadres who had risen through the ranks in the 1970s. There was little if any turnover at the upper levels of the parties during the 1980s, and there were few democratic mechanisms, such as internal elections, to challenge leadership positions. Leadership cabals (or *cúpula*) exercised strong authoritarian control over policy and organization.

Nonetheless, this authoritarian control did not translate into cohesion. Each of the four political forces that seriously competed in elections in the 1980s (APRA, IU, PPC, AP) went through wrenching periods of divisions and factionalizations. These divisions and internal conflicts should be seen as a logical outcome of the lack of institutionalized channels of renewal. Without such channels, internal challengers had little recourse other than to provoke an organizational split.

Dissidence from the party line was generally treated as betrayal, and dissidents were either forced out or left of their own accord to found their own party, as Andrés Townsend did in the aftermath of the 1982 APRA Congress that gave the party leadership to the young Alan García. Much of the division that took place in the United Left after 1988 resulted from frictions between former Lima mayor Alfonso Barrantes and the leader of the radical Partido Unificado Mariateguista (PUM), Javier Diez Canseco. While serious tactical and ideological issues also divided these men, including the relation with the APRA government and the need for confrontational strategies, the divisions were worsened by the well-known antipathy between the two leaders.

A second institution that was often accused of not meeting democratic expectations was the legislature. Although a strong Constituent Assembly that had defined for itself an important political space, albeit for traditional parties, seemed to be a precedent for a strong legislative branch in the new civilian regime, it soon became apparent that the Congress would be a secondary institution. Part of the problem, as mentioned above, was the extraordinary presidentialism of the 1979 constitution. Both Belaúnde and García used their overwhelming party control of the legislature to acquire legislative powers, while Fujimori, who lacked majority control, built a coalition with Right-wing parties until forcibly shutting down the Congress in April 1992.

Although a number of important congressional investigations, particularly in the areas of human rights and corruption, did take place during the 1980s, legislative supervision was severely hampered by a lack of resources and information. For example, congressional committees largely depended upon the executive to provide critical budget information, insofar as the Congress had no independent authority and little technocratic support staff to acquire such information. Some information was restricted on national-security grounds. During most of the 1980s, this included information regarding arms purchases, intelligence, defense expenditures, and foreign-military assistance.

One of the key institutional tests of a newly consolidating democracy is its ability to assert authority over the military institution. Peru's transition, however, did little to increase civilian prerogatives vis-à-vis the military. While the new constitution included mechanisms to delegitimize a de facto military regime, it left untouched a series of military prerogatives in areas such as the budget, arms acquisitions, and ascensions. Efforts to reverse this situation occurred gradually during the 1980s, most notably when the García administration created a unified Ministry of Defense and reformed the police force in 1986. That effort, along with others during the following years, met with significant resistance from the armed forces.

As we have seen, the military's ability to retain for itself the primary role in decisions affecting its corporate interests was in part the result of the negotiated understanding reached between the Morales Bermúdez regime and the APRA-PPC majority in the Constituent Assembly. But it was also the result of an unwillingness by the newly elected government of

Fernando Belaúnde to capitalize on the anti-military feeling during the election period to challenge military prerogatives. Instead, the new regime made it clear, by retaining in place all high-ranking officials even after the formal hand-over of power, that there would be no challenges to military authority.

This situation of military autonomy from civilian authority was worsened considerably after 1982, when the Belaúnde administration declared states of emergency in five provinces of Ayacucho to deal with the emerging insurgency of Sendero Luminoso (the Shining Path). Using vague constitutional language, Belaúnde ceded all governing authority in emergency zones to the military. As the war against Sendero Luminoso expanded, so did the number of provinces governed by the military. By the late 1980s, nearly 60 percent of the country's territory was under a state of emergency. The practical effects of this extensive military control, pointed out by Roberts and Peceny in their chapter of this volume, were the suspension of most civil liberties and one of the worst human-rights records in the hemisphere. Operating with little accountability, Peru's armed forces acted with impunity.

Conclusions

Transitions to democracy tend to be conservative. When transitions are elite-driven, top-down processes, they often reflect the interests of powerful groups in society who seek to protect their interest and carefully circumscribe the limits of political participation. Many of the transitions to democracy in Latin America in the 1980s can be described in this way. However, most Latin American countries that experienced a transition to democracy in the late 1970s and early 1980s had highly repressive conservative governments. By contrast, during most of the military regime in Peru, rulers sought to undertake a radical transformation of the state and society.

The different authoritarian experience in Peru inevitably had an important impact on the nature and goals of the Peruvian transition to democracy. Strong tensions existed between the military's intent to quickly extricate itself from governance, the traditional political elite's desire to restrict participation in the transition by new social actors and reassert its pre-1968 dominance in political society, and the popular sectors' wish to assert a new role in society and politics.

The transition represented a compromise that left many unsatisfied: business and economic elites disliked the inability to revise the economic reforms in the 1979 constitution, while popular sectors felt that the new institutions of democracy that emerged from the Constituent Assembly did not fully represent their interests. Not coincidentally, both of these sectors overwhelmingly supported Fujimori's overthrow of constitutional democracy.

The transition to democracy largely provided a framework for the military to extricate itself from power rather than providing a strong institutional framework for a new democratic order. As in most recent transitions to civilian rule in Latin America, the initiative for the transition began within the military regime as a result of the exhaustion of its political project and was sustained through a series of negotiations with conservative political forces interested in shaping a post-authoritarian political system. Having been divided by the experience of governance, the armed forces had no interest in revisiting the theme of social reform, thus insisting on a constitution that incorporated military reforms.[27]

Yet far from being inclusive, the transition remained an elite-oriented process revolving around the negotiations and understandings reached by the APRA-PPC majority in the Assembly and the military. The Left and much of the popular movement that emerged in the 1970s, in part through its own choice and in part through restrictions on its access to power, opted to press for radical social change through protests, demonstrations, and strikes rather than to focus on the design of civilian institutions. One result of this restricted transition was an undervaluation of institutional democracy by many sectors. One can argue that the view of electoral politics and new institutions as only one (and probably not the most important) "arena" of politics seriously undermined its legitimacy and would set the stage for the high levels of social conflict that would prevail in the 1980s and early 1990s.

Beyond the narrow goals and consensus surrounding the transition process itself, I have argued that the transition did little to reform authoritarian practices and institutions. The common perception among political elites that the election of Belaúnde in 1980 represented a return to nor-

---

27. See Philip Mauceri, *State Under Siege: Development and Policy Making in Peru* (Boulder, Colo.: Westview Press, 1996).

malcy, along with the predominance of conservative forces during the transition and during the Belaúnde government, led to few serious efforts to reform political institutions. The continued reliance on clientelist practices and the lack of elite circulation within political parties failed to take into account the emergence of newly mobilized sectors. Similarly, the persistence of a salient political role for the military and minimal congressional authority vis-à-vis the executive were strong authoritarian characteristics that carried over into the new civilian regime. Given the decade-long inability to increase both the efficiency and representation of these institutions, it is little wonder that Fujimori's attacks on the Congress and the judicial system before the autogolpe of 1992 were applauded by the majority of the population.

Peru's transition put into place a weak institutional structure for the consolidation of democracy. The marvel perhaps is not that that structure would be easily swept away twelve years later, but that it lasted as long as it did. Many authors have pointed out the division that has existed between the Peru "real" and the Peru "oficial" as a way to explain the paradox of Peru in the 1980s, where a functioning constitutional regime coexisted with a daily violation of human rights. The reality of people's daily lives, where police corruption, torture, clientelism, and abuse of power were common, strongly argues that during the 1980s, democracy in Peru, as elsewhere in Latin America, was a limited affair. Those limitations started with the transition.

2

POLITICAL AND ECONOMIC ORIGINS OF REGIME CHANGE IN PERU

THE *EIGHTEENTH BRUMAIRE* OF ALBERTO FUJIMORI

Maxwell A. Cameron

The crisis of the formal economy and the breakdown of the traditional party system were two sides of the same coin. It is impossible to understand the fragmentation of the political parties and coalitions of the Left and Right in Peru without understanding the growth of the informal economy.[1] The instability of class coalitions, in turn, undermined the political consensus around democratic institutions. This chapter examines the interplay between political and economic factors that contributed to the breakdown of democracy in Peru.

The severe economic crisis in the late 1980s, partially but dramatically manifested in the spectacular growth of the informal sector, undermined

A version of this chapter was presented at the annual New England Council for Latin American Studies (NECLAS) meeting, Boston University, 24 October 1992, and it also draws upon arguments developed in Cameron (1994). Talks based on the chapter were given at Carleton University, the University of California at Berkeley, Columbia University, and York University. I am grateful to Henry Dietz, Philip Mauceri, Carmen Rosa Balbi, Julio Cotler, Fernando Rospigliosi, Fernando Tuesta, Alberto Adrianzén, David and Ruth Collier, Charlie Kenney, Shane Hunt, Liisa North, Maureen A. Molot, Arch Ritter, and Michele Dupont, as well as anonymous reviewers of the Penn State Press, for comments and suggestions on this paper and on the topic of autogolpes. I am especially grateful to Cynthia McClintock for correspondence that helped sharpen my analysis of legislative-executive relations. Larisa Galadza provided expert editorial assistance. Initial field work in Peru during July and August 1992 was partially supported by a research grant from the Social Sciences and Humanities Research Council of Canada. Follow-up research in Peru during July and August 1995 was generously supported by Carleton University. Interviews were conducted with senior government officials, members of the armed forces, legislators, and leaders of the opposition political parties. I am grateful for their insights and have preserved their anonymity. The author is solely responsible for the content of this chapter.

1. For an excellent collection of essays on the informal sector, see Rakowski (1994).

political forces based on class coalitions forged in the period of economic expansion in the 1970s. This chapter will show how the inability of Left- and Right-wing parties to adapt to a changing electorate, and the failure of centrist parties in government to stabilize the economy and guarantee public security, created the conditions in which society would coalesce around political outsiders without ties to the traditional party system nor attachments to democratic values and institutions.

From the ashes of the Peruvian party system arose Alberto Fujimori, a self-professed political outsider, who presented himself as a moderate, independent candidate. By occupying the center of the political spectrum, Fujimori was able to win enough support to place in a runoff election against front-runner Mario Vargas Llosa's alliance of Right-wing parties (the Democratic Front or FREDEMO) and then capture the presidency in a second round of voting. However, his political base remained unorganized and unstable, and his improvised party, Cambio 90, lacked a majority in Congress. To those who believed his social base was ephemeral and fickle, it seemed likely that Fujimori would be a weak and vacillating president (Cameron 1994, 138–9).

Fujimori surprised even his own followers with an authoritarian—some said paranoid—style of rule (Gorriti 1994, 12). Cambio 90 had served as a useful political vehicle during the election campaign, and it brought prominent small entrepreneurs into the legislature. But Fujimori did not take his own movement seriously after he was elected (his first cabinet included no members from Cambio 90), nor did he cooperate with the legislature. Instead, Fujimori forged a close alliance with the armed forces, particularly the National Intelligence Service (Servicio de Inteligencia Nacional, or SIN), which he placed under the implicit control of Vladimiro Montesinos (Gorriti 1994, 11–12, 54). During the election Montesinos had boosted Fujimori's campaign by providing polls done by the SIN; he also offered legal advice to the candidate after he was charged with fraudulent real-estate dealings (Burt 1992, 4). Fujimori showed little interest in the legislative process, preferring instead to rely on the willingness of the legislature to allow him to rule by decree. When the legislature began to assert its prerogatives and challenge Fujimori's style of rule by decree, it was closed. Fujimori installed himself, like Louis Napoleon Bonaparte in nineteenth-century France or Oliver Cromwell in seventeenth-century England, as the "savior" of the nation.[2]

---

2. Oliver Cromwell's expulsion of the Rump Parliament in 1652 raised many of the same

Fujimori's spectacular ascent to power was made even more astonishing by the apparent breadth of support for the autogolpe he implemented on 5 April 1992.[3] To explain this, we need to understand why the democratic institutions that were created in the transition from authoritarian rule in the 1970s failed to sustain a consensus around the political rules of the game. The interplay between democracy and changing state-society relations is examined in detail in the chapter by Mauceri in this volume. This chapter focuses more specifically on the political and economic origins of the 1992 autogolpe.

A conceptual map of the chapter, as well as a framework for analysis, is provided by Figure 2.1. The first part of the chapter traces the impact of economic decline and the growth of the informal sector on political parties, showing how the collapse of the party system and the rise of an outsider candidate were facilitated by electoral rules. The second part of the chapter examines factors hypothesized to have contributed to the autogolpe, including the military's perception of threat and the rise of the SIN in response to the Shining Path, opposition to neoliberal reforms led by Alan García, and tensions between the legislature and executive. The final part examines the impact of domestic and international responses on the evolution of the Peruvian political system.

Marx's analysis of Bonapartism provides an appropriate point of departure for this analysis.[4] Marx argued that in certain historical periods when the ruling class in a capitalist society is unable to maintain its dominance through parliamentary or constitutional means, and at the same time the working class is unable to assert its hegemony, it is possible for the state, under the leadership of a dictator, to play a relatively autonomous role (Miliband 1991, 55–56).[5] The purpose of Figure 2.1 is to identify linkages between the effects of a prolonged economic crisis on the nature of class relations and the party system, and the political dynamics—the changing

---

issues as the Peruvian autogolpe: the growing power of the military, corruption, the prerogatives of the legislature and its ability to implement reforms. The literature on Cromwell is vast. For excellent recent sources, see Coward (1991) and Gregg (1988).

3. An autogolpe may defined as "a temporary suspension of constitutional guarantees and closure of Congress by the executive, which rules by decree and uses referenda and new legislative elections to ratify a regime with broader executive powers" (Cameron 1994, 146).

4. For a similar analysis of Boris Yeltsin's crackdown on parliament—which was modeled after the Peruvian autogolpe (Cameron 1994, 164). See Moses (1994).

5. This inspired subsequent work on the "relative autonomy" of the state (Poulantzas 1974).

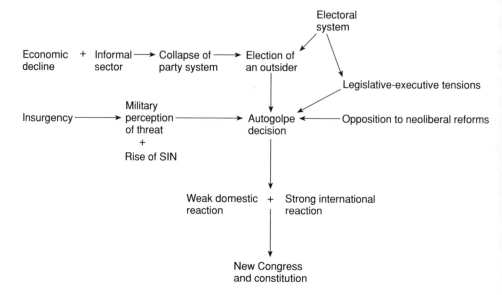

Fig. 2.1. Anatomy of an autogolpe: Peru, 1992

role of the military, the struggle between executive and legislature, and opposition to neoliberal reforms—that created the circumstances in which Fujimori could play a putative "hero's part."[6]

Changes in the Class Structure and the Party System*

Recent studies of voting in Peru have demonstrated the importance of the class cleavage, whether measured by occupation or income, as a determinant of voting for the Left and the Right in elections (Cameron 1994; Tuesta 1994; Roncagliolo 1990, 1980; Dietz 1986–87, 1985; Powell 1976). The Left tended to draw its support from manual workers in the formal sector and also from the informal sector—in other words, from lower-income groups.[7] The Right drew support mostly from white-collar em-

*Parts of this section draw upon Cameron (1994, chap. 6).

6. This expression is used by Marx (1963 [1869], 8).

7. A popular chicha (a blend of Andean and rock music) song, "Ambulante Soy," by Los

ployees, professionals, and business—in other words, from upper-income groups (Cameron 1994; Tueros 1984).

Throughout much of the 1980s Peru had a three-party system with a strong center and two extremist tendencies. Parties that won presidential elections tended to be located at the center or center-Left. At the same time there was a noticeable zigzagging of the electorate, largely due to the failure of successive approaches to stabilization and economic management as well as to the climate of violence and insecurity.

By 1990 the traditional parties of the center (APRA and AP) had been discredited with the electorate. The parties of the Left and Right remained at the extremes and were contaminated by the failure of their allies in government. The dismal experience with radical populism under Alan García lead to a decline in support for the Left. Thus, the Right and Left remained trapped and isolated in ideological ghettos far from the average voter. The center was dangerously vacant, inviting new entrants into the party system. The emergence of an "independent" electorate without partisan loyalties at the center of the political spectrum created uncertainty and instability in the party system.

The volatility of the electorate was due to a number of factors, including the growth of the informal sector and the crisis of the formal economy. Two recessions in the 1980s—a 12.3 percent contraction of gross domestic product (GDP) in 1982–83, then contractions of 8.4, 11.4 and 4.9 percent in 1988–90 (CEPAL 1991, 39)—led to a massive fall in real wages, which reached about half their 1980 value by 1989. Labor's share of national income declined from 37.7 percent in 1980 to 28.8 percent in 1989, while returns to capital rose in the same period from 38.1 to 42.5 percent. A 1989 Ministry of Labor report indicated that 81.2 percent of the workforce in Lima was "underemployed." Roughly 1.5 million could not find full-time work at the minimum wage. "Severe unemployment" (defined as earning below one-third of the minimum wage) afflicted 20 percent of the public sector, 29 percent of the private sector, and 44 percent of the informal sector. Underemployment in 1989 had reached a level "never before observed" (Chávez O'Brien 1990, 59).

As Balbi notes in her chapter in this volume, the effect of the crisis of the formal economy, coupled with the expansion of informal economic

---

Shapis, contains the refrain, "ambulante soy, proletario soy" (I'm a street hawker, I'm a proletarian). In popular culture, the distinction between being a worker in the formal and in the informal economy is apparently insignificant.

activity, was to undermine the basis for collectively organized protest. Collective action and protest was replaced by individual survival strategies, including migration, drug trafficking, crime, and tax evasion. The identity of members of the informal sector, or *informales,* is not captured well by static categories like *workers* or *employers,* terms that imply stable social relations of production. Although they are self-employed, they rarely consider themselves part of the private sector and operate within a complex network of social relations, unstable identities, and shifting alliances. In short, the informalization of the economy undermined partisan loyalties, broke the tenuous linkages between parties and civil society, interrupted traditional channels of communication between ruling elites and masses, and weakened the class cleavage by reducing the militancy of workers, undermining organization, and inhibiting collective action.

For Peru's established political parties, electoral volatility posed the challenge of adapting to voters' evolving preferences. Left and Right-wing parties failed to recognize that most voters were moving to the center of the political spectrum and away from the extremist positions of the late 1970s and early 1980s. The growth of a floating or independent electorate meant that parties had to be more agile in response to the preferences and perceptions of the electorate or become obsolete.

Parties of the Left and Right were too deeply entrenched in ideological positions, and too burdened by reputations for extremism, to be able to capitalize on the growing disenchantment with existing political options. Lacking internal democracy, Peru's traditional parties ran the same candidates in election after election. The attraction of independent candidates was that they represented a break with the established political dynasties: as one street vendor told Javier Diez Canseco, she supported Fujimori because "he hasn't done anything yet" (Guillermoprieto 1994, 81).

In short, Peru's parties failed to play a stabilizing role in the 1990 election. The roots of the subsequent breakdown of democracy can be traced to the failure of the parties to adapt and respond to the electorate's changing identities and shifting preferences. Unsuccessful strategies and errors of judgement made by the oligarchies controlling the major parties—errors rooted in dynamics internal to the parties themselves—played a key role in this failure.

The Right: Old Wine in a New Bottle

Vargas Llosa's campaign operated on a naive premise: FREDEMO (the loose alliance of conservative parties and movements that formed around his candidacy) could win support from those individuals whose interests were served by the policies offered, despite the class and ethnic differences dividing the candidate and his slate from the electorate. Emphasizing the need for a new kind of capitalism that would break the power of rent-seeking oligarchies and create more competitive capitalism, Vargas Llosa anticipated that electoral support would result from the prospect of opportunities such policies would create for the informal sector. The fact that few members of the campaign team had worked in the informal economy, let alone came from working-class or mestizo extraction, was not considered a problem.

Vargas Llosa hoped to capitalize on his image as an independent, while constructing an alliance that included the traditional Right-wing parties. However, infighting dominated the attention of FREDEMO's leader from the outset, creating the impression that Peru's old politicians were carving up the spoils of the proverbial patronage pie even before the campaign had begun. The FREDEMO list read like a who's who of the Peruvian political establishment. Only conspicuous ties to the drug trade prevented one former minister from elbowing his way onto the list.

By failing to position himself near the majority of the electorate, Vargas Llosa created an opportunity for a new competitor to enter the political marketplace. Low barriers to entry were also due to electoral rules that encouraged minor candidates. Peru had an open-list system with runoffs. In such a system, if no candidate wins an absolute majority of the vote, a second round of balloting is held to determine the winner in a runoff contest. Under such rules, it was relatively easy to construct an "anybody but Vargas Llosa" campaign; all that was required was a popular candidate to place second as long as Vargas Llosa failed to win over 50 percent in the first round.

Vargas Llosa repeatedly appealed to the electorate for a first-round victory. This was taken by many Peruvian voters as a sign of hubris, but it was the only way he could win against a more centrist alternative candidate, given how far he had positioned himself from the majority of the electorate. Even so, he might well have beaten Alfonso Barrantes, candidate of the United Left (or Izquierda Unida), in a second round, a prospect for which FREDEMO was thoroughly prepared.

What Vargas Llosa and his team did not (and perhaps could not) anticipate was the possibility that an unknown candidate would emerge with sufficient strength to place in the runoff. Since FREDEMO was an elite organization without a presence in the grass roots of Lima's shantytowns and the provinces, the candidate was unaware of the potential popularity of Fujimori. Fujimori's candidacy spread by word of mouth in a wildfire campaign that was fueled by evangelical churches and informal-sector organizations. Crippled by their inability to comprehend the so-called Fujimori phenomenon, and without reliable information on their opponent, the FREDEMO team was at a loss to respond to his electoral insurgency.

The Left: Reform or Revolution?

The Izquierda Unida had much to win by moderating its image and appealing to centrist voters. By shifting toward the center, it might have substantially increased its electoral support. Moreover, this should have been apparent from the decline of leftist voting in the 1989 municipal elections and the overwhelming success of García in the mid-1980s. Barrantes, perhaps the shrewdest of the Left's strategists, was aware of the electoral opportunity facing the Left, but he encountered stiff resistance from moderates within the Left for his high-handed and *caudillo* style of leadership (the term *caudillo* refers to personalist and dictatorial rule; see Hamill 1992). Radicals thought Barrantes was already too much like García and too interested in winning a seat in the Palace of Government.

The basic problem for the Left was that it failed to build a team. One faction had no serious interest in winning the 1990 election, and it cared less about garnering electoral support from groups like the informal sector than building a popular front for revolutionary change. That faction looked upon Barrantes's desire to win the presidency as a bourgeois fetish. More moderate factions of the Left liked Barrantes's candidacy but were unwilling to accept his leadership unconditionally. Unable to build a consensus around his leadership within the Left, Barrantes opted to compete against the rest of the Left and run independently.

Electoral rules encouraged the division of the Left by fostering rank rather than vote maximization. Candidates realized that it was possible to win less than a plurality of the vote in the first round and then win the election in a second round. Barrantes hoped to run a successful bid for second place in the first round and then unite a broad coalition against Vargas Llosa in the second round. Vargas Llosa's apparent lack of growth potential between first and second rounds encouraged this strategy. Barrantes, on the other hand, had considerable appeal among centrist voters, particularly the informal sector.

The expected contest between Vargas Llosa and Barrantes never occurred. Although Barrantes was perceived to be more moderate than the revolutionary faction, his role in the internecine conflicts with the Left tarnished his image. More important, the division of the Left reinforced the impression that a vote for one of the two leading candidates was a lost vote. Toward the end of the race, polls showed Barrantes's popularity slipping below that of Luis Alva Castro, the candidate of APRA. The runoff system encouraged voters to think strategically and support the candidate most likely to rank second. However, as Barrantes's popularity declined, and the prospect of a runoff between Vargas Llosa and Alva Castro grew, voters began to cast around for alternatives (Schmidt 1996, 328–30).

In short, the Left was less constrained than the Right by the tradeoff between cores supporters and the appeal to centrist voters: a shift to the center would have improved its electoral performance. However, it failed to play a stabilizing role in the party system because of internal factionalism and disunity. The changes in Peruvian society during the 1980s were not reflected in the internal politics of the Left. Orthodox factions remained wedded to the view that the core supporters of their coalition should be organized workers and peasants.

Collapse of the Center and the Rise of Independents

The weakness of the center is crucial to understanding the instability of the Peruvian party system. Timothy R. Scully has convincingly argued that the stability of polarized multiparty systems crucially depends upon the nature and role of center parties (1992, 6–11). The failure of centrist governments (under presidents Belaúnde, 1980–85, and García, 1985–90) to manage the economy and implement a coherent counterinsurgency strategy is well documented in this volume (see chapters by Mauceri, Wise, Roberts and Peceny in particular). Competition for centrist votes would have stabilized the party system, but internal factions within parties discouraged centripetal competition.

Independent candidates managed to emerge because the party system no longer reflected the preferences of the electoral majority. Consider the case of Ricardo Belmont, whose election as mayor of Lima in 1989 marked the appearance of "independent" candidates and presaged the success of Fujimori. Although a prosperous entrepreneur, Belmont was a politician with a common touch who presented himself as an average person's candidate. Belmont's name recognition came not from prior connections with the political establishment, but from his control of a television channel and his role as host of a popular talk show, *Habla el Pueblo*

(The People Speak), as well as of an annual charity telethon. Like most voters, he was hard to define on the Left-Right political spectrum and his movement Obras (Works) focused on ostensibly non-political themes like the need for more public works around Lima.

In the 1989 municipal election, Belmont won 44 percent of the vote across Lima. In most districts, his margin of victory was over 15 percent. FREDEMO only won a plurality of the vote in its traditional aristocratic strongholds, like Miraflores and San Isidro, where it won 56 and 64 percent of the vote respectively. Avoiding polarization and class conflict, Belmont was able to draw support from across social classes and sectors. Occupying the center, he assured himself a plurality of the vote in the shantytowns, without antagonizing the middle class. Belmont built his victory on the same multi-class electoral coalition that supported García's APRA.

Table 2.1 graphically illustrates the growing electoral importance of independent candidates among voters in metropolitan Lima. The phenomenon of independent candidates began with Belmont's victory in 1989. A third of the electorate shifted from established parties in the first round of the 1990 presidential race. That number rose to 50 percent with the disqualification of APRA and the Left. In subsequent elections, even when the Left and APRA competed, the share of the vote going to independent candidates rose as high as 73 percent in the case of the 1993 municipal contest (see data in Table 2.1). The inability of ideological political parties to adjust to changing electoral preferences, and the failure of centrist parties in government to stabilize the economy and provide public security, created an "entry opportunity" for renegade politicians outside the traditional party system. Alberto Fujimori was able to put together a loosely knit movement (called Cambio 90) with backing from small and informal entrepreneurs, protestant evangelicals, and an entourage from the Agrarian University where he was rector. Polls showed that the characteristic that most endeared Fujimori to the electorate was his avoidance of any public affiliation with traditional political parties or politicians.[8] Like Belmont, Fujimori avoided politicized rhetoric. His slogan called for "honesty, technology, and work." He recognized the importance of the informal sector and was influenced by the work of Hernando de Soto (Salcedo 1990, 18), who later became his adviser. Fujimori also knew that informal-sector support could be enough to propel him into a second-

8. *Caretas*, 2 April 1990.

Table 2.1. Voting results from metropolitan Lima 1978–1993

	Left	APRA	AP	Right	Independent
1978[1]	35	25	—	31	—
1980[2]	13	21	46	15	—
1980[3]	29	16	35	20	—
1983[3]	37	15	12	23	—
1985[2]	23	50	4	21	—
1986[3]	33	37	—	29	—
1989[3]	13	11	—	29	44
1990[2]	10	13	—	43	33
1990[4]	—	—	—	50	50
1992[2]	5	—	—	21	52
1993[3]	6	3	9	4	73

N = 25 districts
[1]   Constituent Assembly
[2]   Presidential
[3]   Municipal
[4]   Presidential run off
SOURCE: Calculated from data in Cameron (1994).

round election if the traditional political parties remained locked in polarized competition.[9] The most important coalition partner Fujimori sought was Maximo San Roman, president of Peru's most important association of small and medium-size businesses (Asociación de Pequeña y Mediana Industrias del Peru, APEMIPE).

After the first-round election, Vargas Llosa offered to forge a congressional alliance between Cambio 90 and his coalition, FREDEMO. Such a pact would have given Fujimori a strong congressional majority; indeed, Fujimori would occupy the presidency. Sensing the mood of hostility toward pacts with traditional political groups, Fujimori rejected the alliance and forced a runoff election. Instead, he exploited his superior programmatic mobility. Shifting sharply to the Left in an effort to win votes from APRA and the Left in the second round, Fujimori won a massive 62 percent of the vote to Vargas Llosa's 38 percent. The final result was only 2 percent below the total votes to Fujimori, APRA, and the Left in the first round (Tuesta 1994, 149).

Given Fujimori's unusual political trajectory, it was not surprising that once in power he was unwilling to play by the established democratic

9. As Jochamowitz (1993, 216) notes, Fujimori lost his 1977 bid to be rector of the Agrarian University in a runoff election!

rules of the game. Having never held elected office, he owed nothing to the country's political institutions; as a renegade, or political outsider, he was not constrained by campaign promises—indeed, he had not prepared a written program for government in advance of the election. Yet precisely these attributes were among the reasons for Fujimori's popularity. Voters hoped he would assemble a nonpartisan team of leading technocrats to form a cabinet that would be unconstrained by the need to make compromises and grant favors to special interests. They were rewarded, however, with a president over whom they had very little control. Peru between 1990 and April 1992 became a paradigmatic example of a "delegative democracy."

Guillermo O'Donnell coined the term *delegative democracies* (1992b, 6–7) for a type of democracy grounded on the premise:

> He (or eventually she, i.e., Indira Gandhi, Corazón Aquino and, to some extent, Isabel Perón) who wins a presidential election is enabled to govern the country as he sees fit, and to the extent that the power relations allow, for the term to which he has been elected. The President is the embodiment of the nation and the main custodian of the national interest, which it is incumbent upon him to define. What he does in government does not need to bear any resemblance to what he said or promised during the electoral campaign—he has been authorized to govern as he sees fit. Since this paternal figure has to take care of the whole nation, it is almost obvious that his support cannot come from a party; his political basis has to be a *movement*, the supposedly vibrant overcoming of the factionalism and conflicts that parties bring about.

Thus, Fujimori promised not to impose economic shock measures, but once in power he implemented the harshest stabilization program ever adopted in Latin America. So deep was the yearning for political authority and economic stability that even in spite of such measures, Fujimori's popularity remained stable. It was as if the electorate desired a protector or popular monarch, a twentieth-century Simón Bolívar, who would stand above the political system and establish good government and strong laws.[10]

O'Donnell (1992b, 7) notes that Congress and the judiciary are viewed

---

10. On the authoritarian legacy of General José San Martín ("the Protector"), the fusion of monarchism and democracy in the Bolívarian constitution, and the autogolpes and regimes of exception in the nineteenth century, see Loveman (1993, 209–18).

by presidents in delegative democracies as "nuisances that come attached to the domestic and international advantages of being a democratically elected President. The idea of accountability to those institutions, or to other private or semi-private organizations, appears as an unnecessary impediment to the full authority that the President has been delegated to exercise."

Fujimori saw Congress as worse than a nuisance. He had won only a handful of seats in the Senate and the House of Deputies. The perversity of this result, and its profoundly destabilizing consequences for democracy, should not be underestimated.

Peruvians voted for senators and deputies at a moment in the electoral process in which it was impossible to anticipate the outcome of the presidential race. Thus, they were unable to vote to give their president a mandate in Congress by electing as many representatives as possible from his slate. Fujimori was the first choice of only 25 percent of the electorate; 22 percent elected senators, and 17 percent elected deputies, from his list (Tuesta 1994, 155–56). In the second round, Fujimori won a commanding 62 percent of the popular vote (Tuesta 1994, 149), but by then the congressional results had already been determined. Thus, Peru had a president who could count only on 14 out of 62 senators and 32 out of 180 deputies. The losers of the presidential race had more congressional representation: APRA had 17 senators and 53 deputies; FREDEMO had 21 senators and 62 deputies (Tuesta 1994, 65–66, 68). One can only speculate about how Peruvians might have voted in the congressional competition had they known Fujimori would be their president after the second round, but it is likely that Fujimori would have received more support for his slate insofar as voters wished to provide their president with a governing majority.

Electoral rules (the majority runoff system), combined with the failure of established parties to occupy the political center, created a situation in which an independent won the presidency while controlling less than a quarter of the seats in the Senate and less than a fifth of the seats in the House of Deputies—an unprecedented situation in Peru's fledgling democracy and a potential time bomb in legislative-executive relations. Neither García nor Belaúnde had held executive power with so little control over the legislature. In the 1985–90 Congress, García controlled half the Senate and 105 deputies. Belaúnde, in 1980–85, had 98 seats in the House of Deputies and 26 Senate seats. His coalition with the PPC gave him 10 more seats in the House and six in the Senate. Moreover, Cambio

90 was little more than a loose coalition with neither a program nor an organizational structure, composed of members with no previous legislative experience.

Anatomy of an Autogolpe: Threat Perception, Institutional Gridlock, and Opposition to Neoliberal Reforms

The president announced his autogolpe on the evening of 5 April 1992. The announcement was followed by a statement of support from the joint command of the armed forces. Soldiers parked tanks outside the Palace of Justice and the Congress to enforce the suspension of the legislature and courts, and key legislators were placed under house arrest. On 6 April the government issued a decree (Decreto Legislativo No. 25418) outlining the objectives of the newly established Government of Emergency and National Reconstruction. Under the law, the country was to be ruled by the executive through decrees issued by the president and approved by the Council of Ministers. Using as a pretext for the autogolpe the argument that judges could be bought for five thousand or ten thousand dollars, Fujimori implemented a large-scale purge of Superior Court judges, prosecutors, civil, criminal, and family court judges, and provincial magistrates in an ostensible effort to clean up the judiciary.

Having built his career by attacking major institutions in Peruvian society—political parties and politicians, the bureaucracy, the courts, even the Catholic church—Fujimori's autogolpe was consistent with his anti-political style. Indeed, in the months prior to the autogolpe, opinion polls showed rising support for Fujimori as he assailed the Congress and proposed the need for a major restructuring of the country's institutions (Conaghan 1995, 323). The same polls suggested over 70 percent approval for the emergency measures.

Anecdotal evidence suggested that support for the coup did exist in many sectors. Fujimori was able to walk through the streets of downtown Lima and was greeted enthusiastically by crowds. Business leaders endorsed Fujimori's measures, and those who did not found themselves ridiculed and isolated. People interviewed on the streets argued that Peru needed stronger government to deal with the chaos, insecurity, and corruption that had become a part of daily life in Peru. The breach between the political system and the masses could not have been clearer, nor the public contempt for political parties more palpable. "It's fine with me," said one worker, "they were people who eat while lying on their backs" (*gente que come echado*). How had President Fujimori been able to challenge the power and prestige of all the political parties in the country with the substantial support of the armed forces, business, and a majority of the population? The answer to this requires a discussion of civil-military relations, tensions between Congress and the executive, and political opposition between 1990 and 1992.

The Military in Politics

It has been convincingly argued that the preparations for the autogolpe began as soon as the second round of voting had been completed, in June 1990 (Rospigliosi 1996; Gorriti 1994). A secret Plan de Gobierno (or Government Program, known as the Plan Verde) had been prepared by a clandestine working group within the armed forces prior to the 1990 election (*Oiga*, 12 July 1993, 21–35). The plan outlined a strategy for a military government—including a "guided democracy" and "market economy"—that bore striking resemblance to the initial goals of the 1992 autogolpe.

Attached to the Plan Verde, which had been completed in October 1989, were intelligence forecasts for the period between February and June of 1990, outlining a variety of possible "scenarios" for the implementation of the military coup. One involved negotiating an accord with Fujimori to create a civil-military governing coalition. This negotiation presumably occurred in the period between the election on 8 April and the inauguration of the new president on 28 July 1990, during which time Fujimori was sequestered in military headquarters. Military sources believe that the original authors of the Plan Verde were military officers loyal to the institution, however the plan is assumed to have subsequently fallen into the hands of Vladimiro Montesinos, who showed it to Fujimori.[11]

Fujimori relied on Montesinos and the SIN to co-opt and control the armed forces. He accepted the need to act decisively to counter threats to national security. As Enrique Obando notes (1994, 113), Fujimori's was the first government since the conflict with the Shining Path had begun to design a national counterinsurgency strategy and provide the armed

---

11. This assertion is based on two interviews with senior members of the armed forces who spoke on condition of anonymity. Interviews in Lima, 25 July and 2 August 1995.

forces with "a legal framework with which to prosecute the counterinsurgency war more efficiently."

Fujimori also acted quickly to assert control over the military high command. On the day of his inauguration, in a first step toward the consolidation of a new military leadership loyal to Fujimori and Montesinos, the military hierarchy was shuffled to replace the commanding generals of the navy and air force. A little over a year later, in November 1991, legislation was submitted to Congress that gave the president power to appoint high-ranking generals and admirals and to eliminate term limits on those selected, thus ensuring their personal loyalty to the president (Obando 1994, 114–15).

Fujimori's politicization of the armed forces, his paranoid attacks on political opponents whom he regarded as dangerous, and his contempt for political parties and judicial institutions is, perhaps, more intelligible in the light of the Plan Verde and the clear desire of the military to redefine its role and alter the constitutional order. He may have wanted to discredit and expose the failures and inadequacies of Peru's Congress, judiciary, and political parties, all the while waiting for an opportune moment to implement the autogolpe contingency plan.[12] This behavior is consistent with the desire for political survival in the context of weak institutions.

The growing strength of the Shining Path in the first two years of the Fujimori government was a key factor in firming up support within the armed forces for the implementation of a Plan Verde–type solution. There was a growing sense within the armed forces that they were "doing the politicians' dirty work, and then being asked to pay the bill."[13] The Shining Path was responsible for most of the abuses of human rights, yet the armed forces were continually reminded of such incidents as the massacres of Barrios Altos and Cayara.

When the autogolpe was implemented, the need to fight more effectively against the Shining Path was the principle rationale given by the SIN.[14] In the morning of 5 April 1992, the joint chiefs of staff were assembled in the Little Pentagon building (Pentagonito), a T-shaped leviathan

---

12. See Francisco Soberón Garrido, "Nota Informativa: 'The Peru Report' Revela que golpe de Fujimori es de largo plazo y da a conocer aspectos de sus planes." Lima: Asociación Pro-Derechos Humanos (APRODEH), 18 April 1992.

13. Interview with senior official, Lima, 21 July 1995.

14. This account is based upon an eyewitness account of the meeting. Interview in Lima, 2 August 1995.

in the district of San Borja. With the assistance of sophisticated videos prepared for the occasion, Julio Salazar Monroy, the head of the SIN, and Vladimiro Montesinos, described how the counterinsurgency struggle was failing and a "strategic equilibrium" had virtually been reached with the Shining Path. Montesinos said that the identity and location of many terrorists were well known, but nothing could be done to stop them because the government's hands were tied by the Congress and the courts. Corruption in the courts had reached such an point that fear or money could be used to subvert justice.

Montesinos was followed by General Hermoza Rios, president of the Joint Command of the Armed Forces, who argued that there was no alternative to an autogolpe; a new sui generis path had to be taken involving the dissolution of Congress and the reorganization of the court system. This was the only way of overcoming the obstruction of the government. Not a single member of any of the various branches of the armed forces spoke in opposition to Hermoza Rios's or Montesinos's analysis or their proposed solution. The idea of the autogolpe fell on highly receptive ears within the military.

The capture of Abimael Guzmán in September 1992 seemed to be the best possible vindication of Fujimori's claim that tough authoritarian measures were needed to fight the counterinsurgency war more effectively. The fact that the capture was the result of meticulous intelligence work that began long before the autogolpe was ignored, and the intelligence officer responsible, Ketín Vidal, was quietly shuffled as soon as he began to steal the president's limelight.

In retrospect, many institutionalist officers felt betrayed by the military hierarchy. They believed that General Hermoza Rios was right when he said there was no alternative. They accepted the dissolution of Congress and the reorganization of the courts because "only that way was it possible to overcome the obstruction facing the government." However, it later became clear to some of them that Hermoza Rios, the minister of the interior, and Montesinos had another agenda, which one described as a "personal project" to "seize power for fifteen to twenty years in order to satisfy their own appetites."[15] The split between the institutionalist officers and the coopted hierarchy resulted in an unsuccessful coup attempt in November 1992 (Obando 1994, 115). Much of the dissatisfaction within the army stemmed from the fact that Commander General Hermoza Rios

---

15. Interview in Lima, 2 August 1995.

refused to retire and thereby blocked the assent of other officers, and from the belief that the autogolpe had turned out to be a usurpation of power.

Executive-Legislative Relations

Was institutional gridlock a cause of the autogolpe? There is a debate in Peru, in part between the executive and members of the 1990–92 Congress, over whether the dispute between the two branches of government about their respective powers and prerogatives played a major role in causing the autogolpe (Pease 1994; Blacker Miller 1993; Abad Yupanqui and Garcés Peralta 1993; Torres y Torres Lara 1992a, 1992b; Kenney 1995, 1996).

Conservative legislators believed that it would have been easy for Fujimori to build a stable governing majority within the Congress, but that the president never had any interest in doing so.[16] They pointed to a consensus between Cambio 90 and the members elected under the FREDEMO banner on the liberalization of the economy, the need to reduce inflation, and the imperative to fight effectively against terrorism. The combined votes of each party formed an absolute majority in both chambers. It should be noted, of course, that Fujimori won the second round of the 1990 presidential election after rejecting precisely this option; a pact with the Right in parliament might have undermined Fujimori's popularity with the electorate.

Legislators insisted that the leadership in the Congress made a number of important gestures of goodwill to the executive. For example, in the first year of the new parliament, the presidents of the Senate and the House of Deputies (Maximo San Roman and Víctor Paredes, respectively) were both selected from the ranks of Cambio 90. This, according to one legislator, was "given in exchange for nothing."[17] In the second year, two PPC legislators were chosen, Roberto Ramírez Villar and Felipe Osterling. They represented a consensus among many groups, including half of Cambio 90, APRA, and even some members of the Left. However, the new leaders of the Congress found themselves ignored by the president, and their many requests, reiterated in public, for a dialogue with the executive went unheeded. The presidents of the Senate and the Chamber of Deputies were never invited to meet with Fujimori, except on ceremonial occasions. On one occasion in early 1992, Fujimori ignored a group of law

---

16. Interviews with members of Congress, Lima, 17 July and 21 July 1996.
17. Interview in Lima, 17 July 1995.

makers while on aboard a commercial flight to Asia and during a long stopover in Los Angeles.

According to one prominent law maker, Fujimori did not want to build a majority in Congress. He knew that such a majority would not be unconditional. It would enable him to implement much of his legislative agenda, but it would not allow him to implement his hidden agenda: a constitutional change to permit presidential reelection. That, according to the version popular among opposition law makers, was the real purpose of the autogolpe.

In late September 1991, the executive submitted a package of 126 legislative decrees for approval by the Congress. According to Philip Mauceri (1995, 23):

> Together, these legislative decrees represented the most significant reordering of the Peruvian state since the Velasco era. . . . The decrees were aimed at eliminating the interventionist role of the state adopted during the Velasco years and enshrined in the Constitution of 1979. Most of the strictures in the 1969 agrarian reform on land sales, investments, and management were reversed, along with laws regarding worker participation, union organization, job security, and sales of state property. Meanwhile, neoliberal economic reforms were accompanied by a series of authoritarian political decrees. Arguing that the military required expanded powers over civil society to combat insurgency, Fujimori proposed to grant the armed forces authority to tighten restrictions on journalists, confiscate property on the grounds of national security, create special military courts to try terrorist suspects, and ensure that military officials could not be tried in civilian courts for violating human rights.

The executive was attempting to effectively implement neoliberal reforms within the constraints of a constitution that various officials described as "rigid," "socialist," or "confining" (*encajadora*).[18] The legislative package was regarded as the substantial core of Fujimori's economic reforms.

Congress had previously delegated to the executive the power to submit decrees on an emergency basis, but some legislators argued that the executive had exceeded its authority. In particular, opponents of the legisla-

---

18. Interviews in Lima, 21 July, 1 August 1995.

tion in Congress attacked the "militarization of the country." Expressing exasperation over the inability to control Congress, one cabinet official said: "Once one congressman started to talk about militarization, everyone began shooting down the laws."[19] Fujimori chaffed that congressional attacks on his initiatives were "immature, and out of step with the requirements of modernization" (Pease 1994, 273). In a subsequent speech to Peru's peak business association, the CONFIEP, in November 1991, Fujimori complained that the legislative authority delegated to the executive was not broad enough. He then called for a plebiscite to reform Peru's legislature at a December meeting of Peruvian exporters, CADE (Conferencia Anual de Ejecutivos, the annual conference of executives), and hinted at the need for a strong government with a ten-year tenure in office.

The rhetorical escalation continued in December as the president suggested that the influence of drug traffickers could be the reason why Parliament was holding up his reforms (Pease 1994, 276). In response, the Senate approved a motion to declare the presidency "vacant" due to a lack of moral authority. The House of Deputies was about to do the same when, in an unusual alliance, Ricardo Letts of Izquierda Unida and Lourdes Flores Nano of the PPC worked together to stop the motion and avert a constitutional crisis. The point had come, according to a senior government official, "where either the Congress would kill the president, or the president would kill the Congress."[20]

It has been speculated that measures submitted to Congress in November 1991 were sent in the expectation that they would be vetoed, in order to strengthen the case that a deadlock between the legislative and executive made the autogolpe inevitable.[21] If that was the case, then Congress fell into the trap. As evidence of the need for stronger executive authority, Fujimori used the efforts by the Congress to strengthen its role as a legislative body and to place restrictions on the ability of the executive to rule by decree without congressional oversight.

In early February 1992 the Congress rejected or modified seven executive decrees on pacification and promulgated a law of parliamentary control over executive powers.[22] The clear objective of this law, which re-

19. Interview in Lima, 21 July 1995.

20. Interview in Lima, 8 August 1995.

21. See, for example, the press conference by Peru's foreign minister on 7 April 1992, and his speech to the Organization of American States on 13 April 1992.

22. Disponen derogar y modificar 7 decretos sobre pacificación" and "Congreso promulgó Ley de Control Parlamentario sobre el Ejecutivo," *El Comercio,* 1 February 1992.

affirmed the ability of the executive to issue extraordinary measures and legislative decrees but asserted the right of the Congress to review all executive decrees in accordance with the constitution, was to establish a balance of powers between the executive and legislature, to provide a basis for opposition to some of the legislation the executive had sent to Congress, and to send a clear signal that Congress would oppose excessive centralization of power in the hands of the presidency. Fujimori's cabinet used the law as a rationalization for closing Congress.[23]

The cabinet felt that the law of parliamentary control "exceeded the constitution" and amounted to a "*golpe* with white gloves."[24] In their view, it raised the Congress above the president and imposed one branch of government over the other. At this point, legal options for closing the Congress were actively considered. The president could request that the Congress repeal the legislation or vote on a motion of confidence in the prime minister. A vote of nonconfidence would force the prime minister to resign. This process would be repeated three times. If the Congress still refused to bend and voted nonconfidence in the prime minister on the third occasion, the government would be in a legal position to close the Chamber of Deputies (but not the Senate). This option was discussed with the president, who considered the possibility but did not make a decision or express an opinion.

Instead of closing the Congress, the president authorized secret negotiations between the legislature and the executive, under the leadership of his prime minister, Alfonso de los Heros. The prime minister was instructed to build a parliamentary majority to support the president's legislative agenda. Lourdes Flores Nano was chosen from the Congress to negotiate with the executive, and together the members of each branch went over contentious legislation—on security and judicial issues, not the economic program—letter by letter, until a consensus was reached between the cabinet and the leadership of FREDEMO and Cambio 90. The prime minister kept Fujimori personally informed of progress in the dialogue, and Fujimori always consulted with the military before agreeing to even trivial changes. Among the most important measures that were discussed were reforms to the judiciary, especially the highly politicized Supreme Court and the Tribunal of Constitutional Guarantees, to weed out

23. For a skeptical view of the obstructionism of the Congress as a factor in accounting for the autogolpe, see McClintock (1994b, 308–12).

24. Interview with a cabinet official in Lima, 21 July 1995.

the presence of members of APRA seeking to use these institutions to impede the economic program.[25]

The dialogue between the branches of government was productive and constructive. It was the sense of the cabinet that the progress of the negotiations was due to the recognition by Congress that it had earlier gone too far in its attacks on the president. Thus, it is surprising that the autogolpe occurred on 5 April 1992, just one day before the Congress was to go into session. At that point the results of the negotiations, which had been kept secret from APRA and the Left, would have been introduced for congressional approval.[26] A Machiavellian hypothesis is worth entertaining. Did the success of the dialogue with Congress cause Fujimori to accelerate his plans for an autogolpe? Did Fujimori fear that a new consensus in Congress would undermine the rationale for a coup and weaken public support for his eventual seizure of dictatorial power?[27] On this point there are sharp differences of opinion among policy makers.[28] Those who believed Congress was going to veto the legislative package had difficulty explaining why Fujimori would not wait for such a veto to materialize and then use it as a pretext for his autogolpe.

Enemies of Society: García and Opposition to Neoliberal Reform

To win support for the autogolpe, Fujimori concentrated his attention on two "enemies of society": Alan García and Abimael Guzmán. As far as the Fujimori government was concerned, the former personified inflation, the latter violent death. Two major victories of the Fujimori government were the capture of Guzmán (see Degregori's chapter in this volume) and the political exile of García.

Carlos Boloña, Fujimori's minister of the economy, said (1993, 5), "the names of the two greatest terrorists in Peru begin with the initials 'A. G.': Abimael Guzmán and Alan García." For Boloña, the economic loss under

25. Interview with legislator involved in the negotiations in Lima, 21 July 1995.

26. Indeed, the prime minister had appeared on television on the night of 5 April 1992 to discuss the negotiations with Congress, and he clearly had no idea that a coup was imminent. After the autogolpe, he resigned.

27. Carlos Ivan Degregori (1994, 87) makes a similar assertion: "The possibility that this alternative strategy might be ratified by the parliament in the next legislative session, which was to begin 6 April 1992, was one of the main causes of the autogolpe of the day before."

28. Interview in Lima, 21 July 1995.

García was comparable to the loss of life caused by Guzmán. Both represented the enemies of "property, family, religion, and order," to use Marx's phrase (Marx 1963 [1869], 23). Boloña's comparison of the leader of the most brutal revolutionary movement in Latin American history with an inept, corrupt, populist ex-president could be dismissed as exaggeration, but it provides a measure of the depth of contempt for García among members of the dominant class (who, after all, were rarely the direct targets of Shining Path violence until 1990–92). The chapter by Durand in this volume provides further insight into the antagonism between García and the business community, which is critical to understanding the acceptance of the autogolpe in elite circles.

It might be thought that a key objective of the autogolpe was to eliminate García as a contender in the 1995 elections. However, neither García's sharpest detractors in the Fujimori government nor his closest political allies believed that the autogolpe was intended to eliminate García.[29] García was a convenient enemy, and the rhetorical jousting between the minister of the economy and García created an emotionally charged atmosphere prior to Fujimori's autogolpe, but the events of 5 April 1995, were as much of a surprise to Fujimori's cabinet as they were to García.

For Lima's middle classes, García's malevolent powers verged on the supernatural. The mere prospect of a comeback by García seemed sufficient to shake business confidence, send tremors through the stock market, and threaten to bring down the fragile economic program like a house of cards. "Certainly García had the power to destroy the economic program—this is obvious," said one senior government official, while emphasizing that this was a secondary reason for the autogolpe.[30]

For others, it was García's immunity and his status as a lifelong member of Congress that demonstrated decadence in the nation's institutions and helped to justify the autogolpe. García had been charged with illicit enrichment during his tenure in office. As a senator for life (an honor bestowed upon all former presidents by the Peruvian constitution), García was entitled to parliamentary immunity in perpetuity. In late March 1992, after a lengthy dispute in both the Chamber of Deputies and the Senate in which García was stripped of his immunity, his case was thrown out by

---

29. Interviews with senior officials in the Fujimori government and a prominent member of the APRA party, Lima, 2 and 8 August 1995.

30. Interview in Lima, 8 August 1995.

the Supreme Court. APRA appointees were prominent among the judges who dismissed García's case.[31] For those who were convinced of García's guilt, the results confirmed their worst suspicions about the politicization of the judiciary.

The apparent exhaustion of the legal means of prosecuting García enabled the former president to get an early start on his campaign for reelection. He had been reelected secretary general of the APRA party and was thus well positioned within the party and in the Congress to make a second bid for the presidency. Although García's ability to win reelection was doubtful, some believed he was capable of articulating opposition to the government's neoliberal economic plans in ways that could hurt the president's popularity. One observer, with both business and academic connections, said wryly: "Alan García and a telephone is more dangerous than the Shining Path." On the evening of the autogolpe, police surrounded García's house and attempted to arrest him. García hid in a nearby lot and subsequently escaped to Colombia, where his ability to oppose the Peruvian government was limited.[32]

Just days before the autogolpe, the minister of the economy accused García of "boycotting" the economic program for political ends. He argued that García was using his influence in the auditor general's office to interfere with tax administration, frighten foreign investors, and undermine the reinsertion of Peru in the international financial community. The auditor general had demanded access to the files of the National Superintendency of Tax Administration (SUNAT) to establish whether the remittances of multinational firms were in accordance with the law.[33] The minister of the economy also argued that the auditor general's office was interfering with the privatization process, and he accused APRA of opposing tax-reform measures that were critical to reducing the fiscal def-

---

31. These included Ameli Pereyra Toledo, from the Universidad Federico Villareal (an APRA-dominated university), and Luis Alarcón Quintana, a former adviser to Luis Alberto Sánchez (a founder of the APRA party). "Primera Sala Penal de Suprema orderó archivar cargos en contra," *El Comercio*, 1 February 1992. See also: "Ejecutivo busca preservar interés in el caso del ex presidente García" and "La dañina politización del poder judicial," *El Comercio*, 30 March 1992.

32. García believes that the officers sent to capture him were part of a shadowy paramilitary squadron run by Montesinos called the Colina group, and that it was their intention to kill him. His escape is described in dramatic detail in a novel written in exile (García 1994).

33. "García debe pronunciarse sobre desastre económico que provocó. Ex presidente lidera boicot contra programa económico del gobierno, advierte ministro Carlos Boloña. Tambien acusa a controlora de lo mismo." *El Comercio*, 4 April 1992, A4.

icit. Changes were required, according to the minister, to sales, property, and consumption taxes, without which the government would fall $600 million short on its deficit targets and would be unable to make payments to public-sector employees.[34] Finally, Fujimori's minister of the economy faced a motion of censure from the Congress, lead by APRA, for his management of the economy. The campaign of harassment was deliberately intended to make the minister's position precarious and hinder his economic program.

García responded, literally on the eve of the coup, that he had the moral authority to criticize the government because it had plunged the majority of the country into poverty in order to repay the international debt, and he accused the minister of acting like an employee of the International Monetary Fund. However, neither the motion of censure against the minister of the economy nor the actions of the auditor general were widely supported by legislators outside the APRA party. The war of words between García and Fujimori's minister of the economy was used after the autogolpe as evidence of an incipient campaign, orchestrated by García, in opposition to the economic program of the government, a campaign that could undermine the ability of the Fujimori government to maintain economic stability, attract investment, and stimulate a recovery.

Hostility to García was not limited to the business community. The APRA government had implemented policies that led to a bout with hyperinflation with few historical parallels. Total inflation between 1985 and 1990 is estimated at 2.2 million percent (Boloña 1993, 6). Fujimori's shock therapy was painful, but the government made considerable progress in the area of price stability. Yet, there were disturbing signs that control over inflation had been eluding the government prior to the autogolpe. This fact, combined with growing business opposition, conflicts within the cabinet, and the division of Cambio 90 into three factions, undermined the credibility of the government. The increase in poverty and unemployment, and the failure of the government to implement a social emergency program, left the government vulnerable to populist opposition.

Opposition to the neoliberal economic program was not a central cause of the autogolpe, but dislike for García was part of the glue that held the coup coalition together. Fujimori may have calculated that the autogolpe

34. "Ejecutivo presentó proyectos para garantizar estabilidad tributaria," *El Comercio*, 4 April 1992, A4.

would restore credibility in the government's ability to take whatever measures were necessary to maintain economic discipline and stability. The autogolpe would make it more difficult for García to create economic chaos to discredit the government as part of a strategy to position himself for reelection in 1995. Since inflation has such widespread and draconian effects, such an objective could be expected to be widely supported. By attacking the judiciary and the Congress for corruption and incompetence, Fujimori would also capitalize on the growing disenchantment among the public with these institutions.

Domestic and International Responses to the Autogolpe

The Weakness of the Domestic Reaction

The autogolpe would have been impossible had Peru's political parties been stronger and more capable of mobilizing opposition. The stability of democracy depends on the strength of political parties. Peru's parties were so weak and isolated, so lacking in solid roots in society, and so out of touch with the concerns of the majority of the electorate that they were unable to mobilize any effective opposition to the authoritarian measures. Indeed, some legislators were surprised by how negatively they were treated by the public following the autogolpe.

In an environment of fear and tension, Congress held a secret meeting on 9 April at the home of Lourdes Flores Nano, during which 135 members of Congress unanimously declared Fujimori morally incapable of ruling Peru, and elected Vice President Carlos García to replace him. The lackluster Carlos García was an evangelist from Fujimori's own movement, Cambio 90, and his election was laughable for most Peruvians. Three people were calling themselves the president of Peru: Alberto Fujimori, Carlos García (subsequently replaced by Maximo San Roman, who was out of the country at the time of the autogolpe), and Abimael Guzmán.[35]

---

35. There is a precedent for such a situation in Peru. Brian Loveman (1993, 210) described the civil-military *golpe* that sought to remove Peru's first president, José de la Riva Agüero, and replace him with the Marquis de Torre Tagle, with the comment that "Peru had two presidents, a supreme military commander, a Spanish viceroy, and a royal army—all waiting for Bolívar to play the leading role in the final act of the drama."

From his hiding place, García also called for resistance to the government, a desperate plea that was ignored by the public.

In defense of the coup, Fujimori argued that Peru did not have a real democracy: "The democracy that we had before was just a shell and now we have to give that shell content," he said. The coup was "not a rupture of democracy but rather of rupture of the chain of corruption."[36] Fujimori's idea of a more authentic democracy included direct consultations and plebiscites. He called for a "national dialogue for peace and development," in which business and social groups were invited negotiate "a social pact," and later suggested a "popular consultation" to ratify the need for a new constitution and the restructuring of Congress and the judiciary. The international reaction to these initiatives was cool, and Fujimori did not agree to new legislative elections until forced to by intense international pressures.

As soon as Fujimori agreed to new legislative election, discipline among opposition parties began to disintegrate. Major defections, or acts of open defiance (and in the case of APRA a massive purge), affected virtually all the parties. When Fujimori, under pressure from the international community, proposed a "Democratic Constituent Congress," the political parties were unable to prevent it from becoming a new, servile Congress. Contrary to the wishes of the parties, the new Congress would be a unicameral legislative body that would function until general elections in 1995. The opposition wanted an assembly empowered only to reform the constitution, with a six-month term and the autonomy to call general elections. Fujimori was inflexible on this issue. Not surprisingly, he was not about to agree to a new Congress that could remove him from office as he had removed the congressmen from office in April 1992.

Although many of the major parties—APRA, AP, the PUM—refused to participate in the new congressional elections, a proliferation of smaller coalitions and movements emerged in a bid to fill the void. An ex-minister in the Fujimori government formed a movement (Nueva Mayoria, or New Majority) that later joined forces with Fujimori's Cambio 90. Rafael Rey from Libertad split away and formed a movement called Renovación (Renovation) with Fujimori's apparent blessing. By the time of the elections, the fragmentation of the party system could not have been more complete. Fragmentation carried over into the municipal elections held

---

36. "Fujimori explains why he suspended constitution; seeks to build a 'new Peru.' " *British Broadcasting Corporation Summary of World Broadcasts,* 7 April 1993.

the next year, by which time Peru's mainstream political parties had been essentially wiped out. Parties like APRA and AP were reduced to fringe groupings, unable to win respectable numbers even in their traditional strongholds.

The Strength of the International Reaction

The meeting in the Pentagonito on the morning of 5 April 1992 scarcely addressed the international reaction. The main concern of the officers present was the implications for the border with Ecuador and Colombia. None of the generals worried about the international reaction. As one officer put it:

> The measures were not perceived as a golpe because there was to be no change in the president. The autogolpe did not imply a change in economic policy, or in the ideology of the government. Regarding the reorganization of the courts, the reaction was barely short of applause. Everyone agreed with the need for tough adjustments. Perhaps the advance of the subversive forces was exaggerated. But the external reaction was not taken into consideration because the president was not going to be changed. Perhaps this is a reflection of presidentialism. Closing the Congress was not seen as a serious problem—it has always been looked upon as the "poor sister" of the executive.[37]

Following the meeting with the military, Fujimori called Augusto Blacker Miller, the minister of external relations, to the Palace of Government and asked him to serve as spokesperson for the new government (Blacker Miller 1993, 194–98). They returned together to the Pentagonito, where the rest of the cabinet had been assembled. Fujimori said "watch this cassette, which will be broadcast in half an hour. I'll give you a preview—I'm going to close the Congress." The prime minister, minister of the economy, and the agriculture minister expressed reservations (Daeschner 1993, 288). They were asked to consider their position and report the next morning. De los Heros resigned, but Boloña remained in the cabinet.

The decisions to support the president or uphold the constitution

37. Interview in Lima, 2 August 1995.

raised near-existential angst among some government officials. As one said:

> If I stay, I will be justifying [my opponents]. My [work] will go to hell. If I stay, I am breaking the constitution. I could be imprisoned, sent to jail, persecuted. I could lose everything. If I go, I'll be seen as a great democrat, no one would persecute me; I would not have the stigma of the autogolpe. . . . It was a hard decision, an anguishing one. The insurgency was there, and the autogolpe could be seen as legitimating Sendero Luminoso. I was worried about being taken prisoner, having my property confiscated, and being stigmatized as anti-democratic. Someone said, "when everything closes in around you it is going to be horrible."[38]

A key for government officials involved in the economic program was the likely international reaction. Blacker Miller was concerned that it would be difficult to "convince the world of the rationality of our objectives" (1993, 196). Although he told his cabinet colleagues "don't worry, it is under control,"[39] he and other officials were unprepared for the intensity of the international response. The first delegation to Washington was told by U.S. State Department officials, "We will not allow this. We will close you down."[40] One member of the diplomatic corps tore up his green card, saying:

> In Latin America we always thought that the U.S. had our interests in mind. The younger son you treat with more care. [Assistant Secretary of State for Inter-American Affairs] Bernard Aronson said, "We cannot allow you to take this decision, it could lead other countries to take similar decisions." That didn't leave us much to discuss. They did not try to understand.[41]

Despite the unequivocal signals from Washington that the international community would not tolerate a dictatorship in Peru, Fujimori was reluctant to back down, hoping that Japan would come to his rescue. Japan had not followed the United States in suspending aid to Peru after the autogolpe.

38. Interview in Lima, 8 August 1995.
39. Interview in Lima, 8 August 1995.
40. Interview in Lima, 8 August 1995.
41. Interview in Lima, 1 August 1995.

The minister of the economy, perhaps Fujimori's cabinet official with the strongest international connections, became the focal point within the cabinet for pressure to call democratic elections for a new Congress. Boloña received a hostile reception from international financial institutions and the U.S. government in Washington. Diplomats speculated that Boloña would resign out of fear that the negative international reaction would undermine his economic stabilization program. In an effort to persuade Fujimori to call new elections, Boloña had to call Washington to request that the United States contact Tokyo so that the Japanese ambassador would make it clear that Japan could not support Peru.[42]

Boloña's threats to resign, according to the Fujimori's foreign minister at the time of the autogolpe, Augusto Blacker Miller, were backed by the more serious threat of capital flight. Carlos Rodríguez Pastor, a prominent international banker and former debt negotiator for Peru under President Belaúnde, withdrew $40 million from the Banco Interandino around the time of Boloña's offer to resign. This was immediately followed by a run on the sol in the Banco Wiese. Blacker Miller interprets this as evidence of pressure from international financial markets to support the position of the minister of the economy (Blacker Miller 1993, 213–14).

The minister of the economy ultimately prevailed. As the dates for a meeting at the Organization of American States approached, and a growing chorus of nations began calling for sanctions against Peru, Fujimori became increasingly agitated. The president's advisers worked late into the morning night after night, in an effort to convince Fujimori of the need to restore democratic institutions through some sort of Constituent Assembly. A key turning point came when one adviser came up with a phrase that appealed to the president: "You are not going to Nassau as a repentant dictator," he said, "but as a lecturer on the partyarchy" (*catedratico de la partidocracia*).[43] The idea of *partidocracia* captured Fujimori's imagination, and from that point onward he became enthusiastic about speaking before the OAS and agreed to the idea of a Constituent Assembly. This was enough to "get that democratic feeling back," to use the phrase of a U.S. State Department official.

42. Interview with government official, Lima, 8 August 1995.
43. Kenney (1996) has documented how parts of Fujimori's speech, including his criticisms of "partyarchy," were taken, without attribution, from Coppedge (1994) prior to its publication.

The New Congress and Constitution

The 22 November 1992 election for a Democratic Constituent Congress (CCD) gave Fujimori a majority of forty-four seats in an eighty-seat, single-chamber Congress that had little independence from the executive. The CCD, which was charged with drafting a new constitution as well as serving as a legislative body until the 1995 presidential election, consolidated a new regime with broader executive powers.

The weakness of the CCD was demonstrated by two events. In April 1993 it established a Special Commission of Inquiry to investigate the disappearance and assassination of nine students and a professor from La Cantuta university. When the commission began to pursue allegations that the paramilitary death squad Grupo Colina was responsible for the massacre, General Hermoza Rios sent tanks and troops into the streets, and the congressional majority quickly backed down. In June 1995 an amnesty law (No. 26479, dubbed the "Colina law" in reference to its principal beneficiaries) was approved with little debate and went into effect forty-eight hours later. It provided amnesty to all police, military, and civilian personnel sentenced or charged with assassination, torture, rape, disappearances, or other civil or military crimes in the course of the fight against subversion in the period between 1980 and 1995.

Fujimori was reelected in 1995, despite the militarization of the political regime and the centralization of power in the executive branch, because his autogolpe decision was supported by a broad, multi-class consensus on the need for exceptional measures to confront terrorism and restore economic discipline (Cameron 1994). The strength of this consensus provides a key to understanding Fujimori's success, for unanimity is as inimical to democracy as are irreconcilable differences. Democracy failed because, after a decade of violence and decline, the cacophonous plurality of interests organized by parties was no longer seen by the majority of Peruvians as necessary or desirable. The system of checks and balances built into presidentialism was considered inessential to democracy by the vast majority of the public, and Fujimori's repeated attacks on parties and politicians resonated with an electorate that associated partisan politics with corruption, excess, and irresponsibility.

Antipolitical attitudes became so widespread that credible opposition candidates—such as unsuccessful presidential candidate Javier Pérez de

Cuellar and Lima's successful mayoral candidate Alberto Andrade—were both compelled to avoid even the appearance of partisan opposition to the executive, and both sought to cast themselves as independents. Only one candidate, Meche Cabanillas of the APRA, ran under the banner of a traditional political party in the 1995 presidential election, and she won only 4 percent of the vote nationally. The combined 1995 congressional vote for all parties that had participated in the 1978 Constituent Assembly—namely, the APRA, Acción Popular, Partido Popular Cristiano, and Izquierda Unida—was 15 percent (Palmer 1995, 20). It would be hard to imagine a more complete breakdown of a party system.

Conclusion

In his preface to the second edition of *The Eighteenth Brumaire of Louis Bonaparte,* Karl Marx compared his writings with Victor Hugo's *Napoléon le Petit* and Proudhon's *Coup d'État.* Marx criticized Victor Hugo for presenting the 2 December 1851 coup d'état of Louis Bonaparte, the nephew of Napoleon I, "like a bolt from the blue" (Marx 1963 [1869], 8). By implying that the coup was "only the violent act of a single individual," Hugo "does not notice that he makes this individual great instead of little by ascribing to him a personal power of initiative such as would be without parallel in world history" (Marx 1963 [1869], 8). Proudhon, on the other hand, presented the coup d'état as "the result of an antecedent historical development." However, Marx faulted Proudhon's history for providing "an historical *apologia* for its hero." "I, on the contrary," said Marx, "demonstrate how the *class struggle* in France created circumstances and relationships that made it possible for a grotesque mediocrity to play a hero's part" (Marx 1963 [1869], 8).

The challenge facing analysts of Fujimori's role in Peruvian politics is similar to that confronted by Marx more than a century ago. If the autogolpe of 5 April 1992 is interpreted as the act of a single individual, the analyst unwittingly ascribes to Fujimori an excessive power of initiative. The autogolpe was the product of a complex set of conditions, including economic distress and violence, the decay of institutions and the collapse of political parties, the assertiveness of the military, and the reactions of the international community. On the other hand, if the autogolpe is presented as the inevitable consequence of objective historical forces, then history becomes an *apologia* that ignores the role of choices and denies free will or responsibility. Marx's own view was best captured in his famous phrase: "Men make their own history, but they do not make it just as they please; they do not make it under circumstances chosen by themselves, but under circumstances directly encountered, given and transmitted from the past" (Marx 1963 [1869], 15).

In the spirit of Marx's analysis, a full account of the autogolpe must make a place for both agency and structure. My study leads to the conclusion that the autogolpe was largely the product of a growing perception of threat among a group of military officers, allied with an outsider president who shared their contempt for Congress, the judiciary, and political parties as well as their ambition to perpetuate themselves in power. Structural conflict between the executive and legislature was exacerbated by electoral rules that resulted in a president with little direct control over the legislature, but evidence of dialogue between the branches of government suggests that Fujimori could have negotiated much of his legislative agenda short of changing the constitution to enable reelection. Opposition to neoliberal reforms played a secondary role as a cause of the autogolpe but was a critical factor ensuring the post-coup coherence of the authoritarian coalition.

Fujimori could not have succeeded in his "heroic role," with its collateral damage to the body politic, were it not for a perception that Peru's decline was caused by political parties that cared only for partisan gain and placed narrow interests above the national interest. Traditional political parties were seen not as channels for representation but as vehicles for the political ambitions of corrupt politicians and self-serving interests. As class solidarities dissolved under the stress of economic decline, class-based parties suffered corresponding electoral losses. No longer seen as valid representatives of different interests and values within a framework of agreed-upon rules, and unable to respond to changing electoral preferences due to internal factions, parties were ultimately unable to mobilize opposition to authoritarian measures that attacked the political system within which parties operated. Under these circumstances, Fujimori was able to rise to near-absolute power. Had Marx been writing in 1992, he would probably have said something like: "as Peruvian society is convulsed by changes, it conjures up the most conservative forces from the past: *caudillismo,* militarism, and the jousting ghosts of Bolívar, Riva Agüero, and Torre Tagle."

3

STATE POLICY AND SOCIAL CONFLICT IN PERU

Carol Wise

Always somewhat out of step with political and economic trends in the rest of Latin America, Peru still continues on a track of its own. On the one hand, the country joined its neighbors in 1990 by adopting the same market-oriented policies that have swept the region in the wake of the debt crisis. Yet, with the 1992 "self-coup" by President Alberto Fujimori, Peru was the first country in South America to officially break ranks with the region's decade-long thrust toward political democratization. At face value, the reasons underlying this turn toward markets and authoritarian rule were obvious. President Fujimori's embrace of a neoliberal economic program in 1990 can be seen as a response to the excessive and reckless government intervention of previous administrations—the most striking example being the highly distorted hyperinflationary economy inherited from the preceding García administration—and to new demands for state cutbacks imposed by the prolonged recession of the 1980s. Though unfashionable, the turn toward authoritarian rule in 1992 can be understood

The research for this article was completed while the author was a visiting scholar at Grupo de Analisis para el Desarrollo (GRADE) in Lima during May 1992 and during a follow-up field visit in July 1995. Funding for the research was provided by the John D. and Catherine T. MacArthur Fellowship in Conflict, Peace and Security; the Institute for the Study of World Politics; the Organization of American States; and the John Randolph Haynes and Dora Haynes Foundations. The author thanks Douglas Chalmers, Francisco Durand, Robert Kaufman, Mark Kesselman, Robin Kirk, Cynthia McClintock, Manuel Pastor, Orin Starn, several anonymous reviewers, and the editors for their helpful comments on earlier drafts. Also, Patricia Arregui, Sally Bowen, Carlos Bustamante, Javier Escobal, Juan Larco, Alberto Pasco-Font and Juan Zuñiga provided many insights during the Lima field visits. Thanks also go to Monica Garaitonandia, Julia Holman, Deborah Hudson, Lori Snyder, and Carlos Westerman for their highly capable research and technical assistance.

against the backdrop of extreme levels of national violence and political uncertainty that have prevailed in Peru since the early 1980s.

While the causes may be readily apparent, a full understanding of Peru's recent political economic trajectory begs two larger questions. The first has to do with the reasons for the extreme gravity of the Peruvian situation, in the sense that Peru's trials and instability have outstripped those of any of its neighbors. In this chapter I argue that these trends are the result of a distinct pattern of state-led development in Peru that evolved over the post–World War II period. Unchecked for some thirty years, this pattern eventually gave rise to what has now frequently been referred to as a "political economy of violence" (Figueroa 1995). As anxious as President Fujimori has been to restore an image of normalcy since his carefully maneuvered "reelection" in 1995, the very drama of the Peruvian case merits more reflection than it has heretofore received in the political-economy literature. The second question explored here is whether the present combination of neoliberal reforms and a tightly circumscribed return to civilian rule since 1995 can provide the necessary backdrop for addressing longstanding development challenges that have yet to be resolved.

The analysis is presented in three parts. The following section elaborates on the ways in which Peru's increasing resort to a state-led development strategy had evolved into a political economy of violence by the time of President Fujimori's election in 1990. The next section explores the extent to which the Fujimori administration has succeeded in addressing these complex problems. The final section comments on the institutional backdrop in Peru and emphasizes a long-term pattern of mutual aggravation between economic policy making and domestic institutions. The conclusions touch on the policy implications of these trends for the present administration, and on those institutional arrangements that appear to offer the most promise for ameliorating a pattern of state policy and social conflict that has been one of Peru's distinctive characteristics since the outbreak of the 1982 debt crisis.

Peru's Political Economic Problems: Critical Turning Points

In a long view of the evolution of Peru's political economy, perhaps most puzzling is the country's transformation from a fairly successful exporter of mineral and agricultural products in the 1950s—reflected in its high growth rates, low inflation, and balanced budgets—into a deficit-ridden, hyperinflationary wanderer in the late 1980s (see Table 3.1).[1] There was little in Peru's early post–World War II history to suggest that it would

Table 3.1. Public-sector behavior and overall economic performance in Peru, 1950–1990

Years	(2) G/Y[a]	(2) GCI/Y	(2) D/Y[b]	(3) Inflation	(1) Y/Y	(4) NF/Y	(4) DBT/Y
1951–62	15.2%	N/A	− .06%	7.6%	6.1%	0.7%	7.7%
1963–68	18.0	N/A	− 3.0	9.4	4.6	2.2	10.4
1969–73	20.1	25.2	− 1.8	9.5	4.8	1.7	13.9
1974–75	30.2	38.5	− 7.0	9.0	7.1	5.5	19.3
1976–77	34.5	41.6	− 8.7	21.6	0.3	3.7	24.9
1978–79	37.6	42.8	− 3.2	38.6	1.3	3.6	37.1
1980–82	40.0	47.8	− 6.0	67.1	3.6	2.5	29.8
1983–85	41.1	48.5	− 6.1	90.2	− 2.3	5.8	46.3
1986	32.6	38.0	− 5.0	62.9	7.7	2.9	52.8
1987	29.0	33.5	− 6.7	114.5	9.8	2.5	43.0
1988	27.5	31.1	− 6.9	1722.1	− 8.2	2.8	49.5
1989	22.0	25.2	− 6.6	2775.3	− 11.8	2.8	57.5
1990				7649.7	− 4.4	2.1	60.7

(1) Figures are compiled from Richard Webb and Graciela Fernandez Baca, *Peru en números, 1991* (Lima: Cuanto, April 1991), 737.
(2) Figures given are from Cuanto, except for the periods 1951–62 and 1963–68, which are from the International Monetary Fund's *International Financial Statistics (IFS)*, various years, and from CD-ROM, June 1993. The IFS figures are for the central government only; the Cuanto figures are for the public sector as a whole.
(3) Figures given are from Cuanto.
(4) Figures given represent data from Cuanto as % of GDP, based on World Tables calculations for dollar GDP, except for the periods 1951–62 and 1963–68. The debt data are from Cuanto as % of $ GDP, as calculated using IFS exchange rates.
[a]The 1951–62 figure for this column is actually 1953–62.
[b]The 1951–62 figure for this column is actually 1957–62.

G/Y = Public sector's current expenditure as % of GDP.
GCI/Y = Public sector's current and capital expenditure as % of GDP.
D/Y = Public sector's deficit as % of GDP, including both current and capital balance.
Y/Y = Annual rate of growth of GDP.
NF/Y = Net flows on public debt (disbursements minus repayments and interest payments) as % of GDP.
DBT/Y = Total public-sector debt as % of GDP.

1. In-depth historical overviews of the Peruvian political economy can be found in Gonzales and Samame (1991), Wise (1990), Fitzgerald (1979), and Thorp and Bertram (1978).

plummet thirty years later into the region's worst performer in terms of growth, income gains, and productivity, let alone display such alarming outbursts of political violence.

There is no shortage of opinions as to just what went wrong. I argue here that the general patterns underlying Peru's gradual political and economic decline date back to the demise of a development model based on raw-material exports in the late 1950s, when relations between the state and the private sector first turned sour, and when the popular sectors became more of a social force to contend with. As subsequent governments searched for alternative solutions, the tendency was to turn increasingly to state-sponsored development strategies. Although many Latin American states have responded to development crises in a similar fashion, what appears to distinguish the Peruvian case from the experience of other countries in the region is a particular pattern of state-led development that took root in the early 1960s and that remained steady regardless of the application of five different economic-management models between 1963 and 1990. (The presidential administrations, development models, and accompanying economic policies are displayed in Table 3.2).

In broad terms, this pattern has consisted of the following: (1) the state's over-reliance on external borrowing, which made it easy to ignore the sound macroeconomic policy management necessary to secure domestic savings and investments (Paredes and Sachs 1991; Kisic 1987); (2) the increasing use of state enterprises to provide employment and to channel subsidies to the private sector, but with little regard for their productivity or profitability (Alvarez 1991); (3) continuing conflict with domestic capitalists, who have benefited greatly from the state's economic largesse, all the while holding back their own investments and resources due to macroeconomic uncertainties and the state's obvious administrative ineptitude (Durand 1994, 1992); and, finally, (4) the low priority given to social welfare and redistributional policies, because of chronic balance-of-payment crises and the pressing need to stabilize the economy and shore up development funds for infrastructure (Abugattas 1991).

In the end, the analysis points to an unfortunate interplay between politics and economics, on the one hand, and between domestic institutions and these same political economic trends, on the other hand. While Peru's dismal economic performance until the mid-1990s makes it tempting to lay blame on the domestic front, the argument here is that this development pattern is best understood by analyzing the impact of global forces in interaction with domestic state and societal structures in Peru.

Table 3.2.

Presidential Administration	Development Model	Economic Policy
1963–68 Fernando Belaúnde	Import substitution industrialization (first phase)	• Infant industry protection • Public infrastructure investments • Fiscal expansion • Redistributive rhetoric • Overvalued exchange rate • Erratic monetary management • Increased public borrowing
1968–80 Revolutionary Government of the Armed Forces (RGAF) Phase I Juan Velasco (1968–75)	State capitalism	• Secondary import substitution • Public infrastructure investments • Widespread nationalism • Land reform • Redistributive policy • Overvalued exchange rate • Erratic monetary management • Increased public borrowing
Phase II Morales Bermúdez (1975–80)	(Adjustment phase—shift toward outward expansion)	• Promotion of nontraditional exports • Trade liberalization • Currency devaluation • Fiscal tightening • Debt renegotiation and increased public borrowing

1980–85	Fernando Belaúnde	Neoliberalism and populism	• Promotion of primary exports • Public infrastructure investments • Privatization • Fiscal expansion • Overvalued exchange rate • Erratic monetary management • Debt renegotiation and increased public borrowing
1985–90	Alan García	Neostructuralism	• Wage and price controls • Consumer-led economic reactivation • Trade protection • Redistributive rhetoric • Overvalued exchange rate • Expansionary fiscal and monetary policy • Unilateral debt moratorium
1990–96	Alberto Fujimori	Stabilization and liberalization	• Tax and banking reform • "Industrial reconversion" • Privatization • Financial liberalization • Deregulated labor markets • Land reform • Trade liberalization • Overvalued exchange rate • Tight monetary policy • Resumption of debt-service payments and debt renegotiation • FONCODES safety net

The remainder of this section looks briefly at each trend mentioned above. I wish, first, to highlight the critical turning points in this rise of a political economy of violence in Peru; second, I intend to set the backdrop for understanding the origins and content of the neoliberal program that was implemented as yet another remedial response to this pattern when the Fujimori administration was elected in 1990.

External Financing and Macroeconomic Neglect

Although this first theme applies to all of Latin America in varying degrees, the question here is why Peru fared so poorly in coordinating its borrowing on foreign money markets with a sound set of macroeconomic policies. A large part of the answer has to do with timing. The country turned to a strategy of promoting industrial production, through the financial support and protection of local "infant" manufacturing concerns, much later than the rest of the region. Yet neither the strategy nor the domestic political alliance needed to back it had been fully consolidated when private international bank loans became so readily available in the early 1970s. Furthermore, because of a historical bias against state intervention on the part of the country's elites, and a strong dependence on foreign direct investors that had prevailed for most of this century in Peru, no initiative had been taken to create a main development institution that could foster the macroeconomic coordination and government-business cooperation demanded by a more sophisticated industrial strategy.

As Tables 3.1 and 3.2 show, the 1960s marked the end of the "small state," pro–private sector ethos that had prevailed prior to this period. The more specific reasons for the state's assumption of a direct leadership role were at least twofold. First were the shrinking opportunities for raw-material expansion, particularly in mining and petroleum, without large economy-of-scale commitments that local private investors were not able to undertake, and foreign investors—dubious of the slowing growth trends and populist political tone of the 1960s—were increasingly less willing to. The standoff with private investors in the traditional export sectors left the government little choice but to initiate industrialization, and in Peru this task was rather haphazardly assigned to the state.

Second, the need to address Peru's highly skewed patterns of income distribution could no longer be ignored. Although social demands from the working classes and popular sectors had previously been too weak to extract substantial subsidies from the state, increasing urban migration and the growing modern-sector workforce in manufacturing and industry converged to create further pressures for state spending.

Peru's first phase of import-substitution industrialization (ISI) during the 1960s became rapidly swept up in a misdirected nationalism, as both local and foreign capital soaked up the generous incentives and tax concessions in the name of indigenous industrial development, but continued an investment strike in related raw-material exports. As the first Belaúnde administration mounted a massive infrastructure and industrial drive, but with insufficient regard for the sources and supply of financing, public spending ultimately tipped over into much higher levels than had been expected or intended. It was during this period that Peru's total investment coefficient began its long decline, mainly because the private sector's share of investment began falling disproportionately (Thorp and Bertram 1978, 288–91). By the late 1960s a state-led development strategy had evolved mainly as a matter of default, and the combined results were an increasing resort to external financing and a much greater difficulty in achieving sound macroeconomic policy management.

It was the need for debt refinancing and macroeconomic adjustment that went to the heart of the crisis that preceded the military coup of 1968. By implementing such reforms as land redistribution, widespread nationalization, new private investment laws, and worker ownership schemes, the Revolutionary Government of the Armed Forces (RGAF) broke with Peru's past in dramatic ways when it took command in 1968. Nevertheless, this period also solidified a pattern of debt-led state intervention and chaotic macroeconomic policy management that would persist until 1990 (Wise 1990).

The first phase of this pattern consisted of active external borrowing, which continued through the easy times of unmonitored Euromarket lending in the early 1970s and ended with Peru's final $100 million foreign bank loan in 1984. Even though a strong reliance on external borrowing was not an option after 1985, the newly elected García administration launched the second phase of this pattern by obtaining de facto financing through its policy of limiting Peru's debt payments to just 10–20 percent of export earnings until 1990 (Lago 1992).

Despite five separate administrations between 1963 and 1990, all of which embraced markedly different development strategies, there remains an intriguing continuity over this time period in both the willingness of each to go to any extremes to avoid adjustment, and in the accompanying macropolicy patterns and economic indicators. The final section of this chapter ties these problems in with the institutional backdrop in

Peru, and in particular with a long-term pattern of mutual aggravation between economic policy making and domestic state structures. For the sake of this argument, what follows are some of the general results of this negative interplay between external financing and macroeconomic policy making.

On the debt side, only one-third of the loans disbursed to the public sector between 1970 and 1985 were invested, and those that were typically went toward large capital-intensive projects that contributed less than 10 percent of public investment for export or industrial activities. The remainder of the funds were spent on food and defense imports, on budget and balance-of-payments support, and on penalties for refinancing (Kisic 1987). The accompanying macroeconomic policy trends, although spanning development strategies as diverse as state capitalism and neoliberalism, are congruous in the sense that they remained erratic and unpredictable for thirty years. The entire time period saw just two brief attempts at adjustment, in the throes of the 1977 and 1983 debt crises; as noted in Table 3.2, fiscal, monetary, and trade management policies have fluctuated greatly, while exchange rates—for varying reasons—have been largely overvalued since 1963 (Gonzáles and Samamé 1991).

The State-Owned Enterprises and Disarticulated Capitalism

After 1968, Peru's state-owned enterprise (SOE) sector quickly became the cornerstone of the RGAF's state capitalist strategy, which, at least theoretically, was designed to kick off heavy industry through the expansion of primary exports. As a result, the SOE contribution to GDP jumped from 1 percent in 1968 to nearly 20 percent in 1975. This intensely compressed expansion, which has normally occurred over four or five decades in other Latin American countries, came about in three basic ways (Fitzgerald 1979, 192–95). First, there were those firms in mining and oil that had been expropriated from foreign capital under largely ideological ("antiimperialist") guises; second, there was the reorganization and expansion of firms that were already publicly held to form new SOEs in mining, steel, and electricity; third, there were inadvertent takeovers of domestically owned companies that had fallen too deeply into the red. In hindsight, the legal and administrative backdrop against which the Peruvian state undertook these new entrepreneurial responsibilities could not have been more vague (Saulniers 1988). While the RGAF did begin circulating a draft version of a public-enterprise law in 1971, a comprehensive code endowing SOEs with a coherent legal and administrative structure would not be passed for another twenty years.[2]

Given this state of legal and administrative limbo, as early as 1975, Peru's SOE sector had already succumbed to two of the classic pitfalls most mentioned in the literature on SOEs (Glade 1986). First was the constant tension between the pursuit of a firm's microeconomic investment goals and the more macroeconomic and social objectives of the central government; second was the chronic tug-of-war between the attempts at managerial autonomy on the part of individual firms and excessive control exerted by the various ministries. Looking back over the twelve years of military rule, it is still difficult to explain this disjuncture between the SOE sector's critical importance in the transformation of the political economy and the totally insufficient effort that was made to harness the SOEs to this task.

In recognition that the SOEs had come to play a pivotal role in the economy, all of the subsequent administrations since 1975 stressed the need for serious SOE reform. However, rather than tackle the difficult legal and administrative problems within the SOEs, almost all of the reform efforts between 1980 and 1992 centered on ambitious and highly unrealistic privatization drives. For instance, in line with its goals of reviving private-sector participation to pre-1968 levels, the second Belaúnde administration placed top priority on the reduction of the SOEs and the stimulation of private investment. However, despite a highly vocal privatization and investment campaign from 1980 to 1985, Belaúnde's second term closed with just a few insubstantial liquidations and with private investment at a new historical low of 12 percent of GDP.

The García administration paid some lip service early on to SOE reduction and reform and even passed a long-overdue Entrepreneurial Law of the State, which more concisely defined the legal and administrative terrain of the SOEs.[3] But when it came to implementing this legislation, or rationalizing and shrinking the SOEs, the García team was no more politically committed than its predecessor had been.[4] Instead, García and his

---

2. Oddly, Peru's 1971–75 national development plan, for all its emphasis on the state's new entrepreneurial role, devoted just a few lines to SOEs in a buried section on the central government organizational structure (Wise 1990, 177).

3. "Ley de la actividad empresarial del estado (Ley No. 24948)," Casa del Congreso, Lima, 1 June 1988.

4. The García government did announce a divestiture plan in 1986 that targeted the sale of $400 million in company shares over two years. But, similar to the pattern under the

party perfected the practice that began in the early 1980s, of blaming most of Peru's economic ills on the SOEs, while technocrats and politicians close to the administration openly employed them for private benefit.

By 1990, the debate over privatization in Peru had degenerated to the level of panel discussions where state functionaries and private-sector representatives each summarized the problems in the SOE sector from their own viewpoint, and then shelved the recommendations for reform. In fairness to both administrations, during the 1980s none of the major Latin American countries outside of Chile made any better headway with privatization than did Peru.

State and Private Sector: An Approach-Avoidance Relationship

Underlying Peru's long downward trend in private investment has been a standoff in domestic public-private relations that has persevered in one form or another since the decline of the traditional primary-export model in the early 1960s. Contrary to the explicit kinds of investment deals that had been forged between public and private actors in other Latin countries (Sikkink 1991), Peru's private sector viewed the state as a passive partner for guaranteeing the profits of domestic capital and its foreign allies. In fact, the winner-take-all attitudes of domestic and foreign capital partially prompted the military intervention of 1968. But, while the RGAF's state capitalist model factored in a high level of private investment, the regime's ambiguous stance was such that this period now stands out as the key turning point in the decline of private-sector participation in Peru (Paredes and Pasco-Font 1990).

There are two main legacies from the 1970s with respect to this theme of public-private relations in Peru. First was the transfer of the investment burden from the private to the public sector, but without any improvement in the latter's ability to finance this effort and with amazingly little initiative taken to gain access to the substantial private-sector profits that registered over the decade (Fitzgerald 1979). Second was the emergence of a cross-sectoral alliance of domestic capitalists in the mid-1970s, who found themselves united against the military and what was widely per-

---

second Belaúnde administration, the entire García period saw a divestiture of just several small shareholdings, plus one physical plant, all of which sold for about $1.5 million. This information is reported by Alvarez (1991, 68) and by Joseph Borgatti, *Divestiture Program of Inversiones COFIDE S.A. (ISCA),* Washington, D.C.: U.S. AID Bureau for Private Enterprise, 21 March 1988, 50/2–50/3.

ceived as the "crowding out" effect of state expansion, but not at all unified in pursuit of a coherent alternative. After having gone through several reincarnations, it is this alliance that in 1984 went on to form CONFIEP, Peru's major business organization (Durand 1992, 249–50).

As eager as Peruvian business has been to catch up from the crisis of representation that it experienced under the RGAF, both the Belaúnde and the García administrations during the 1980s succeeded in alienating the private sector early on. In the case of the former, part of the problem was the administration's unrealistic goal of turning the country back into a primary exporter spurred by FDI (foreign direct investment). The second Belaúnde administration simply misread the interests and needs of domestic capital, which had by now succeeded in reorganizing around a mixed economy, forming more modern groups based in the financial system. The diversification of local private capital into banking, real estate, manufacturing, agro-industry, and other non-traditional exports made for a more complex set of policy demands from the private sector, something the badly managed Belaúnde economic program failed to address and the administration failed to grasp (Wise 1989, 171).

The García team clearly understood these new realities vis-à-vis the Peruvian private sector but never followed through with the appropriate set of policy responses. To his credit, García sought a national-industrial alliance with the private sector that centered on the promotion of new export-oriented projects (Durand 1992, 243). Given the context of severe economic crisis and explosive political violence, domestic capital accepted García's invitation and entered into its first explicit development pact with the state. But no sooner had the deal been struck than it became clear that the state itself lacked a core constituency with the initiative and vision to uphold its part in the alliance. State policy making post-1985 was plagued by the president's highly impulsive behavior and by the paucity of sound administrative follow-up on many of the promised economic reforms. The grand finale, of course, was García's impetuous decision in mid-1987 to nationalize that portion of the financial system that still remained in private hands, thus rendering state-capital relations highly acrimonious for the remainder of the decade.

Social Policy and the Bottom 75 Percent of the Income Pyramid

Most administrations since the 1960s have engaged in some form of redistributional policy or rhetoric. Yet, amazingly, Peru entered the 1990s with a dualistic pattern of production and income shares no less polarized than that of thirty years ago (Abugattas 1991; Gonzáles and Samamé 1991). Dualism refers to a pattern whereby a small segment of the workforce in the modern sector of the economy accounts for the bulk of national production and income, while the mass of the population is employed in traditional economic activities that generate very little income. By the early 1980s, for example, the traditional rural and urban informal sectors still comprised 75 percent of all workers, while the value-added contribution to GDP of these workers was just 36 percent. In other words, the remaining 25 percent of the modern-sector workforce accounted for 64 percent of the value added to GDP at this time.[5]

Efforts at redistributional policy reached new heights in Peru during the Velasco period in the early 1970s, but the outcomes were just the opposite of the RGAF's vision of a more equitable society regrouped into benign corporatist units. The military's inability to follow through on its many social and economic promises, and the mass rejection of the hierarchical corporatist structures imposed by the RGAF, gave birth to a new horizontal network of base groups that became better organized and more capable of defending their interests than ever before (Sanborn 1991; Stokes 1991). Part of this new highly politicized faction led the return to civilian rule in 1980 and went on to form the broad spectrum of Left-leaning political parties that began making strong electoral headway after 1983.

Another part of this faction, embittered by the persistence of almost ancient forms of poverty and by the fact that a large percentage of the population was still excluded—by sector and by region—from fully participating in the national political economy, has since 1980 turned underground and taken up arms against the state. A full account of the various debates and explanations surrounding the rise of Sendero Luminoso and Peru's other militant insurgencies lies beyond the scope of this analysis.[6] For the purposes of this argument, suffice it to say that the political economic trends and outcomes analyzed above have both contributed to and perpetuated the nihilistic attitude and ready resort to violence on the part of this second faction.

---

5. The figures are cited from an unpublished table compiled by Richard Webb, president of Peru's Central Reserve Bank from 1980 to 1985.

6. For a more thorough treatment of the rise of Sendero Luminoso and the various debates over the roots of political violence in Peru, see Degregori (1990) and Gorriti (1990). See also Starn's (1992) first-rate review of the growing body of literature on this subject.

Returning more specifically to the theme of social policy, distributional patterns during the 1980s in Peru could hardly have done more to fuel the domestic violence. The first half of the decade saw an outright neglect of social policy, under the guise that the second Belaúnde administration's neoliberal program would prompt a redistributive trickle-down. It was the synergistic effect of economic crisis, an increasingly polarized distribution of income, and staunch popular resistance that helped pave the way for García and his neostructuralist experiment (Lago 1992; Pastor and Wise 1992). García made it clear that his sentiments lay with that lower rung of the workforce that still encompassed 75 percent of the working population. But the reliance on debt non-payment and reckless deficit spending to boost real wages, not to mention García's alienation of the private sector, quickly led to hyperinflation. In the end, the measures hit hardest at those whom they were most intended to help: the number of Peruvians living below the poverty line slipped from 17 percent to 44 percent over the course of the García administration.

Looking back, both Belaúnde and García bent over backward to avoid the necessary macroeconomic adjustments, ostensibly because of the high social and political costs. The result, as inflation was left to perform the dirty work of stabilization, was a severe deterioration in the wage share of national income and a correspondingly sharp increase in the proportion of national income accounted for by gross profits (profits, rent, and net interest) (Pastor 1992, 8). As guerrilla insurgencies capitalized on these miserable trends, expanding their presence from the highlands into the streets of Lima and other major Peruvian cities, it was the failure to properly adjust the macroeconomy that proved much more costly than ever imagined.

The Fujimori Track Record: Markets Without Politics

When President Fujimori was inaugurated on 28 July 1990, the country was at a particularly painful juncture. A break with this failed statist approach had become a prerequisite for reestablishing Peru's relations with the international financial community, not to mention for fending off a full-blown guerrilla campaign. Given the unenviable task of repairing South America's most desperate economy, Fujimori followed in the footsteps of Venezuela's Carlos Andrés Pérez and Argentina's Carlos Menem by reversing earlier campaign pledges to carry out a gradual adjustment and instead launched an ambitious set of market-oriented reforms (the so-called Fujishock).

Besides starting out with a severe economic handicap, Fujimori had his hands tied politically in that this was the first civilian administration since 1963 that did not command a majority vote in Congress, and thus could not easily will its way in the policy-making arena. It was this early standoff between the president, his backers, and the political opposition that quickly led to policy paralysis, and that the president used as grounds for dissolving Congress and suspending the constitution in April 1992. With Fujimori's victory in the 1995 presidential election, as well as the installation of a new Congress and constitution, a democratic regime has now been restored in the formal sense.

However, because of the president's refusal to delegate authority, his continued reliance on the military as a source of legitimacy, and his insistence on circumventing established institutional channels when dealing with the main groups and sectors of Peruvian society, the country's return to democratic rule has been eerily apolitical. For example, the president recently passed a law forbidding judges to interpret the new constitution, and Congress has taken to approving key economic measures, such as Latin America's most unrestricted land-tenure law, in the midst of all-night legislative sessions. Because other chapters in this collection address this theme, my purpose in this section is to examine the extent to which the Fujimori administration's neoliberal reforms have reversed the trends reviewed above, while taking this depoliticized backdrop into account.

Turning to the Fujimori track record on economic reform since 1990, the results have been mixed. Most of the headway thus far has been made in restoring ties with the foreign financial community, particularly the multilateral lenders, in stabilizing the macroeconomy, and in the privatization of state assets. With regard to its foreign financial ties, Peru has now renegotiated $1.7 billion in arrears with all of the main multilateral funding agencies, a hurdle that had to be crossed before policy makers could proceed in rescheduling some $8 billion in debt held by the western-country creditors, also known as the Paris Club. The Paris Club rescheduling took until mid-1993, as Fujimori and his advisers—caught off guard by the vehement rejection of Peru's authoritarian persona by the industrial-bloc countries—were basically given the quid pro quo of producing a credible timetable for the return to civilian rule. As a result of the Paris Club deal, Peru received 60 percent relief on the $3.1 billion it was due to pay during the 1993–95 period, some of the most favorable terms given yet by the Western creditors.[7]

While the Fujimori team still must face the music in renegotiating another $7 billion in commercial-bank debt, this initial victory with debt rescheduling and reduction enabled the administration to attract some $500 million in FDI in 1993, thus providing some badly needed credibility for the government's privatization effort. However, even with these favorable payback terms, Peru's annual debt-service payments are running at around 20 percent of export earnings, which still places extremely tight constraints on the financing of the government's ongoing macroeconomic adjustment program.[8] Nevertheless, now having faced its creditors, under the leadership of President Fujimori the country has finally buckled down in implementing its most rigorous macroeconomic stabilization and structural adjustment program to date (see Table 3.2).

On both counts, the Fujimori administration has relied on a combination of liberalization, deregulation, and an ambitious set of market-oriented structural reforms (Gonzáles 1993; Sheahan 1992; Paredes and Sachs 1991). While local policy analysts applaud the efforts of the current economic team to finally tackle the long-overdue task of economic adjustment, there is some concern over the administration's failure to articulate a medium-term development strategy. Moreover, in the shorter term, although inflation had dipped below 20 percent and Peruvian growth rates had rebounded to 12.9 percent of GDP by 1994—led primarily by fishing, mining, and the privatization of state assets—policy makers now find themselves facing the same medium-term macroeconomic challenges that have plagued other neoliberal reformers in the region, such as Argentina and Mexico.

These medium-term challenges, which are documented in Table 3.3, have clustered together into the following pattern: given the stubborn persistence of inflation through the 1980s, all of these market programs finally turned to unilateral trade liberalization as an anti-inflationary strategy in the early 1990s, the hope being that the combination of exchange-rate stability and foreign competition would impose price discipline on domestic producers (Pastor and Wise 1994b; Naim 1993). As a result, in-

---

7. Paris Club Agrees Rescheduling," *Latin America Monitor: Andean Group*, June 1993, 1159.

8. "Trend Report," *Peru Report*, December 1993, 2.

flation has dropped but trade deficits have quickly expanded, leaving governments in a pinch to cover the shortfall. Most states, including Peru, have succeeded in attracting offsetting capital flows by maintaining high interest rates and by liquidating public firms.

Such strategies, however, are merely stopgaps in the sense that earnings from privatization provide a one-shot infusion of capital, and today's capital flows, although responsible for the recent boom in the Lima stock market, have also contributed to the increasingly overvalued exchange rate that appears in Table 3.3. As much as these trends cry for a debate over the need to adjust the exchange rate and redirect incoming capital flows into productive ventures, such debate has been hampered by today's highly autocratic decision-making style, which concentrates power almost entirely within the executive.[9]

Although the current economic team's tight insulation and unchecked commitment to the market may become so rigid as to jeopardize the recent gains that have been made with macroeconomic stabilization, this elite-level decision-making style has thus far worked well on the privatization front. Given an almost complete collapse in public finances and annual SOE losses of around $3.2 million shortly after Fujimori's election in 1990, the administration succeeded in passing a new privatization law in late 1991. Having sidestepped the staunch congressional opposition to privatization that prevailed up until the 1992 coup, and despite a cold-feet response by private domestic producers who were reluctant to give up whatever state subsidies still remained, the government's newly created privatization commission (Comisión de Privatización, or COPRI) began trying to quickly unload state assets in late 1992.[10] With its mandate to sell everything it possibly could and liquidate the rest, COPRI has simultaneously pursued several strategies.[11] First, and this is something new for Peru, COPRI staff have been actively involved in the restructuring of companies to make them more attractive to potential buyers, and in helping to put together the necessary financing schemes to support privatization. Second, apart from better preparing state firms for sale, COPRI started its

9. Although the president's inner circle of economic advisers insists that the Peruvian exchange rate is freely floating and will therefore adjust automatically, local Central Reserve Bank officials readily admit that the current regime is one of a "dirty float" where the bank has been intervening regularly to maintain the exchange rate. Based on confidential author's interviews, Lima, July 1995.

10. "Promulgan la ley de promocion de la inversion privada en las empresas del estado (Decreto Legislativo No. 674)," *El Peruano*, 27 September 1991, 100325.

11. Interview with Carlos Montoya, COPRI's chief operating officer, Lima, 25 May 1992.

Table 3.3. Economic trends under Fujimori, 1990–1994

	GDPGROWB	CHGDPRPC	XCSGDPC	MGSGDPC	TBGSGDPC	CURGDP	INVGDP	PRIVING	PUBINVG	RER02NRM	DECINF
1990	−4.9	−6.8	12.6	11.9	0.7	−3.8	14.7	12.2	2.5	100.0	7,649.7
1991	2.8	0.9	9.7	11.6	−1.9	−5.6	14.3	11.8	2.5	80.9	139.2
1992	−2.4	−4.2	10.3	13.3	−3.0	−7.1	15.3	12.4	2.9	75.6	56.7
1993	6.5	4.4	10.6	13.7	−3.1	−5.4	16.7	13.5	3.2	82.4	39.5
1994	12.9	10.8	9.4	11.5	−2.2	−3.5	NA	NA	NA	74.5	15.4

GDPGROWB = Growth of real GDP.
CHGDPRPC = Growth of real GDP per capita.
XGSGDPC = Exports of goods and nonfinancial services as % of GDP.
MGSGDPC = Imports of goods and nonfinancial services as % of GDP.
TBGSGDPC = Trade balance of goods and nonfinancial services as % of GDP.
CURGDP = Current account as % of GDP.
INVGDP = Total domestic investment as % of GDP.
PRIVING = Private investment as % of GDP.
PUBINVG = Public investment as % of GDP.
RER02NRM = Real exchange rate (1990 = 100); calculated using period average exchange rates, US WPI, and domestic CPI.
DECINF = December to December inflation.

Most data from the World Bank's World Tables, 1995 (CD-ROM).
Data on December to December inflation from International Financial Statistics, CD-ROM, 12/9.
Data on investment from the World Bank's International Finance Corporation.

sell-off campaign with smaller firms, which are easier to unload; the strategy with the larger SOEs, which currently dominate mining, petroleum, agriculture, communications, transport, and electricity, has been to offer stock options in a more piecemeal fashion. This latter approach is another departure from past efforts, which have hinged on grand privatization schemes that simply never paid off.

Although COPRI set out on this aggressive privatization drive at a time when no one was certain as to the actual size of Peru's SOE portfolio,[12] and when most SOEs were technically bankrupt (Webb 1991, 3), optimism is now warranted on the privatization front for several reasons. First, the legal guidelines for privatization are finally in place, the most important being an explicit set of instructions for assessing the value of individual firms and concrete procedures for divestiture. Second, there is an unprecedented consensus in favor of the SOE sell-offs among policy makers within the major state financial and economic institutions. Finally, COPRI is widely seen as the most professional and authentic attempt yet at bringing together the kinds of technical expertise and financial know-how that have been prerequisites for successful privatization drives in countries like Chile and Mexico.

By the end of 1993, just $317 million in state assets had been sold under the Fujimori administration, despite COPRI's optimistic goal of "selling everything by 1995." The government's unrealistic timeline aside, 1994–95 proved to be the turning point. Lower inflation and higher growth rates sent the most convincing price signals in years; moreover, the president showed investors that he was willing to go so far as to suspend democratic rule in order to secure his victory over recession and hyperinflation. By mid-1995, some seventy-two privatizations had been completed in such sectors as electricity (Edelnor, Edelsur), telecommunications (ENTEL-CPT), mining (Tintaya, Cajamarquilla), industry (Cementos Lima), and banking (Banco Continental), bringing the total proceeds up to $3.6 billion.[13]

While the present privatization program stands out as the most successful and broadly agreed-upon aspect of the Fujimori reform effort, the

12. Counting all the various categories of companies with some state shares, estimates of Peru's SOE sector on the eve of the 1992 privatization drive range from 135 SOEs (Alvarez 1991, 124) to 182 ("Privatization," *Peru Report*, July 1991, 7).

13. The data cited here stem from an internal COPRI report entitled "Avance del proceso de privatizacion," 17 July 1995, and from my interview with director of COPRI Manuel Llosa, Lima, 18 July 1995.

administration has been criticized by the political opposition for acting too hastily in its attempts to liquidate those state firms that provide crucial public goods (for instance, water, electricity, transportation) and could thus play a key distributional function in channeling more affordable services to the poorest sectors of society (Gonzáles 1993, 70–71). It is this distributional shortfall and the continuing tensions between the government and the domestic private sector that constitute the downside of the Fujimori program. The discussion now turns to that downside.

With regard to the changing relationship between the public and the private sectors, Peru in the 1990s finds itself in the same position as the rest of Latin America (Durand 1994; Wise 1993). That is, governments are more in need of private investment than ever before, but they are no longer in a position to offer the kinds of subsidies and financial incentives that have traditionally been used to cement alliances between the state and domestic capitalists. At the same time, for all the private sector's calls for a small, efficient, hands-off state in the 1990s, the data show that public investment has actually played a complementary, "crowding in" role for private investors in Latin America over the post–World War II period (Pastor 1992, 28).

As much as the state and the private sector still need each other, the long recession of the 1980s has forced domestic policy makers to devise alternative means for courting the private sector. In the 1990s, a productive public-private relationship has come to rely increasingly on the state's ability to establish and maintain a more level macroeconomic playing field, and on the initiation of a serious dialogue with domestic capital geared toward the negotiation and promotion of greater private investment. Having spent the bulk of its time since mid-1990 on macroeconomic stabilization and its international economic "reinsertion strategy," the Fujimori administration has moved slowly in terms of strengthening the relationship between the public and the private sector. In fact, when compared with most of its neighbors in the large middle-income Latin American states, Peru is off to perhaps the latest start of all in attempting to launch a more constructive and productive working alliance between the state and domestic capitalists.

On a positive note, the privatization program is now operating with a sound legal and technical framework, and an estimated $2 billion in repatriated deposits have been registered in Peru since 1991.[14] The early

---

14. However, the bulk of these repatriated funds appear to have been spent on daily

1992 appointment of former CONFIEP president Jorge Camet as finance minister is also seen as a favorable step toward building a healthier rapport between the public and the private sector. Yet, there are still complaints across the Peruvian private sector that CONFIEP and its twenty-four-member groups have, in fact, had little input or say about the present economic approach.[15] An even deeper concern is that, in view of the lack of a concrete medium-term development strategy, it is not at all clear what the state and domestic capital would be negotiating toward, should the former step forward again and more formally solicit the cooperation of the latter.[16]

Thus far, the development catchwords of the Fujimori administration have been "industrial reconversion," which suggests a Chilean-style approach of increasing value added in natural-resource exploitation and forging stronger backward and forward linkages with industrial and other non-traditional export projects.[17] Clearly, with the uncertainty of external capital flows, a public-private alliance acted out through the CONFIEP and geared toward leveraging local investment along these lines is a logical path forward for Peru. It remains to be seen whether the administration will be able to articulate these goals more concretely and to better coordinate the kinds of macropolicy (particularly exchange rates, interest rates, and the tax code) that would make them obtainable. Six years into the market-reform effort, private-sector representatives have placed some very concrete demands on the negotiating table—for example, the need for export promotion incentives, the expansion of public infrastructure, and further economic deregulation—yet they claim to still be waiting for the government to respond.[18]

Finally, there is the challenge of income distribution, which has been the Achilles' heel for all of the market reformers in the region. By the time of Fujimori's election in 1990, the unmet basic needs of the population, including everything from food and housing to education and

operating costs by companies trying to make it through the economic adjustment program without going bankrupt. See "Political Interview," *Peru Report,* November 1993, 4.

15. Interview with Luis Abugattas, director, Instituto de Estudios Economicos y Sociales de la Sociedad Nacional de Industrias, Lima, 17 July 1995.

16. El rol de la CONFIEP: Mas alla del corto plazo," *Peru Economico,* May 1992, 4–8.

17. This interpretation is derived from interviews in Lima with Guido Pennano (May 1992), minister of industry during the first eight months of the Fujimori administration, and with José Valderama (July 1995), special adviser to the finance minister.

18. Interviews in Lima with Arturo Woodman, president of CONFIEP, and with Augusto Alvarez, APOYO, July 1995.

health care, had accumulated into a social deficit of crisis proportions (Abugattas 1991, 148). In its eagerness to cement the international reinsertion strategy, the Fujimori administration went ahead with the stabilization program knowing full well that the anticipated short-term social costs of the reforms were higher than those of a well-designed stabilization program, particularly given the highly distorted price structure that the administration had inherited in 1990 (Paredes 1991, 303). Thus, whereas by July 1990 working Peruvians were earning half of what they had earned in July 1985, in the wake of the August 1990 adjustments, even this dismal purchasing power was again cut in half.[19] Startlingly, in the short time between Fujimori's election and the April 1992 coup, the real income of all Peruvians had dropped by another third (Gonzáles de Olarte 1993, 52).

Despite the availability of multilateral financing to launch a credible social emergency program to complement its highly regressive economic adjustment effort, the Fujimori administration was quite slow to act on this front. After a first year of false starts in formulating a desperately needed social policy, the government finally announced the establishment of a National Fund for Development and Social Compensation (FONCODES) in August 1991. Similar to compensatory social programs that have been implemented with multilateral support in Bolivia, Chile, Colombia, and Mexico, FONCODES is an attempt to redefine the state's role in the provision of public goods under a market-oriented economic model that still faces serious resource constraints. In doing so, all of these programs combine traditional social-welfare policies with new "demand-based" criteria requiring that communities generate specific proposals for assistance. Moreover, all of these programs make some effort to integrate marginal and/or crisis-ridden sectors into the productive economy (Graham 1994).

Since its founding in 1991, FONCODES is finally coming into its own. Having suffered initially from a high level of turnover at the top and from the president's tendency to treat the agency as a mechanism for pursuing his own political objectives (Graham 1993), FONCODES has gradually become more independent and more professional, due partially to the support of various nongovernmental organizations and the multilaterals. Beginning in 1994, for example, both the World Bank and the Inter-American Development Bank kicked in $100 million each for social-sector

---

19. "Trend Report," *Peru Report*, September 1990, 1–2.

loans, which have enabled the establishment of competitive salaries for FONCODES staff.[20] To its credit, the Fujimori administration has now joined other market reformers in the region in targeting desperately needed compensatory resources, the bulk of which have gone toward economic infrastructure (like road-maintenance projects, irrigation, deforestation) and social infrastructure (such as health and education facilities and basic housing).[21]

Despite these advances, Peru's social policy is still running distinctly in the red, as reflected in the following four problems. First, the cuts in spending for traditional public goods like health and education have been the steepest among the top six Latin American countries, a trend that is readily apparent in Peru's continuingly dismal social indicators (Figueroa 1995). As a temporary safety net, FONCODES has provided some immediate relief, however, none of today's compensation schemes can substitute for an ongoing social policy proper, which Peru still lacks. Second, FONCODES has been implemented in the absence of a concrete development plan, and with weak coordination between the sectoral ministries responsible for the activities that FONCODES has overlapped with (health, education, housing), which makes it difficult to maximize on scarce resources or to measure the efficacy of the program.[22] Third, even if social policy were better planned and coordinated, "the project evaluation skills within the government are nil,"[23] a weakness to which FONCODES staff readily admit.

Finally, although FONCODES is less under the reach of the president than before, Fujimori still controls the bulk of social policy through his newly created Ministry of the Presidency. Thus, through the establishment of various mini-entities within this powerful new ministry, the president has succeeded in streamlining some of his social initiatives and in maintaining the option of designating these resources toward his own political ends. This highly presidential institutional arrangement is reflective of how the entire policy-making apparatus has been managed through the 1990s, a point to which the analysis now turns.

20. Interview with Rosa Flores, executive director of Evaluation Department at FONCODES, July 1995.

21. FONCODES: Nota Mensual (November 1994–April 1995).

22. According to one of the finance minister's principal advisers, Iván Rivera, the Fujimori administration has no intention of producing a development plan, as this runs counter to the administration's belief that the economy should be guided by the market. Interview with Iván Rivera, Lima, July 1995.

23. Interview with Roberto Abusada, executive director, ECONSULT, Lima, July 1995.

The Institutional Backdrop: Whither Civil Society?
The Limits to a Strong-Executive, Weak-State Approach

Because of the weaknesses in Peru's own institutional landscape, it is useful to establish a reference point for analyzing the country's organizational makeup by considering some of the more successful development
scenarios. Several of these are cited in the recent comparative political-
economy literature on state institutions and political capacities in developing countries (Geddes 1994; Sikkink 1991; Gereffi and Wyman 1990;
Haggard 1990; Evans 1989). From this literature, which focuses on both
Latin America and East Asia, certain broad features of the state and society stand out as facilitating a given country's ability to extract a longer-
term commitment from private investors, and to reconcile complex social
and political demands with a designated set of development goals. The
range of institutional structures that emerge from this literature has been
summarized in Table 3.4.

The table points to bureaucratic autonomy and economic institutional
consolidation as two key structural features that have enabled some states
to devise a convincing set of market-supporting reforms; it also shows the
importance of a stable leadership coalition and the coherence with which
organized interests are tied to the state. Because institutional capacity can
vary over time and across a number of policy tasks, the framework in
Table 3.4 is best viewed as a continuum that allows for a more nuanced
assessment of a given state's ability to generate market-supporting measures and gather sociopolitical consensus.

At the more successful end of the continuum (Chile, Colombia, Mexico), effective states are characterized by the ability to join well-developed
bureaucratic internal organizations with a sophisticated network of public-
private ties (Evans 1989). In the less-effective states (Argentina, Brazil,
Peru), undisciplined internal bureaucratic structures are controlled by the
same public-private network, but chaotically, leading to the kinds of erratic policy shifts that ultimately undermine the investment confidence of
those same private interests that helped give rise to them.

Turning to the evolution of state and societal institutions in Peru, it
helps to point out that any serious attempts at state building did not get
under way until the early 1970s. The 1960s did see the creation of the
National Planning Institute and the laying down of professional recruit-

Table 3.4. The political capacity of the state to intervene

	More Effective	Less Effective
State planning and economic institutions	A few powerful economic and planning institutions Decisional and operational authority linked to strategic policy areas Technically skilled civil service governed by merit procedure	Lack of major planning or economic institution, or existing agencies marginalized or made ineffectual for political reasons Narrow decisional leeway with policymaking ad hoc and dispersed Hiring and promotion within state bureaucracy governed primarily by personalistic ties
Degree of bureaucratic autonomy within the state	Insulated political structures with regulated access Clientelistic exchanges minimized State goals not easily subverted	Loosely linked administrative structures permeated by special interests Clientelism main form of exchange State goals not clearly defined
State-business relations	At the level of the state, stable leadership in the executive able to legitimate itself through skillful use of incentives and disincentives A sophisticated network of public-private ties capable of steering policy without directly interfering in it	Frequent changes of government and/or regime with unpredictable swings in policy Undisciplined internal bureaucratic structures easily captured by private actors
Interest intermediation	Policy mediated through peak organizations (industry associations, trade unions) that are recognized and respected by the state	Fragmented and competing interest-group organizations Attempts by the state to forge policy by circumventing key societal interests or through haphazard mediation

ment and hiring standards at the Central Reserve Bank. Policy making, however, was controlled by Peru's other main economic institution, the Finance Ministry, where favoritism and corruption flourished. Thus, Peru launched its first state-sponsored industrial drive without any one planning or financial entity that was capable of taking the lead, which meant that the import-substitution industrialization program more or less lurched forward at the hands of those private interests that came to control it. As with other ISI experiments in postwar Latin America (Haggard 1990; Sheahan 1987), this transmission of the public good into private hands was asymmetrical, with the state giving, the industrialists taking, and labor for the most part assigned the role of junior partner. Although Peruvian workers were well organized by the 1960s, government-labor mediation at this time has been described as a "nonconsensual structure of coercion" (Astiz 1969, 69), whereby economic concessions were granted by the state around election time and most other labor demands or strife were met with political repression.

It was ostensibly in response to the obvious economic failures and institutional shortcomings of the first Belaúnde administration that a reform-minded military intervened in 1968 and launched one of Latin America's more anomalous efforts at state building, particularly given the lateness of the effort and its military sponsorship. Thus far this analysis has mainly credited the RGAF with more firmly institutionalizing the difficult state-led dynamic that has plagued the country since the early 1960s, and surely most Peruvian elites would bristle at the suggestion that this period did anything but multiply the rent-seeking and predatory costs of state intervention (De Soto 1989). As true as these last statements may be, upon closer inspection, the early 1970s also stand out as the country's first and only serious attempt at upgrading and modernizing certain parts of the state apparatus.

To elaborate on this point, the upside of the RGAF program under Velasco was the regime's explicit attempts at bureaucratic innovation, the strengthening of state planning and economic institutions, and the establishment of a framework for mediating interests between the state, capital, and labor. Having witnessed all the factions and infighting that had over-whelmed his presidential predecessor, Velasco and his cohorts moved quickly to restructure channels of access to the executive, and they reorganized civil society into state-chartered corporatist units. Along with the creation of a more autonomous executive, the central-government ministries saw their first major administrative overhaul, and two of the main economic institutions (National Planning and the Finance Ministry) were bolstered with greater decisional and operational authority. By 1975 the Peruvian bureaucracy was finally beginning to take the more professional shape that other central governments in the region had assumed since the 1950s (Fitzgerald 1979), and with the entry of a highly capable corps of technocrats, state-sector employment briefly came to be considered a prestigious and economically appealing endeavor (Giesecke 1985).

The downside of this ambitious state-building effort, already implicit in the analysis presented in the preceding section, was the haste with which the development program was launched, the lack of clarity in goals, and the built-in tensions of a strategy that merged military and civilian policy makers into a top-down relationship on the latter's own bureaucratic turf. Moreover, the regime went overboard in ensuring the autonomy and influence of an elite executive-level team of advisers, while neglecting to cultivate sectors of the state bureaucracy that were capable of actually carrying out executive policy directives. Bureaucratic autonomy, as it is referred to in Table 3.4, implies that officials who constitute the state not only have preferences that are more than simple reflections of those expressed by powerful societal groups; in order to implement these preferences, autonomy also entails the cultivation of organizational cohesion, expertise, and extractive capabilities within strategic sectors of the state bureaucracy (Geddes 1994; Sikkink 1991).

As the state capitalist program ran into its first balance-of-payments difficulties and the Velasco coalition began to unravel over policy differences, the regime's lack of a broad constituency—both within and outside of the state—proved to be its ultimate undoing. The military's network of state-dominated peak associations, created originally to quell conflict and to gather support for its program, later proved more effective for setting in motion the organized opposition to the regime (Sanborn 1991).

It was during the transition to civilian rule in the late 1970s that domestic institutions were cast into the mold that persisted until the end of the García administration. A main response to the 1977 debt crisis was the massive layoff of public-sector personnel, with the unfortunate result that those employees in the highest job grades and with the longest civil service tenures were let go (Giesecke 1985). The elimination of this core policy-making segment, and the military regime's inability to consolidate a "super ministry" to coordinate and manage the development program, reversed much of the momentum that had been gained earlier. Relations between the main state planning and financial institutions became increasingly conflictual, as each squared off in the competition to control economic policy making. Paradoxically, and in direct contrast to what the RGAF had envisioned, labor and the private sector emerged from the 1970s more vocal and assertive, while the state was weaker and highly ineffectual.

With an eye toward rectifying those political and economic aspects of the institutional setting that appeared to play a strong part in thwarting the success of civilian rule in the 1960s, the framers of Peru's 1979 constitution passed two key clauses. The first provision redressed the policy gridlock between the executive and the legislature that had preceded the 1968 coup: it granted the president the power to legislate by special decree on certain issues and for set periods of time. The second provision, in line with the intentions underlying the governance of the U.S. Federal Reserve, mandated increased autonomy for the Central Reserve Bank and a set five-year term for its director, so as to buffer economic policy making from political interferences. With the return of civilian rule in 1980, these two reforms quickly meshed with the numerous structural transformations handed down from the RGAF, setting the institutional stage for the pattern of policy making that has prevailed ever since.

Beginning with the second Belaúnde administration, this pattern has consisted of the following. First has been the persistence of an almost purely presidential management style not unlike Velasco's, whereby the executive and a small, insulated team of technical advisers have ruled by decree, basically disregarding inputs from other parts of the state policy apparatus. Originally intended to mitigate the destructive influence of party politics, this practice of ruling by legislative decree has completely overshadowed the need to foster pockets of expertise within the state bureaucracy to carry out the executive will. While some explanations for Fujimori's suspension of Congress in 1992 have hinged on the battles surrounding the president's abuse of this decree-making authority, in fact, Fujimori exercised this legislative power no more than did his predecessors.[24]

The main difference between the present administration and those of Belaúnde and García is that the respective political parties of the latter two held a majority vote in Congress and thus supported each president's actions. In contrast, Fujimori was the first civilian president since 1963 to take office without a majority in Congress. Overall, the cumulative toll of this highly presidential management style since 1980 has been drastic shifts in economic policy between each administration, with virtually no accountability in implementation. Furthermore, given the absence of re-

24. Congress Defies Fujimori Policies," *Latin American Weekly Report*, 5 December 1991, 11; "Conflict of Powers in Peru Worsens As Fujimori Defies Vote of Censure," *Latin American Weekly Report*, 26 December 1991, 1.

liability checks and technical staff support, none of these insulated executive management teams since 1980 have proven adept at shifting course or making necessary corrections midway into the adjustment program. This is the very juncture at which the present economic team now finds itself.

In line with the pattern just described, a second major aspect of the policy-making process in the 1980s was the marginalization of state financial institutions and the abandonment of any pretense at national planning. The earlier commitment toward creating a more autonomous policy-making apparatus within the Central Reserve Bank rapidly rendered the bank a political scapegoat for economic policy failures. Moreover, this commitment was violated when the García administration fired the bank's president in 1987 and then rotated the office three more times. Similarly, President Fujimori dismissed his first Central Bank president and the bank's board of directors long before their designated five-year terms had ended. Apart from this basic disregard for standing legislation, the tendency has been to rely heavily on patronage and the meager expertise of those with close personal ties to the executive, practices that both Belaúnde and García refined to an art. The combined impact of this strong executive–weak state approach to managing the political economy since 1968 is the low correlation between the espoused development models, the actual polices that have been embraced, and the final outcomes that appear in Tables 3.1, 3.2, and 3.3. The gaps between all three drive home the importance of state structures as intervening variables, in the sense that in order to be successfully realized, prevailing development ideologies and strategies must have somewhere to lodge themselves institutionally within the state (Sikkink 1991).

By 1990 Peru's state institutions had collapsed. With the eventual drying up of external credit, foreign reserves, and tax revenues, per capita government spending fell by 83 percent between 1975 and 1990 (Webb 1991, 2); the state sector has now shrunk to just a quarter of its previous size. The Fujimori government has fired thousands of state workers who entered the bureaucracy through party patronage in the 1980s and has set an overall target of paring public employment by five hundred thousand. Thus, Peru now has the small state that the private sector has been yearning for since 1968, but it is still a far cry from the realization of an efficient, market-supporting state that has dominated national-policy debates since the late 1970s.

The present administration has moved gradually to at least resurrect and reconstruct the extractive capabilities of the state. For example, along with the new privatization secretariat, both the tax administration and customs offices have been revamped and staffed with more highly paid and professional technocrats. Furthermore, efforts have been made to restore the operational autonomy and sophistication of key institutions like the Central Reserve Bank and the state oil company (Petro-Perú).[25] If successful, today's attempt at launching a tax shock will constitute the first major fiscal overhaul since 1968. Similarly, if the present regime is able to finesse the international economic-reinsertion strategy, this will be the first full follow-through on debt renegotiation since 1971. Nevertheless, as important as these advances are, these reforms still lack any vision of the overall need for more constructive state action.

Since the dissolution of a democratically elected Congress in 1992, the gutting of the ministries, and another major turnover at the Central Bank, economic policy making has been governed by just two poles of influence: on one side is a tightly insulated executive who has given up on delegating responsibilities outside of his Ministry of the Presidency, and, on the other side, a handful of isolated technocrats in the Finance Ministry intent on applying a somewhat purist interpretation of neoliberal economics. For all the technical backup that could still be tapped by the government from within Lima's impressive network of private economic think tanks, the Fujimori administration has made few attempts at outreach. At this point, it is these overriding characteristics of the state itself, as opposed to the size or the perceived weight of the state on the economy, that is making it difficult to establish productive ties between the public and the private sectors.

At the risk of understatement, the final trend surrounding the policy-making framework since 1980 has been the inability of those civilian groups that supported the transition to democracy in 1980 to enjoy adequate representation in the aftermath (Sanborn 1991). Clearly, the country's historically undemocratic character and weak record of institutionalized political participation cast a dark shadow over the return to civilian rule in 1980. Out of frustration, President Fujimori redrafted the constitution and turned his wrath on the traditional political parties on the grounds that the system had bogged down from the chaotic input of too

25. I thank Javier Escobal at GRADE and Oscar Zaldívar at the Central Reserve Bank of Peru for their insights concerning the institutional transformations now under way within the state sector.

many political and social actors. Since 1992, the president has derived legitimacy by pointing to his majority support within the national public-opinion polls (Conaghan 1995). Yet the polls also show that a majority of the population opposes the remaining vestiges of authoritarianism—for example, within the judicial system—since the highly controlled return to civilian rule in 1995. So Peru's public-opinion polls support Fujimori, which can be safely interpreted as the populace's endorsement of anyone who convincingly commits to clamping down on the various terrorist groups, drug traffickers, and state security squads that ruled de facto over large parts of the country until quite recently (Webb 1991, 4).

Yet, underpinning the Fujimori administration's effective use of public-opinion polls to garner support is another stark reality: the present thrust toward more executive-level insulation, and less dialogue and inclusion of a broad range of political and social actors, represents an intensification of the very circumstances that gave rise to Peru's highly explosive situation in the first place. The fact is that Peru's system is suffering from far too little input, both at the level of high politics and economic-policy decision making and at the everyday level of accommodating the needs and demands of those groups that span civil society. Though the crisis and chaos of the past decade in Peru have left groups within the popular sectors, labor, and business weakened economically and exhausted politically, out of this experience has emerged a more organized, responsible, and level-headed set of base groups, workers' organizations and producer associations (Stokes 1995; Durand 1994; McClintock 1989).

In other words, although Peruvian civil society appears to be more prepared than ever to participate in an authentic consolidation of democratic rule, it has been largely written out of the present institutional blueprint. Even in authoritarian Mexico, the lesson of the last decade is that more sustainable solutions to economic reform were finally found in an overhaul of key state institutions and state-society relations, which partially entailed greater dialogue and collaboration between state managers, political elites, and the representatives of powerful societal interests (Pastor and Wise 1994a).

To reiterate, in Peru, the lesson over the past three decades is that without a consolidated institutional backdrop to facilitate the redefinition and implementation of state goals, or a well-defined relationship between the state and civil society, alliances have fragmented and with them the capacity of the executive to steer policy in the desired direction. The 1980s saw the eruption of this pattern into a violent standoff between state security forces and those who have been marginalized historically, in both political and economic terms. As appealing and expeditious as the present strategy of greater exclusion may be for those now responsible for restoring law and economic order, it is difficult to envision how a full transition to democracy could actually be completed without harnessing to this task the energy of those legally sanctioned groups in civil society and a better-developed set of internal bureaucratic state organizations.

Conclusions

This chapter has identified a pattern of state-led development in Peru that took root in the early 1960s and became problematic by virtue of its over-reliance on external borrowing, high dependence on public firms, alienation of the local private sector, and chronic neglect of social policy. The analysis traced the manner in which these political-economic trends have both stemmed from and been perpetuated by domestic institutional arrangements, and it argued that the adverse interplay between these trends, the state's weak internal organizations, and its poor ties with organized societal interests all go a long way toward explaining Peru's political and economic turbulence over the past decade. What stands out is the paucity of hard-policy decisions that have actually been made since the early 1960s, as well as the lack of follow-through on those steps that have been taken to strengthen the Peruvian state as a more viable actor in the country's development.

The present period finds the country at a compelling juncture, in which the resolution of the worst vestiges of this state-led pattern has finally gotten under way. As noted above, much progress has been made in the areas of macroeconomic stabilization, liberalization, and deregulation, and the Fujimori administration has advanced considerably in reestablishing Peru's relations with the international financial community. Growth rates, moreover, have moved briskly under the impulse of privatization and more favorable commodity prices over the past few years, and this has clearly won the government the good political will necessary to forge ahead further with its market-reform program. Yet, as Peru now moves firmly into the medium-term phase of economic restructuring, there are some worrisome signs on the horizon.

While all of the major market reformers in the region face tough me-

dium-term challenges in terms of achieving sustainable growth and rendering free markets and liberal politics more compatible, countries like
Chile and Colombia have promoted the successful sustainability of their
market reforms by renovating state economic institutions, initiating a serious dialogue with the private sector, and formulating credible social
compensatory programs. In Peru's case, as the president and his small
circle of advisers deepen their ideological commitment to neoliberal approaches and continue to rely on an increasingly autocratic and exclusive
policy-making style, the general resistance to institution building—both
within the state and between the state and key societal groups—could
itself become a bottleneck in the reform process. Against this backdrop, at
least two main challenges are at hand.

The first has to do with the fact that the earlier period of market reform from 1990 to 1995 has itself given rise to the need for new policy
responses. Nowhere is this more apparent than in the rural sector, where
on the one hand the rapid liberalization of land-tenure laws and food
prices has created the necessary conditions for the long-overdue modernization of Peruvian agriculture; yet on the other hand, these measures
have also provoked greater levels of migration from the countryside to the
city, with very little but the urban informal economy awaiting these migrants—no housing, few educational opportunities, and at best perhaps
some temporary safety-net kinds of relief. Although trends such as these
reflect a tremendous demand for public policy—that is, a "second phase"
set of reforms to better link favorable macroeconomic performance with
the difficult microeconomic adjustments that are also occurring—the
stance of the Fujimori administration has been to leave these microeconomic adjustments up to the free hand of the market.

Given the current economic team's aspirations toward replicating the
Chilean model, technocrats within the Ministry of Finance would do well
to give that model closer scrutiny. Although President Fujimori's own interpretation of what it means for Peru to follow in Chile's footsteps appears to rest on the combination of free markets bolstered by a benevo-
lent authoritarianism, the Chilean case also offers some powerful lessons
in the use of innovative public policies to make its market program more
politically and economically viable (Bosworth, Dornbusch, and Laban
1994; Meller 1992). These have ranged, for example, from the use of
temporary tariff hikes, to export promotion for nontraditional products,
to partial restrictions on incoming capital flows, to aggressive investment
in basic and technical education. The point is that even in the case of the

region's most highly touted market reformer, public policy played a key role in facilitating the adjustment to more open markets.

Finally, the second main challenge related to the medium-term phase of market reform is that President Fujimori and his small circle of allies are eventually going to have to face up to the question of policy efficacy. In fact, underpinning Peru's impressive growth rates over the past three years are dismal patterns of per capita GDP growth, income distribution, and productivity gains (Figueroa 1995). These lackluster returns, combined with the country's burgeoning trade deficit and overvalued exchange rate, do not bode well for the viability of the current economic model. Again, the analysis points to the need for a more coherent public-policy framework to help bridge the gap between high GDP growth rates at the macroeconomic level and the continuing stagnation at the microeconomic level.

As tempting as it might be to point to the combination of the president's thin base of support and the poor progress on distributional gains as the possible catalyst for the collapse of Peru's market model, or to the deepening of authoritarian politics, I would phrase today's challenge in slightly different terms. That is, the more likely risk is that Peruvian policy makers will succumb to economic mediocrity and throw away the opportunity to vastly improve the nation's welfare and the country's position in the international economy, which are ostensibly the main reasons for launching a sweeping set of market reforms in the first place.

PART II

SOCIAL ACTORS
AND
POLITICAL CHANGE

PEASANTS, WORKERS, BUSINESS

4

THE RURAL LANDSCAPE AND CHANGING POLITICAL AWARENESS

ENTERPRISES, AGRARIAN PRODUCERS, AND PEASANT COMMUNITIES, 1969–1994

Christine Hunefeldt

In the 1950s Peru's rural landscape was often described by social analysts as "dualistic," with small producers and peasant communities coexisting beside large landholdings (plantations and haciendas). The first ones were described as essentially self-sufficient and eventually producing for small local markets, the second ones as sending their products to the regional and international markets. On the extremes of such a dualistic interpretation, few links existed between the self-subsistence small land-holdings and the internationally oriented large plantations beyond the occasional need of labor. The concentration of land in the hands of a few had resulted from the gradual encroachment of peasant lands by large landowners.

In the past, such a diagnosis formed the basis for proposals with varying degrees of radicalism to address land distribution and ownership, conflicts over boundaries, and technological development. An expanded role for the state was perceived to be key to solving such abysmal disparities. The result of the dualistic characteristics of the agrarian landscape were some timid agrarian reforms in the early 1960s, and finally the more radical agrarian reform decreed by General Velasco in 1969. Since then, however, dualism has been replaced by a better-informed vision of the heterogeneity of the rural landscape and by a critical assessment of state

Many Peruvian and non-Peruvian colleagues will find that some of their ideas, data, and interpretations have been included in this chapter. Thus, the only merit here is that their work has in some way been reassembled to provide to an English-speaking audience a general picture on the evolution of the agrarian sector in the last twenty-three years.

intervention in general. The depopulation of the countryside, militarization, and a steady long-term decline in production have challenged traditional power structures, created new development options and strategies, and, more generally, realigned social groups within society. Gradually, technocratic optimism has given way to uncertainty; state intervention has been replaced by self-help; and the fight over land has become a forum for political and economic bargaining. Today we see a deeply transformed vision of the role of the state, a changed social spectrum, and a different relationship between state and social actors. Although changes have deep historical roots, it seems that the pace of change increased in the years following the Velasco agrarian reform.

Since the beginning of President Velasco's agrarian reform in 1969, peasant and small agrarian production, as well as rural enterprises, have undergone dramatic changes, further increasing Peru's rural heterogeneity. Traditional forms of production coexist side by side with technologically developed rural enterprises, and in between there is a whole array of new and old ways of organizing rural production. The rural sector is characterized by a multiplicity of diverse responses to macroeconomic policies, local problems, and national political pressures. In part, this is due to the fact that successive governments have implemented contradictory and often drastic policies[1]—a fact that certainly also holds true for President Fujimori's current neoliberal program.

This chapter examines the changes of the last three decades in order to convey the diversity and heterogeneity of Peru's rural landscape and the varied responses such heterogeneity has created, in sharp contrast to the goals the agrarian reform designed during General Velasco's presidency between 1969 and 1973. The first section of this chapter explains the objectives of the 1969 agrarian reform and the changes it brought about in the last three decades. Following this descriptive section, the second part examines the most salient outcomes of the agrarian reform: parcelization and privatization (mainly on the coast), and the violent confrontations between cooperatives and peasant communities (in the highlands). The final section summarizes the long-term consequences of Velasco's agrarian reform and presents some of the economic and political options available today in Peru's agrarian sector.

---

1. See Carol Wise's chapter in this book.

The Agrarian Reform: Conflict and Contradictions

The 1969 agrarian reform was preceded by guerrilla warfare in the southern highlands, syndical radicalism on the coast, and an overall growing peasant movement throughout the country. Unrest signaled that long-standing patterns of development based on oligarchic domination were no longer viable.[2] In this context, the reformist military government led by General Velasco regarded agrarian reform as a necessary first step toward more encompassing reforms throughout society. Within these broader economic and political changes, the role of the state and the agrarian sector were crucial. In contrast to what actually happened, the military expected to gain popular support, destroy oligarchic domination, control conflict and rural discontent, improve income distribution, stop massive migration to the cities, and create a stable agrarian sector for an expanding internal market. During the implementation of its reform program, the state's involvement grew and—paradoxically—became increasingly out of touch with popular (and rural) demands.

The cornerstone of the agrarian reform was the associative enterprise, in which former workers and peasants would become members of different kinds of cooperatives. (These included the CAP, or Cooperativa Agraria de Producción; SAIS, or Sociedad Agrícola de Interés Social; and ERPS, or Empresas Rurales de Propiedad Social. For a description of the internal organization of these entities, see Carter 1984, McClintock 1981.) The military government was ready and willing to invest huge amounts of money to achieve a transition toward socialized patterns of ownership and management. In part, these expenditures explain the enormous increase of the external debt at the beginning of the 1970s. The growing state deficit was partly caused by cheap credit, subsidies to buy agrarian inputs, and massive administrative expenditures in the agrarian reform. These policies were implemented in a period when prices for traditional export crops were falling and much of Latin America was pursuing import-substituting industrialization.

Critics (particularly those representing the New Right, see the chapter by Durand) abounded when the agrarian reform was first implemented. In retrospect, however, the agrarian reform achieved some measure of

---

2. For a more detailed discussion of oligarchic power and decay, see Durand's chapter in this book.

success, not only in creating a wider political consciousness but also in economic terms. Overall, a total of 2,889 units of production, involving 429,384 beneficiaries (roughly 30 percent of all peasants and agrarian producers), were allocated 9,672,017 hectares of land (out of a total of 23 million). About 40 percent of the economically active population (EAP) was directly or indirectly affected by the agrarian reform process (Mejía 1990). The hiring of temporary workers within the newly created associative enterprises expanded the number of beneficiaries by about 25 percent (Carter 1990, 72).[3] In no other country in Latin America (and few in the world) was land distribution so far-reaching.[4] However, this reorganization of the rural landscape was not without many conflicts.

A chronology of agrarian changes in the presidential periods since 1969 shows that land distribution did not end after the reform, although it almost came to a standstill between 1980 and 1985 (Mejía 1990, 21–22). Each government following the Velasco regime since 1973 adopted a new attitude toward the agrarian issue. Attitudes in turn were tinged by different political ideologies and priorities, and at least three periods of rural development are discernible.

The first period (1969–80) encompassed Velasco's agrarian reform itself and included the presidency of General Morales Bermúdez (1975–80). By 1980, after twelve years of military rule, 8.6 million hectares of land and 2.2 million head of livestock (representing 39 percent of the land and nearly 8 percent of livestock) had been granted to 390,684 peasants, that is, about 60 percent of all beneficiaries up to 1990. Paradoxically, land redistribution between 1969 and 1980 involved a process of land concentration and the centralization of decision making. The previous 16,000 haciendas were transformed into 2,252 reformed (cooperativized) units of production under state tutelage. Public-sector technocrats and bureaucrats were in charge of managing these new enterprises.

3. The urban implications of this same phenomenon are discussed at length by Carmen Rosa Balbi in this volume.
4. The scope of land distribution appears even more impressive if patterns of land tenure in Peru before 1969 are remembered. Prior to Velasco's reform, haciendas and peasant communities were the core entities of agrarian life and production. Haciendas represented 3.9 percent of existing units of production and controlled 56 percent of arable land. Four thousand Indian communities, which represented 96 percent of existing agrarian units of production, controlled only 44 percent of the land. Moreover the land peasant communities controlled was located essentially in the less-fertile highlands.

The state also monopolized commercialization, for which new enterprises were created.[5]

At the political level, Velasco dissolved the National Agrarian Society (SNA, Sociedad Nacional Agraria) in 1972; for decades it had been the bastion of oligarchic political organization. He sponsored the Peruvian Peasant Confederation (CCP, Confederación Campesina del Perú) and the National Agrarian Confederation (CNA, Confederación Nacional Agraria). The CCP and CNA were vertical organizations designed to re-build state-rural sector relations; they were political instruments of the military regime.

From the beginning, the agrarian reform was part of a more ambitious plan of national development in which agriculture would assume its tradi-tional role: producing cheap food and labor. In the initial stages, opti-mists speculated that export-oriented agrarian production (the former plantations on the coast) would generate profits high enough to repay the so-called agrarian-debt, thus fueling other investments, particularly in industry. The 1971–75 plan was based on the assumption of a 4.2 percent increase of agrarian production. Debt payments could go to former *hacen-dados* and plantation owners, who then would invest at least half of their revenues in industrial development. Another portion of the expected profits were meant to repay credits to the state.

Few of the newly created cooperatives were able to repay their accumu-lated debts. In most cases debts skyrocketed, production stagnated, and exports declined. Shortly after implementing the agrarian reform, Peru was forced to spend 25 percent of its annual budget on food imports, in spite of the fact that peasants, smallholders, and medium-size entrepre-neurs, were—at least in the first years of the agrarian reform—still pro-ducing cheap food for urban consumption. Industrial investments, on the other hand, had been steadily declining after 1960 and continued to do so after the implementation of the agrarian reform.[6]

5. EPSA, EPCHAP, ENCI, ENATA, ENACO.
6. For an evaluation of how and when capitals were—or were not—transferred, see Caballero and Alvarez (1980). See also Wise and Durand in this volume, and the overview on available literature by Eguren (1989) and Revesz (1986). However, little research has been done on what happened to former hacendados. Apparently, at least some of them managed to rebuild their power through a sectorial transfer of capital (into services, insur-ance, and banking). But there are few indicators that show when and how this transfer occurred. This absence of information is striking because the agrarian reform was imple-mented to parallel industrialization based on import substitution.

State control was meant to increase grassroots support. However, it also had negative consequences: in many places patronage resulted, as well as corruption, misuse of funds, and managerial inconsistencies; clientelistic relationships were reinforced; real and artificial scarcities of basic consumption products for the urban population soon became commonplace; some groups acquired preferential treatment based on their links to the power structure; and regional distortions were accentuated. Rage on the part of those left out, or those whose expectations had been raised by the reforms, created a disposition to accept radical discourses (see Degregori's chapter in this volume) by both those promoting terrorism and those demanding privatization. Although the agrarian reform could register a few successful undertakings, the overall picture looked quite gloomy.

A second period of rural development, 1980–85, involved the dismantling of the associative enterprises. A new political outlook of monetarist and liberal inspiration emerged with the second presidency of Fernando Belaúnde Terry. Following a worldwide trend, liberal technocrats believed that the only way to increase productivity was through private ownership. This implied a shift in the focus from global political change and land distribution to a more narrow concern with better and higher output rates. Efficiency, not social justice, preoccupied policy makers. State subsidies were eliminated.[7]

"New" agrarian options were created in order to incorporate more beneficiaries into the process of agrarian transformation and thus ease social and political pressure. Traditional communal rights of peasant communities in the highlands were made more "flexible." For example, land could be sold or mortgaged. This greatly benefited the richer peasants within the peasant communities and alienated those who did not have the resources to purchase land. Through costly colonization projects, a narrow agrarian frontier was expanded into the Amazon basin. However, this last option exacerbated ethnic conflicts. The expansion into the jungle region touched upon traditional land rights of several Amazonian Indian groups.

In the first two years after 1980, statistics registered an increase of agrarian output. This was more a result of climatological conditions than of the policies implemented. A decrease of output followed in the third year. Opposition to the government and the growing financial and administra-

---

7. Some analysts have defined this period as neo-reformist or a counterreform (Mejía 1990).

tive problems in the cooperatives resulted in the first national agrarian
strike and the formation of the CUNA (Congreso Unitario Nacional
Agrario).

In 1982 Peru was hit by several natural catastrophes with disastrous effects on agrarian output: a decline of 9.3 percent was registered in 1983.
In 1984 and 1985 agrarian production increased again, in part because
international development agencies opened new avenues for private capital (above all on the coast and in the jungle region). Growth was accompanied by the reemergence of power claims by the former landowners
who had lost their land under the agrarian reform.

As a result of these developments, privatization (or "parcelization") of
the associative enterprises began in spite of very widespread resistance
from both members of the cooperatives and ideologues of socialist development. The government countered this resistance with the idea of a new
"agrarian developmentalism." This new approach would seek higher productivity, participation from the producers, and broad consensus (Mejía
1990, 50). Thus, the social and political components were brought back
in. Changes in this direction were accompanied by more private initiatives
in commercialization that challenged existing state monopolies.

The specific problems of peasant communities were not addressed under military rule or the civilian government of Belaúnde. These peasant
communities (approximately five thousand) encompassed more than one
million *minifundistas* (smallholders, most of them with less than three hectares of land). The SAISs were intended to incorporate peasant communities, but they did so in only very limited ways. And it was particularly in
these production sites that the most appalling demographic indicators
were recorded. Life expectancy averaged 46.6 years, and the infant mortality was 145 in 1,000 births.[8]

A third period was inaugurated with Presidents Alan García (1985–90)
and Alberto Fujimori (1990–95). This period witnessed the intensification
of the privatization process. Like Velasco, García put the agrarian sector at
the forefront of his economic policy of self-reliance (or, as stated in his
electoral campaign, "*aprendiendo a vivir de lo nuestro*"). He believed in the
possibility of reactivating the agrarian economy,[9] and he felt it necessary
to reduce Peru's dependency on food imports, to incorporate the so-

8. The national infant mortality average is 101 to 1,000. See the Banco Central de Res-
erva del Perú report on poverty, "Mapa de Pobreza." These indicators look alarmingly like
comparable indicators in the colonial period and on slave plantations.
9. See the 1986 Plan de Reactivación Agraria y Seguridad Alimentaria.

called Indian regions in the highlands, where peasant communities and small landholdings were concentrated. His plan included a new land-distribution program, particularly for peasant communities, and economic policies designed to strengthen small-scale producers. The economic policy package included price controls, state subsidies, credits (in some cases with negative interests), and privileged exchange rates to favor the purchase of capital goods.

The García government initially supported and promoted associative enterprises. Between 1986 and 1990, however, it sponsored privatization of the CAPs and the SAISs, very much sanctioning what had been happening before as a result of the cooperatives' financial and political problems. In 1985 *parceleros* (the owners of plots in the associative enterprises) met for the first time in the context of their newly founded association, ANAPA (or Asociación Nacional de Parcelaros). The shift in the government's outlook created uncertainties and deepened rural and political schisms, because there were already divisions regarding parcelization. From its inception, ANAPA defended private property within the cooperatives and opposed state interference altogether. This was probably the first time in Peruvian history that organized sectors of rural workers directly imposed their will on a government.

Notwithstanding the vicissitudes of policy under García, relative prices tended to favor agrarian production. Food supply increased, and higher levels of mechanization were achieved. However, this positive situation would not last: a decline in agricultural production was registered again in 1987. The public-sector deficit reached appalling heights, fueling desperate currency emissions. An increased money supply led to inflation, which was exacerbated by the cutoff of new external funds.[10] Social discontent, delayed payments to producers, and price increases finally led to strikes in several provinces (Puno, Cusco, Huaraz, Ucayali). An initially promising interaction between producers and government came to a standstill.[11]

10. At this point the government had stopped paying interest to international creditors.

11. Paramonga, once a part of the Grace empire, one of the world's largest agro-industrial enterprises, and now a CAP based on sugar production, is often used as an example of the agrarian reform's failure in modernizing agrarian exports through state intervention.

With the implementation of agrarian reform, the state divided Paramonga into two different types of enterprises. The first one was to control the sugar mill and the land on which sugarcane was produced (Cooperativa Agraria Paramonga), and the second was to be in charge of its formerly complementary industrial complex (Sociedad Paramonga Limitada).

The state became the new owner of the industrial complex, whereas six thousand hectares

In sum, policy shifts, from collectivism to market-oriented solutions and back to heterodoxy, deeply disturbed rural processes. Each shift increased distrust and alienation among agriculturalists and eroded the credibility of the state. The rural sector had witnessed extensive state intervention followed by a virtual withdrawal of the state from rural affairs. Two different processes, both causes and consequences of state action, intensely marked the rural landscape throughout these years: the first was the privatization process in the big associative enterprises, concentrated (but not exclusively) on the coast; the second was the invasions of the SAISs, carried out by peasant communities in the highlands. Both were the consequence of policy makers' incompetence and laissez-faire attitude. It was the state's conflicting policies and the lack of solutions that made the emergence and strengthening of the Shining Path possible and explains the increasing mobilization of rural interest groups, including peasants.

Confronted with hyperinflation and widespread terrorist attacks, Fujimori's government did not have much time to plan rural development or to think about how to deal with rural problems. Most of his policy decisions were geared toward solving these issues considered to be of primary importance. Rural producers were left to themselves, often manipulated by the military and the Shining Path. In the meantime, parcelization and invasions continued to be options for a whole set of different reasons.

Cooperatives and Privatization

The first parcelization processes took place in the highlands (Andahuaylas in 1974). Peasants invaded cooperative land but refused to organize along prescribed associative lines, signaling the limits at this early stage of the state-imposed agrarian transformation. Peasants remained on their

---

of land belonged to the members of the CAP and one thousand additional hectares producing sugar for the mill belonged to smaller ERPSs and some private owners. As production and industry had formerly been integrated, this arbitrary division created severe organizing conflicts (see Novoa and Morelli 1990).

Distortions—always meant to favor the state-controlled industrial complex—were created through price controls in the production of sugar, waste pulp, molasses, steam, and electricity. Through price controls, dependency was reinforced on state subsidies to continue production.

In a similar fashion, the state intervened in the distribution of scarce water, in many instances neglecting sugar-producing areas and privileging rice growers, who by this time were lobbying very strongly through their organized representatives.

own individual plots of land. At this early stage, parcelization also occurred on those haciendas that had satellite functions for the CAPs. These occurrences gave weight to the warnings of some agrarian experts that the model of associative enterprises was not a suitable solution for every situation in a very heterogenous agrarian world. As varied as the agrarian landscape were the reasons for which members of the cooperatives opted for privatization.

In the 1980s many members of the cooperatives opted for privatization as a result of the failure of cooperatives to cope with internal conflicts and the demands of their members. Among the many problems facing the cooperatives was that previously organized (since the 1920s) syndicates had not disappeared when the coastal cooperatives had been instituted.

Instead, the cooperative members were formerly unionized workers. Now owner and worker were combined in one person. In most cases, the result was undisciplined labor, lack of managerial skills, squandering of resources, nonreplacement of decaying infrastructure, and lack of coordination. Soon differences among cooperative members were evident, not only because resources were unevenly allocated, but also because the members came from different former haciendas, had different political outlooks, and lived on scattered locations within the cooperatives (Valdivia 1987, 54).[12]

At the decision-making level, the state appointed managers for the cooperatives who, in turn, sought to expand their internal power and legitimacy by enlarging their bureaucratic clientele within the cooperative. This provoked fights over the management of resources. Under such conditions, the lack of continuity in entrepreneurial decisions became evident as production decisions were subordinated to political maneuvering.

Many workers showed increasing dissatisfaction and declining identification with the cooperatives' mandates. However, resorting to parcelization was not always an economic issue, nor did it necessarily reveal a clear preference for private property on the part of those involved. Sometimes parcelization merely represented a strategy to conceal corruption and mismanagement.

Internal conflicts were matched by disastrous government macroeconomic policies. The repercussions from those policies also explain the decay of cooperatives: price controls decreed by the government resulted

---

12. In the Ica valley, 182 production sites were turned into twenty CAPs. In the valleys of Lambayeque, 154 became forty-two CAPs. See Portocarrero (1987, 78).

in a distorted relationship between prices and costs; exchange-rate policies encouraged food imports. Members of the cooperatives soon recognized that cooperativization was not the best solution for their interests.
Many thought it safer to get a hold on a piece of land within the cooperatives. As more and more members of the cooperatives severed their relationships with the associative enterprise, the process of land privatization
within the cooperatives accelerated.

Parcelization was also encouraged by the fact that many former hacienda workers, now members of cooperatives, had already worked on land
given to them by hacienda owners to cultivate their own crops. In some
places parcelization of the cooperatives reflected the workers' success in
defending plots they believed belonged to them by ancestral rights.

Parcelization further intensified in the 1980s. President Belaúnde allowed cooperatives to change their entrepreneurial model when members
petitioned for such change. Thus, a legal opportunity was created to
channel pressures toward parcelization.[13] According to the Agriculture
Ministry in Lima in 1988, the number of families living in CAPs and SAISs
was 141,583—2.44 percent of the EAP and 6.83 percent of the farming
population. These families received 303,491 hectares of irrigated land,
229,933 hectares of land for dry farming, 2,665,107 hectares of natural
pasture land, and 681,877 hectares of forests and barren land (Fernández
de la Gala and Gonzáles Zuñiga 1990, 42–3).

In 1989, the Board of the Agrarian Reform (Dirección General de Reforma Agraria) claimed that 430 out of 609 associative enterprises had
been subdivided by parceleros. In 234 of the cases, official recognition
had already been granted, 69 were still being processed, and 127 had
proceeded to divide land with no consultation whatsoever (Fernández de
la Gala and Gonzáles Zuñiga 1990, 46; Mejía 1990, 96–7). Parcelization
occurred in the most fertile areas on the coast.

Land privatization in the cooperatives had far-reaching consequences.
It diminished the associative enterprises' capacity to produce enough for
urban and industrial needs, for agro-industry and exports, and for the
smaller internal market (Caballero and Alvarez, 1980). Particularly within
the cotton and sugar production, the smaller holdings of parceleros were
not competitive in the international market. They tended to be less efficient in terms of technological innovation and renovation, their transac-

___

13. The law that allowed for this reorientation was the Ley de Promoción y Desarrollo
Agrario (Decreto Legislativo No. 002). See Portocarrero (1987), 80.

tion costs were higher, and it was also more difficult to achieve collective action among individual producers to provide common agrarian or industrial projects. The former members of cooperatives also lost some of the social benefits previously guaranteed by bigger enterprises. The loss of social benefits is estimated at approximately 25 percent of their real income.

Another important consequence of parcelization was the narrowing of the labor market. Prior to parcelization, cooperatives had provided temporary and even permanent jobs to migrants from the cities and the highlands. Migrants sold their labor—in some cases they had done the same while the haciendas and plantations still existed. The cooperatives employed a huge pool of temporary, landless workers. Although in some cases the use of temporary labor has not diminished (Figallo 1988; Vergara 1986), parceleros tend to prefer family labor (Fernández de la Gala and Gonzáles Zuñiga 1990, 47) to minimize costs. The impact of privatization on employment depends on what parceleros produce and what kind of relationships they establish with enterprises, with the market, and with temporary laborers.

Overall, parceleros are victims of the same economic environment the associative enterprises faced at an earlier stage: fluctuating international and controlled domestic prices, credit problems (both with state banks and private capital), inefficient systems of commercialization resulting from an overabundance of intermediaries, the delay in payments coming from state agencies, and the lack of storage facilities.

Notwithstanding this, some authors underline positive aspects of parcelero production. Carter (1990, 73) points out that parcelization is an imperfect solution, for large-scale production is more efficient, but the parceleros are more efficient than the former CAPs in terms of social benefits and the ongoing use of temporal laborers. A definitive assessment of the advantages and disadvantages of small-scale production must ultimately take into consideration the location of parceleros, the type of crops they produce, and the facilities with which they are provided by either the state, commercial banks, or international agencies.

Roughly 30 percent of the parceleros are concentrated on the coast, in the Lima, Cañete, Huaral, Chillón, and Huaura valleys in Lima's rural hinterlands. The departments of La Libertad, Piura, and Lambayeque on the northern coast, and Cajamarca in the northern highlands—also with large coastal areas—are a second group with important levels of parcelization. In these areas the average number of hectares per family is 6.6, and the land is highly fertile. Thus, in terms of land redistribution, the ongoing process of parcelization in some way fulfills the agrarian reform's goal of creating many small producers. Some authors claim that parcelization—a consequence of the agrarian reform—may be even more important than agrarian reform itself (Fernández de la Gala and Gonzáles Zuñiga 1990, 52).

Yet even the most ardent proponents of parcelization recognize that there are limits to the capacity of parceleros to expand production. As demographic pressure increases, land fragmentation seems to be unavoidable given the limitations on alternative means of subsistence. As soon as the parcelero's property is legalized (meaning that the state recognizes his property and extends property rights to parceleros), he is entitled to sell and divide his land. Without official recognition, property rights remain blurred and hamper transactions of landed property. The land market remains restricted, and state credit is not available without official recognition. Control over official recognition and credit still give the state some say in the viability of associative enterprises and the emerging new patterns of land distribution.

In spite of evidence that parcelization is an ongoing process in the rural landscape, already some new developments have emerged. After living through cooperative experiences, peasants and smallholders now know that there are social services and tasks that cannot be obtained through individual efforts. As a result there are new cooperative efforts among parceleros aimed at joining forces to achieve higher levels of schooling, health services, and infrastructure. The idea of cooperativization thus has been rescued and redefined by the parceleros, but this time the active agent is the agrarian producer himself, not the state. This tendency brings them close to what peasant communities in the highlands have been doing for centuries.

In several provinces, cooperatives have been diversified. The formation of loosely defined organizations such as CAUs (Cooperativa Agraria de Usuarios), CATs (Cooperativa Agraria de Trabajadores), ETAPs (Empresa de Trabajadores Agrarios Permanentes), and even new peasant communities suggests a willingness to solve problems that reach beyond the organizing capacity of smaller units of production or of individual producers. More than two hundred CAUs have been founded throughout the country, 80 percent of which even have communal lands (from 6 to 297 hectares) that serve for the payment of common services and sometimes include land that cannot be subdivided. Each new entity defines its own commitments. Thus, after subdividing the land, new and original processes of cooperative reorganization are visible. In some cases these new processes have demonstrated great success in solving managerial problems. This is particularly true where capital and technological support are present (De Wit 1990, 151).

At a different level, parcelization has produced political polarization. Whereas in some areas the liberal option—parcelization and privatization—has been successfully implemented, in other areas it has led to land invasions under the aegis of Peru's Left, clearly opposing privatization efforts (Portocarrero 1987, 82). Initially the National Agrarian Organization (ONA, Organización Nacional Agraria, the organization that congregated landowners of medium-size and big farms) favored the formation of ANAPA in 1985 in order to strengthen privatization efforts. In the course of recent years, however, these two organizations have stood for quite distinct conceptions of agrarian development: a rural sector populated with small producers versus the market deciding the size of landed property. Although the best solution tends toward small producers, in many places a new process of land concentration—decried by the weak remains of Peru's Left—has begun.

Conflicts in the Highlands

Parcelization occurred within the CAPs located in the coastal region, but also in the highlands. In the heterogeneous rural landscape of the highlands, the effects of the agrarian reform were even more varied. Whereas on the coast the agrarian reform intervened on behalf of salaried laborers by assuming production decisions and later by granting land property, in the highlands agrarian reform was basically a result of ongoing fights between unevenly strong *comuneros* and *hacendados*. Peasant communities and agrarian workers (many of them laboring under sharecropping arrangements) had been involved in struggles with *hacendados* and the big agro-industrial bourgeoisie for decades (Caballero 1990, 98). The solution brought forward by the agrarian reform was to create the SAISs. These were aimed at consolidating enterprises on expropriated haciendas by incorporating their labor forces and the surrounding peasant communities.

Places like Ayacucho, Apurímac, and Andahuaylas in the heart of the central-southern highlands have received little scholarly attention in the last decade. The activities of the Shining Path accounts for the lack of research in this area, and, beyond general indicators and anecdotes, we know little about the processes of rural realignment in the region. Peasants there have clearly been victims of both the Shining Path and military repression. When the Shining Path controlled production, few links to the market existed, and links to the state were more tenuous. Many people fled or were killed—although nobody knows for sure how many.[14]

The peasant communities and smallholders of these highland departments were not only neglected by the agrarian reform, but had never had any political participation rights in preceding decades, indeed centuries. It has been among these producers, and in their name, that the Shining Path started its terrorist activities. Only then did these regions move to the center of political (if not economic) attention.

The diversity of changes may be illustrated by looking at three other regions of Peru's rural highlands: Junín (located in the central highlands), Puno (in the southern highlands on the frontier to Bolivia), and Cajamarca (in the northern highlands). Although quite distinct in terms of the size of the units of production, demographic composition, and land-tenure patterns from the core region of the central-southern highlands, a look into these three regions helps us understand rural responses in the highlands.

Cajamarca

In Cajamarca, modernization took place prior to the agrarian reform through links to sugar production in the coastal departments of La Libertad and Lambayeque and the presence of a multinational enterprise, Nestle. By 1972 Cajamarca had one of the highest average plot sizes per household in the highlands: 1.58 hectares, or about five times more than in Ayacucho and other highland regions. Between 1940 and 1981 the rural population decreased only from 86 percent to 79.8 percent. Nearly 3 percent of all the communities incorporated into the new SAISs were located in Cajamarca. By 1988, 70 percent of the agrarian enterprises had

14. By 1981 the proportion of Peruvians living in the Andes was 36 percent. In the 1970s, less than 1 percent of the public monies invested in Peru reached Ayacucho (the department in which the Shining Path originated). According to Amnesty International's 1985 report on Peru, the number of "disappearances" and extrajudicial executions "could be much higher" than the estimated 1,005, due to the difficulties in collecting reliable information. See Kirk (1991, 7, 11). See also the chapter by Roberts and Peceny in this volume.

undergone parcelization in Cajamarca (De Wit 1990), following a pattern of already prevalent tendencies toward smallholding with high levels of productivity. With a predominantly mestizo population and few peasant communities, the conflicts with surrounding peasant communities were almost nonexistent.

Puno

In contrast to Cajamarca, Puno and Junín accounted for 25 percent of all peasant communities in Peru.[15] Puno's haciendas varied in level of internal organization, depending on market proximity and labor availability. In general, the haciendas had undergone a very slow process of modernization. Only a few were successfully integrated into expanding wool-export markets. Land had been divided among many heirs or had been sold to other landowners and even peasants before the agrarian reform. Thus, the hacienda system—quite in contrast to coastal plantations and Cajamarca's haciendas—had already been weakened. Under agrarian reform, the larger remaining haciendas were merged into new administrative units.

Puno had the highest percentage of family beneficiaries through the formation of SAISs[16] between 1971 and 1988.[17] Seventy-six peasant communities received 46,454 hectares of land, which represented 11.7 percent of all the land given to peasant communities. In Puno, prior to the agrarian reform, peasant communities controlled 19.5 percent of the department's land. After agrarian reform this percentage jumped to 30.4 percent: the big associative enterprises controlled 49 percent and medium-size properties accounted for the remainder. Inside the peasant communities, more land was divided among families. Thus, in spite of the increase of available land, a tacit and rapid parcelization occurred (Caballero 1990, 115). Out-migration affected 13.3 percent of peasant families annually. This was the highest out-migration rate nationwide. Average plot size in Puno's peasant communities was 0.4 hectares. Natural disasters periodically accentuated poverty so that even those peasant communities that were part of associative enterprises suffered.

15. Of a total of 3,312 recognized peasant communities in 1986, 348 were in Junín and 487 in Puno.

16. At a departmental level, SAISs were distributed as follows: Cajamarca 2, La Libertad 13, Ancash 8, Junín 6, Huancavelica 1, Cusco 2, Puno 23, Arequipa 2, Tacna 1.

17. In Junín, sixty-six peasant communities obtained 146,433 hectares of land.

The result was increasing conflict with SAISs over land. Even before the government intervened to solve the land problem, the SAISs had already given away 7.8 percent of their lands to peasant communities by 1982. García's government recognized the potential political threats. When the restructuring process began between 1986 and 1987, forty-four agrarian enterprises were affected, most of them through the direct invasion carried out by peasant communities and without official permission.[18]

Nationally, only 6 percent of all legally recognized peasant communities participated as members in SAISs. Given the low participation of peasant communities in SAISs and CAPs, many demands for hacienda lands (the most fertile in the respective areas) forwarded by peasant communities remained unfulfilled. Given these patterns it is not surprising that conflicts arose between new associative enterprises and peasant communities (Caballero 1990, 102).

The few peasant communities in Puno and Junín that gained access to land in the new SAISs soon encountered unsurmountable problems in their relationships to SAIS management. Typical of Puno was the *via huacchillera,* a traditional cattle-raising pattern by which workers on former haciendas, sometimes linked to surrounding communities, would graze their own creole cattle on the hacienda pasture lands.[19] The incorporation of more community members into the SAISs meant that more cattle had to be fed than the meager pasture lands could afford. Soon the new SAISs found themselves confronted with excess labor and declining sal-

---

18. Of the 1,765,038 hectares these agrarian enterprises controlled, 57 percent was distributed among 591 peasant communities, 58 peasant groups, and 30 other individual producers or state agencies. In Puno, 74,783 families benefited from this overturn, representing 44.5 percent of rural families in Puno (Quispe and Araca 1990, 131–2). The results were the following:

Table 4.1. Restructuring by invasion in Puno until 1987

Enterprise	no.	total hectares	restructured by invasion	remaining enterprises
SAISs	23	1,024,475.32	599,387.23	425,097.00
CAPs	14	498,417.44	334,584.56	163,832.88
ERPSs	5	217,345.84	71,919.88	145,425.96
Total	42	1,740,238.69	1,005,882.67	734,355.93

SOURCE: Caballero (1990, 129).

19. As opposed to the fine breeds raised by the enterprises. Cattle were competing for pastures, but at the same time, as it was hard to keep them apart, no continuous fine-cattle breeding could be upheld.

aries. This provoked conflicts between ex-hacienda laborers and community peasants.

In a similar vein, longstanding disputes over land with the former haciendas and among peasant communities had not been solved prior to the creation of the SAISs. These quarrels made concerted action in the SAISs practically impossible. Furthermore, these disruptive forces acted as an invitation to the Shining Path. In siding with one of the contending parties, the Shining Path asserted new political loyalties.

Junín

Long-term changes in Junín were less dramatic than in Puno. The reform created cooperatives in which much of the haciendas' former internal organization was retained, and even administrative personnel continued in charge after 1969. This provided continuity in management dating back to the 1920s. In contrast to those of Puno, Junín's haciendas were prosperous and intensively linked to coastal markets. Nevertheless, even in Junín, demographic pressure steadily increased. In some peasant communities, annual population growth was at a rate of 2.69 percent; the average size of plots was one to two hectares, and people had to emigrate for seven months in a year to supplement their income (Caballero 1990, 114). Junín peasants were doomed to look for alternative sources of income: commerce, artisanship, urban employment in Huancayo (Junín's capital city) and Lima, or work in the cooperatives.

In Junín, pressure was exerted by peasant communities in SAISs searching for changes in entrepreneurial leadership. The state proposed that communal and multicommunal enterprises should be constituted on the lands of the SAISs (Caballero 1990, 129), thus strongly linking peasant communities to the associative enterprises. In Puno, pressure originated in peasant communities that were not part of the agrarian enterprises, and changes were forced through invasion.[20]

20. A few observations on the nature of the peasant economy are in order. As peasants, comuneros have nonmonetary components in their incomes and expenditures it has been shown that only some peasant products have a productivity that is high enough to compete in market conditions, unless peasants are willing to sell their products below production costs (Golte 1980, 69–71).

Their competitiveness is also defined by the ways which prices and salaries are formed. Some peasant products have to compete with imported goods. Intermediaries manipulate prices, and peasants also suffer from price controls (including salaries).

On the other hand, subsidized industrial products create positive rates of exchange for

In summary, reactions in the three highland regions depended on the kind of relationships that had developed between small producers and haciendas, and between small producers, haciendas, and peasant communities. In Cajamarca the hacienda system was firmly consolidated, small producers had reasonable portions of land, and peasant communities were almost absent. Parcelization, thus, followed a long-term pattern of smallholding in the region. In Puno the haciendas were in decay, peasant communities were strong but had few resources, and many entered litigation with former haciendas over boundaries and land. The result was violent conflicts between the associative enterprises and surrounding peasant communities. In Junín, modern haciendas and peasant communities had found ways of conflictual coexistence. Similar interests made the peasant communities' incorporation into SAISs a relatively smooth process, further facilitated by the fact that associative enterprises in this region were—at least in their initial stage—economically successful. Conflicts in Junín resulted from mismanagement. As illustrated in the next section, these broadly regional disparities led to different political options.

Drifting Toward New Political Turf

The manifold outcomes of the agrarian reform, political violence, and macroeconomic policies have radically changed the rural landscape over the last three decades. Many new processes are visible, which in turn challenge former patterns of political consciousness and action. Many problems in the rural sector are based less on economic considerations than on political conflict, and in some cases on very narrow and immediate political interests. Although extremely fragmented, political debates concerning the rural sector have become more polarized.

---

peasants (Gonzáles de Olarte 1987, 27–9), fomenting industrial consumption and the neglect of traditional self-consumption crops. In the labor markets, more often than not only temporal salaried labor is possible. In this setting, peasant economy defies conventional theories of inflation analysis. Rural rates of inflation are different from urban ones.

In considering microregions, Gonzáles de Olarte has found that there is no uniform national inflation rate as a result of the presence of peasant production. A reverse effect is also visible. As inflationary pressures originate outside the peasant economy, peasants react by reducing and even withdrawing from the markets. As a result, production patterns, occupational structure, and the levels of monetary incomes and expenditures have changed, reducing—from a national perspective—agrarian production for urban consumption.

In the past, workers in the large coastal plantations were organized either by the populist APRA or by parties of the Left. In the wake of the agrarian reform and the creation of associative enterprises, former workers have learned varied patterns of cooperative entrepreneurial and labor organization under state tutelage.

ANAPA today represents an initiative geared toward improvement and progress, not just growth, for the parcelero. The organization—in spite of internal disagreements and schisms—articulates an alliance between industry, agriculture, and ranching. The importance of this small and medium-size peasant organization has grown to an extent that former presidential candidate Mario Vargas Llosa optimistically believed that parceleros could be convinced to support his ticket. The 1990 elections proved otherwise. Through the election of ANAPA's founder and leader, Germán Gutiérrez Linares, as a deputy for Lima's provinces, the leftist groupings (IU) demonstrated that political manipulation was no longer as easy as it had been in the past (Mejía 1990, 155).

CAPs, SAISs, and ERPSs are continuously reexamining their internal organization and, as a result, changing the ways in which their members are represented and their interests defended against external conditions and pressures. Mixed cooperatives that tend to combine the advantages of individual effort and associative administration have been able to reassess levels of economic efficiency.[21] Other CAPs have completely changed their legal composition by now calling themselves a Sociedad Anónima de Accionariado (Joint Stock Company), whose members not only have a differentiated status, but in some cases have joined the agrarian bourgeoisie's political organizations.[22] Other forms of agrarian reorganization proposed by the state (like the multicommunal enterprises) have not achieved acceptance among agrarian producers.

The Peruvian Left sees legislation to promote private investment in agriculture and encourage medium-size and big landowners to expand their agricultural frontier (Supreme Decree 029–AG in 1988)[23] as a potential danger leading toward a new cycle of land concentration. If parceleros

21. Examples of this success are analyzed in Mejía (1990, 168–80), when he looks at CAP Casimiro Chumán in Ferreñafe and Lambayeque, at the valley of Chancay-La Leche, and at CAT Fonupe-Vichayal. For this last case also see Arroyo (1988).

22. See Mejía (1990, 168–80) for a presentation of the cases of the Sociedad Agropecuaria Industrial Luis Pardo S. A. and the fruit growers in Santa Rosa and Sayán.

23. See Figallo (1990, 156 n. 4).

are allowed to sell their plots—so runs their argument—hardships and dependency on credit and markets will create the conditions in which creditors and mortgage holders are able to either recover or buy land (Letts 1990, 64).[24] Moreover, demographic pressure will lead to land fragmentation and dispersal of the existing *parcelas* and consequently to a further weakening of individual owners. This process implies a definite and more complete reversal of the initial objectives of the agrarian reform.

In other political spheres, these worries are dismissed with the argument that the parceleros' last choice is to sell their land. In the central coast, where average plots are relatively large and land is fruitful, parceleros first resort to leasing out their property, and then to borrowing money from merchants or agrarian-industrial enterprises. Sharecropping is another option. In other words, the parcelero's options suggest that he is willing to share profits or obtain a rent rather than sell his land.

Although such hopes have little real basis in a liberal economy, the same macroeconomic conditions also explain the reproduction and even expansion of the amount of land under parcelero cultivation, because such an economy offers few if any other productive alternatives. Thus, small producers are dependent on their own resources and capacity to organize.

This does not mean that parceleros have started to behave like "typical" peasants—they have not retreated into subsistence consumption. Parceleros tend to link their production to the cooperatives and nearby urban markets, and to diversify their income sources.[25] For parceleros, labor is the second most important production cost, after agricultural inputs. If they wish to reduce costs, they lean not toward hiring additional labor but to exploiting family labor more intensely, thereby restricting employment for temporal laborers. Although this reduces labor opportunities, it is often a marginal savings that permits commercial production to be maintained.

24. It has been noted that in Huaura, for example, land has been transferred to merchants (Valdivia 1987, 57).

25. In the Chincha, Huaral, and Santa valleys, only 40 percent of the parceleros are permanently laboring on the plot, 47 percent are there occasionally, and 9 percent never work the land. Seventy-seven percent of their income is produced through salaried labor. This clearly reflects options taken by the parceleros' children. They do not see themselves as "merely" agricultural producers; they want to become professionals and live in the city, in spite of the restrictive labor market (Figallo 1990, 164–5).

These assertions, while true for some parcelization processes, should not be overgeneralized. There are wide disparities among regions and even within valleys, from family to family. In some regions "peasantization" is well under way, whereas in others, higher productivity, proximity to markets, and access to credit have permitted parceleros to continue to produce commercial crops.[26]

In the case of the Chancay-Lambayeque valleys, there has been a consolidation of medium-size owners (ten to fifty hectares). They have expanded agrarian boundaries, sometimes beyond the maximum extension (fifty hectares) permitted by agrarian reform laws. They have incorporated new agrarian producers, among them professionals, bureaucrats, and others linked to the government. These producers also propitiated the acquisition of peasant communities' lands, the invasion of non-cultivated areas of the associative enterprises, and the reincorporation of non-

26. If we retake the Lambayeque case analyzed by Torre (1990), we find that in the rice-producing parcelas, "peasantization" is rising. These producers have not been able to increase their levels of productivity, because they are far removed from access to commercialization, investments, technological assistance, and the provision of services. Rice parceleros have decided to live on their plots, because transport costs are increasingly expensive. As their relation to the markets is restricted, they have also resorted to the cultivation of alternative crops complementary to their diet and destined toward self-consumption ("campaña chica"), in spite of the fact that there still is a tendency to use salaried labor (Torre 1990, 187).

But inside Lambayeque, another tendency is also visible in the Motupe and Olmos valleys. Here the use of family labor is very intense, and it has been accompanied by an increase of production of 196 percent between 1985 and 1988. After benefiting from large irrigation projects, these maize and fruit producers do have private ownership over their lands, but commercialization, water distribution, and machinery maintenance are collectively organized. In spite of their relative success, Torre believes (1990, 189) that there are signs of internal differentiation that may lead to land sales.

Some other scattered examples may also be referred to, examples that tend to show that in some places the parcelization process has been quite weak. In the four valleys of the department of Lambayeque, four CAPs were formed on the lands of the former huge agro-industrial sugar haciendas, and so were thirty-eight CATs on the lands of more than 150 smaller haciendas. By 1980, 54 percent of the irrigated land had been allocated to 21,771 beneficiaries of the agrarian reform, and 72 percent of that 54 percent corresponded to four CAPs.

Thus, the new cooperatives controlled 40 percent of the irrigated land in the department (Torre 1990, 175). Between 1980 and 1988, the agrarian scenario had changed again. From the forty-two cooperatives, twenty-nine have been parcelized and thirteen remain as integrated units. The four big CAPs have strenuously resisted parcelization (Torre 1990, 175), whereas on the other side we have a persistence (as prior to the agrarian reform) of small and medium-size plots. This in part is the result of the fact that these producers are dedicated to the labor-intensive growth of rice.

adjudicated lands. Some of these owners have bought land from parceleros (Torre 1990, 191).

These producers have also regained political control by occupying the
hierarchies of local agrarian organizations (OAL, Organización Agraria
de Lambayeque). Such trends tend to change the local power structure.
The smallholders (with an average of six hectares) participate in the elections of the OAL and have integrated smallholders that survived the
agrarian reform. Through participation, they have improved their ability
to bargain for better rice prices, for credit, and for water distribution.
With higher political participation, new political alliances are struck, as
shown by their support in the early 1990s for state employees' strikes.

New cleavages are also visible in commercialization. Regional agrarian
federations have taken up competition with longstanding power groups
with great success. Since 1984 the Federación Regional Agraria in Piura
and Tumbes (FRADEPT), composed of small and medium-size producers,
communal units of production, peasant communities, and agrarian cooperatives, has managed to successfully compete with one of Peru's most
important power groups, the Grupo Romero. Although the federation
controls only 30 percent of cotton production, the FRADEPT has managed to set cotton prices, greatly benefiting many producers. Thus, new
associative models and new redistributive patterns are emerging.

In the highlands the picture is more confusing. Until 1990 only 4 percent of the peasant communities who benefited from land distribution
after invading the SAISs lands had organized communal enterprises.
Much disorder resulted from the abandonment of invaded land; in part
this was a result of the longstanding boundary disputes between haciendas and peasant communities, between peasant communities, between
associative enterprises and peasant communities, and between peasant
communities and small landholders both within and outside peasant communities.

In Junín—in the SAIS Cahuide—the Shining Path, after completely
devastating the existing infrastructure, reorganized peasant production
with addressing neither conflicts over land nor the distribution of land.
Peasants reacted by trying to reorganize their communities to confront
the Shining Path (Manrique 1989, 71), even amid treacherous political
unrest.

The government has found no lasting solution to the variegated field of
conflicting interests in the rural sector. Occasionally the state has orga-

nized (with poor equipment) peasant self-defense groups (*rondas campesinas*). Rondas first appeared in Cuyumalca (Cajamarca) in 1976 as a peasant response to increasing cattle theft. Around 1991, there were 3,435 ronda committees (*comités de ronda*) in a 100,000–square-kilometer area on the coast and in the northern highlands, where few peasant communities existed. Rondas were officially recognized in 1986, whereas in previous years they had suffered from persecution at the hands of local state authorities.

In 1989 the church—particularly Monseñor Dammert, Cajamarca's bishop—helped organize the first regional ronda organization, in spite of (or maybe because of) the fact that many ronda leaders are local evangelical catechizers or coordinators. Rondas have always had an undertone of popular justice or "direct democracy," as their anger was often directed against corrupt local judges and political authorities. They represent a new political culture, one that in the eyes of some analysts—and of the peasant communities—has aided the government in resisting the Shining Path.[27] Peasant communities and rondas have acted as a counterforce to the Shining Path for two reasons: they reject the Shining Path's authoritarian verticalism, and they represent two of the few civilian organizations left.

Imitating the ronda model, the government tried to institute similar self-defense organizations (sometimes called the *rondas falsas,* or "fake self-defense units") in other parts of the country. Some leaders—especially Comandante Huayhuaco—received much journalistic coverage decrying the threat of an imminent civil war.[28]

SAISs no longer seem to represent a viable alternative for peasant communities. Peasant communities still organized within the CCP and the CNA have turned their eyes back to the state. This has been reinforced by President Fujimori's promise to support and defend peasant communities (Mejía 1990, 216). However, in the course of the last two decades, and due to the experience of the agrarian reform, their expectations have increased and so has their capacity to exert pressure on the government. If the government does not listen, they are now more ready to act

27. For a more detailed discussion of oligarchic power and decay, see Durand's chapter in this book.

28. In Puno's RIMANACUY (regional agrarian Congress) organized by García's government, the president publicly asked the peasant community leaders whether they were willing to resist the Shining Path's incursions. The leaders shouted yes. García even promised arms, which evidently never reached peasant hands (personal observation).

in defense of their interests, either militarily by forging self-defense groups and invading lands they have long been asking for, or by seeking to participate in the government's decisions about fiscal and monetary policies.

At the other end of the social spectrum, the agrarian bourgeoisie—in somewhat changed composition—has survived the agrarian reform and has reorganized itself. It has moved into export crops on the coast and in the jungle region and obtained access to cheap credit and export subsidies. CONAGRO (Confederación Agrario) today has incorporated ONA and CONFIEP and has thus expanded its bargaining power with the government.[29] Their problems today are restrictions on land tenure and the Shining Path, which continuously menaces their crops and industrial plants. The land-tenure problem has partially been solved through an alliance with cooperatives, and as a result, industry in rural areas is emerging. For both problems state support is vital and has persistently been used, in spite of the popularity of rhetoric about liberalization and privatization (García 1990, 299; see also Letts 1990, 66).

In the highlands, there are clear signs that former *hacendados* (and their progeny) have regained access to portions of their property and are becoming—with state aid—a part of a new and more dynamic landed highland bourgeoisie. The reduction of their landed estates, and suspicions about Indian and mestizo laborers, have obliged them to mechanize their lands. Some are working in close connection with international agencies and development projects. In some areas a complete new spectrum of modernizing owners—some of them of foreign origin—have created new projects (including trout, shrimp, cheese).

New trends are also visible in the jungle, a region we tend to forget is part of the rural landscape as well. The jungle region has never been a priority for agrarian reform nor for any government policy since 1969. Nevertheless, colonization projects were started to ameliorate the pressure on land in the highlands given the scarcity of land for all agrarian producers. In the lower jungle (*selva baja*), seven special developmental projects carried out one of the most ambitious colonization projects ever initiated.

In spite of this, today it is estimated that 180,000 hectares of land (roughly 15 percent of the land redistributed through agrarian reform in the last two decades) are planted with coca. Coca, in fact, is one of Peru's

---

29. They represented one of the backbones of Mario Vargas Llosa's candidacy for the presidency in 1990.

most important export crops.[30] In 1982 coca exports produced $850 million, which represented approximately 25 percent of the total value of agrarian and animal production. Coca transactions carried out in Peru in 1988 amounted to between $1,500 million and $2,000 million, from which around $600 million to $800 million remained in Peru.[31] This indicates that a growing number of coca producers are marginal to any kind of state control and immune to state-structured incentives. Different options predominate in this area.[32] The Shining Path, the military, and drug lords compete for control.

In tandem with this process, native groups in the Amazon have begun to organize. For the first time they have gained status as a social force through organized action under the political leadership of the CUNA and the CCP (Letts 1990, 66).[33] Violent struggles between the state and Indian organizations, as well as between the military, the police, and drug lords, are today a vivid part of the redefinition of political boundaries and actions.

Conclusions

Rapid changes in Peru's rural landscape over the past three decades make it difficult to identify an overarching trend of political development. In the past, immediate economic considerations and political pressures defined agrarian policy. The urgency of change left little room for anything but improvisation.[34] In spite of (or maybe because of) differing governmental policies and bureaucratic inefficiencies, patterns of land tenure and rural organization have irrevocably changed. An overwhelming feature of these changes is the trend toward privatization of the associative

30. Declaration of Minister Agustín Mantilla, *El Peruano*, 6 July 1989, cited in Fernández de la Gala and Gonzáles Zuñiga (1990, 50).

31. In contrast, investments coming from the United Nations to promote alternative crops amounted to only $1.5 million (Salcedo 1989, 42).

32. Salcedo (1989, 43) argues that there are two "coca-poles" in Peru, one located in the central and northern jungle (encompassing Tarapoto, Juajui, Tocache, Uchiza, Aucayacu, and Tingo Maria), and the other in the southern highlands (Quillabamba and Cusco).

33. For a complete list of Indian organizations in Peru's Amazon, see Ballón (1987, 105–19, especially 107).

34. Remarkable and important exceptions to this assertion are the long-term irrigation projects. See Seminario (1990, 73–97). For a particular case—Majes—see Beltrán (1987, 85–104).

enterprises created in the wake of the agrarian reform. Nevertheless, privatization does not imply the dismissal of cooperative efforts. In some cases cooperative initiatives represent a successful answer to commercialization challenges, in others to better public services.

Any socially responsible solution should be based on the continued existence of peasant communities, which were reinforced by the agrarian reform and the varied outcomes that followed it. Peasant communities organized land invasions to assert their rights on disputed hacienda and associative enterprises' lands (Puno); they resorted to their traditional organization to confront the Shining Path (for example in Junín); and they developed and expanded entrepreneurship to successfully manage their associative enterprises (as in Cajamarca and Junín).

As a result of highly heterogeneous long-term rural processes, Peru's political landscape has also dramatically changed. What is obvious today is that there is no state-guided transformation of the agrarian sector, but several quite distinct initiatives brought to the political forefront by Indians, peasants, small producers, and rural enterprises. The initiative has shifted to society's organized social groups. An optimistic attempt to read the agrarian landscape's future, taking into consideration its heterogeneity, indicates that peasants and rural workers, and a different kind of bourgeoisie, especially in the highlands, are taking the lead in asserting a social project that reaches beyond the state and beyond the Shining Path. There are visible, long-term rural processes of change that were not explicitly designed. In this commitment, peasants have been joined by a different landed bourgeoisie, especially in the highlands. This is a vision of Peruvian society far removed from the cooperative enterprises General Velasco had in mind.

It is probably true that the Shining Path has understood the meaning of this shift much better than the Peruvian government. To gain power and exert its devastating influence, the Shining Path not only took sides in rural conflicts, it also tried to disarticulate Peruvian society at several levels of civil organization. It is not by chance that members of the Shining Path encountered extensive resistance in those areas with strong self-organization—the rondas in Cajamarca and the peasant communities in Puno—and that from very early on, the Shining Path moved its headquarters to Lima. People's distrust of the state has increased, but the developments in the rural sector demonstrate that this does not necessarily imply the victory of neoliberalism or terrorism.

5

POLITICS AND TRADE UNIONS IN PERU

Carmen Rosa Balbi

Trade unions in Peru in the 1990s have undergone an acute ideological and organizational crisis.[1] The rank and file no longer see many of their leaders as legitimate representatives, and the union movement as a whole has proven unable to put forth alternatives to the neoliberal agenda. The strength of organized unions in Peruvian society has diminished dramatically.

In the past, the Confederación General de Trabajadores Peruanos (CGTP) was the main political representative of organized labor. The CGTP was consolidated during the 1970s in a struggle for workers' rights and for improved labor legislation. This struggle occurred in the favorable context of the reformist military government of General Juan Velasco Alvarado, which sought to incorporate workers and sponsor the formation of new trade unions. When the military shifted toward more repressive policies after the ouster of Velasco in 1975, widespread work stoppages between 1977 and 1979 precipitated the end of military dictatorship under Morales Bermúdez. Yet by the early 1990s, labor was in disarray.

Many factors have contributed to the weakening of labor, including structural changes in the composition of the labor force, more dynamic growth of small businesses, and an explosive expansion of the informal sector (estimated at around 40 percent of the EAP) to the detriment of the wage workers in large and medium-size businesses. Another key variable was the prolonged recession of the 1980s and the sharp drop in salaries. Economic stabilization failed to revitalize employment in the for-

---

1. This chapter was translated by Carlos Rosales.

mal sector of the economy, resulting in structural unemployment and underemployment.

A major cause of labor's weakness—which was not sufficiently well understood by union leaders—was the creation of a more flexible work force. Flexibilization involves the elimination of institutional rigidities in the labor market, including legislation on job security. There has been a massive expansion in the number of contract or temporary (casual) workers. The flexibilization of the labor market, a product of significant changes in labor relations in response to global economic trends since the mid-1970s, has become a major theme in debates over economic and social policy. Its implications in Peru are the subject of this analysis.

Changes in the Workplace in Peru

In an effort to address the crisis of Peru's heavily protected industry, there have been adjustments in policies regulating labor contracting. The requirements of the economy and the needs of the business community have shifted from a stable workforce based on permanent labor contracts to temporary hiring in order to create a more flexible labor market. The number of workers unable to engage in collective bargaining has increased, and the number of union members in the workforce has declined. The increase of temporary labor has created a precarious workforce and led to uncertainty and instability in the workplace. This process was exacerbated as the neoliberal program of the Fujimori government was being implemented in 1990 and 1992, and it has radically changed labor relations.[2]

A key piece of labor legislation in the fight over the flexibilization of

2. Fujimori's policies resulted in a dismantling of industry through closures, bankruptcies, forced reductions in shifts or in workloads. Yet this did not result from a process of industrial restructuring, nor was it due to the introduction of new technologies or a more rational administration of firms. Rather, in Peru, large corporations (such as Nissan and Toyota) that have automobile-assembling operations and that employ a good number of metal-bending workers have sought to become more export-oriented. The same has happened in the field of manufacturing home appliances. Little technological change has occurred. Instead, given the abrupt opening up of the markets and the lowering of tariffs, a turn toward the import of vehicles has taken place. This accelerates the recessionary process, causing the reduction of countless workers. Unions have been unable to provide an alternative to either government policies that weaken labor or to the liberal model of development.

the labor market was the Labor Stability Law (Decreto Legislativo No. 18594). Promulgated in 1970 during a period of steady economic growth, strong state protection, and high levels of employment, the law created a regime of nearly absolute job security that was described as "traumatic" by the business community (Ermida 1991; Durand in this volume). It gave workers absolute security after three months of probation; all dismissals from that point on had to be based on strictly justifiable causes. The negative reaction that the law provoked in the business sector was largely due to the fact that it limited employers' disciplinary power in the factories and transferred that power to the state. Not only were grounds for dismissal required, but the legal system determined the fairness of employers' decisions. The notion of "faults by the employer" was given new legal status; it referred to ways in which employers could be held responsible for mistreatment of workers.

In an unprecedented step, the military government made noncompliance with resolutions issued by the labor authorities an offense punishable by a sentence of no less than three years in prison. Furthermore, any substantial modification in the conditions of labor relations would be subject to complaints, so that an infringed right might be restored. In the process of extending and redefining rights of workers, the Industrial Communities were created. This institution became a key element in promoting a new type of trade unionism that sought to channel the demands of workers for participation in the workplace.

The demand for flexibilization emerged initially out of business opposition to labor stability. The law was seen as a source of a lack of discipline among workers, theft in the workplace, and declining productivity. Unlike in Brazil, Mexico or Argentina, where labor market flexibilization has been driven by technological restructuring, in Peru no substantial technological innovations had occurred that required a more flexible worker. Efforts to roll back job security originated in the insistent demands by business to eliminate labor stability in order to promote investment. The demand for a more flexible workplace intensified when the boom phase of the 1970s was replaced by a period of bust and recession. Contractions in the market led to a decline in production, closure of plants, and personnel slashing. Maintaining a payroll of fixed workers in an economy with wildly fluctuating demand implied an excessively burdensome cost.

Changes in Labor Legislation:
Precarious Employment and the Law

Diverse legal steps encouraged temporary employment after the Velasco government ended. During the Morales Bermúdez government, new labor legislation was introduced to deal with what were seen as worker attitudes responsible for declining production and productivity. Rules were liberalized giving employers greater leeway regarding worker discipline. These liberalizing tendencies continued during the subsequent governments of Fernando Belaúnde Terry and Alan García Pérez.

In 1985, under the García administration, a new law was enacted that restored labor stability after the three months' probationary period; however, a year later an emergency temporary employment program (PROEM) was implemented that conflicted with the goal of job security. PROEM permitted employers to hire workers without giving them job security. Under the government of Alberto Fujimori, inaugurated in 1990, greater coherence was achieved in building a liberal market economy.[3]

The major complaints voiced by the Peruvian business community were centered on the rigidity of the labor-stability laws that impeded personnel reductions during periods of recession, and on the lack of discipline among workers that management attributed to the existence of job security. Recent research (Paredes 1988) confirms that the rise in employment between 1986 and 1987—a period of economic boom—was caused by the hiring of temporary personnel under PROEM.

As a result of the institutionalized proliferation of temporary hiring, about 45 percent of wage workers within the private sector in Lima are currently in an unstable situation (307,000 workers out of a total of 687,000). The highest incidence is among blue-collar workers (Paredes 1989). It is estimated that 430,000 of these are wage workers from the private sector, of whom approximately 50 percent are temporary or precarious workers. These are not part of the unionized population.

Sixty-seven percent of unionized workers are thirty-five years of age or older, 27 percent are between twenty-five and thirty-four, while only 6 percent are younger than twenty-four. These numbers are in sharp contrast with the age distribution of workers in companies with fewer than twenty

3. The legislation is created in some cases by laws that are approved by the parliament. However, the most important laws have been created by decree as a result of special powers held by the executive branch.

employees, where by law workers are not allowed to organize in unions. Within this classification, 37 percent of the workers are younger than twenty-four and 33 percent are between twenty-five and thirty-four years of age; adding the two age groups totals 70 percent. At the same time, three-quarters of those who comprise that 70 percent work in companies with no unions, which means that today the younger labor force is not unionized.

Liberal Politics and the New Rules of the Game

After years of structural-adjustment policies, flexibilizing tendencies have been accentuated. Structural adjustment seeks a restructuring of the productive apparatus to eliminate restrictions on the free market. To that end, the dismantling of regulatory and interventionist legislation is required. Collective negotiations and collective rights in general—such as unionism and the right to strike—must be profoundly modified within this framework.

Thus, a number of presidential decrees were announced to accelerate flexibilization of the labor force. Just three months after the inauguration of the Fujimori government, Supreme Decree 077 was proclaimed. It provides new rules regarding the hiring of full-time permanent workers. These rules extend the grounds for hiring temporary workers (according to the needs of the market, the beginning of new projects, and so forth) without any obligation to justify it before the Labor Ministry. Indeed, employers do not even have to show that they are not hiring temporary workers for jobs other than those of a temporary nature.

A package of 119 executive Supreme Decrees in November 1991 led to even more radical changes in employment. The number of workers that management is allowed to hire on a temporary basis has been dramatically increased (whether for needs of the market, restructuring, incidental or other reasons). As a result, the principle of stability is rendered practically meaningless. Temporary hiring was sought by business to reduce costs in a recessionary environment, and precarious employment is becoming an institutionalized reality in Peru.

Supreme Decree 077 also modified labor stability. It effectively ended absolute job security by stipulating that the replacement of workers no longer fell under the jurisdiction of labor judges. Job security is now a matter for the discretion of the employer.

Employers are allowed to dismiss annually up to 5 percent of the workforce without any justification. Also, the meaning of "grave offenses" has been widened to facilitate dismissal. Lack of loyalty and diligence were made sufficient grounds for dismissal; likewise, untimely work stoppage in or out of the workplace or attempted theft (even if frustrated), regardless of how little the cost involved, are sufficient grounds. Other decrees provide the finishing touches to the flexibilization crusade by clarifying the power of employers to modify workers' schedules and holidays.

Finally, a drastic Supreme Decree, enacted in December of 1992, extended the authority of the employer even further. Under this decree, a stable employee may be suspended temporarily; his or her contract may be modified or rescinded if the company sees fit. Likewise, a worker may be freely transferred or substituted. The company may unilaterally suspend or alter work shifts. These measures effectively end job stability. The 1993 constitution, approved in a 1993 referendum by the Peruvian people, specifically modified the article guaranteeing job security.

Part of the goal of flexibilization is to obtain higher diligence and precision in manufacturing work. The more fundamental purpose is to deregulate bargaining over collective work contracts; flexibilization is not merely a technical or organizational requirement of the productive process.

The Bill of Collective Relations promulgated in July of 1992 seems to confirm the conclusion that the goal of the government is to deregulate collective bargaining to undermine job security and labor rights. At the same time, it signals the intention of the government to pursue market-oriented solutions that give maximum latitude to the private sector. This law seriously restricts the right to unionize. Unions have complained before the International Labor Office (ILO) of violations of already ratified agreements in Peru. But the government attained greater control over the Union Registry, which decides what unions may be dissolved. Restrictions on the right to strike and regulations concerning procedures for calling a strike have been established. Moreover, The law bans strikes in "essential services."

The new law of collective bargaining represents a compromise between state intervention and deregulation. It provides protection for certain basic labor rights such as the eight-hour shift, minimum wages, the thirty-day vacation, and severance pay. Despite an enormous weakening of labor rights, the state retains an active role. This role has been weakened with regard to protection of the rights of individual workers, but strengthened in its ability to intervene in unions, strikes, and collective bargaining.

Declining Capacity of Trade Unions for Political Action

This section explores the role of labor organizations in the context of changes in state-society relations under the Fujimori government. By early 1990 the Peruvian labor movement was severely weakened; unions comprised only 48 percent of the total number of wage earners (Yañez 1992). That represented a decline from 80 percent in the 1970s. The most important union organization in Peru remained the CGTP, but it only represented stable workers. Currently the EAP is 7,800,000 people, and wage earners make up only 30 percent of that total.

Peak worker organizations suffered a gradual loss of legitimacy and credibility. In the decade of the 1970s, when important labor mobilizations took place, a vigorous, class-conscious, and combative labor movement emerged among the Peruvian working class. This movement became a leader in many sectors, as well as among urban neighbor-based and regional associations.

The rise of organized labor was spurred by a new Left, which sought political power based on a worker-peasant alliance. The centralization of the labor movement around the CGTP, and the legitimacy that it acquired in labor and popular circles, allowed the Left to lead district shantytown federations and regional movements, principally through strategies of confrontation. By the late 1970s, the labor movement led massive national strikes. The most important of these occurred in 1977 and 1978, and they threatened the stability of the military regime. The withdrawal of Morales Bermúdez was forced by the convergence of multiple social actors opposed to his military dictatorship and its economic adjustment policies. Labor was central to these forces.

The 1980s saw a decline in labor's capacity for collective action and its leading role as a social actor. A key factor in this change was the strengthening of the capacity of each grassroots organization to negotiate with the state through the channels of representative democracy. This eventually led to a rupture in the alliance of unions and neighborhood and regional movements that had emerged during the national strikes.

Thus, the combined effect of the transition to democracy and the economic crisis in the 1980s undermined organized labor as a political force. The labor movement had been consolidated during a dictatorial period, and now the radical ideology of labor leaders led to their intransigently defending worker rights rather than proposing socialist alternatives within the context of democracy. Excessive and recurrent stoppages were encouraged, and strikes proliferated. Labor leaders had little experience with conciliation and a search for understanding, and management contributed to labor unrest by refusing to enter into dialogue and reconciliation with labor groups.

Beyond the deepening of the economic crisis and growth of precarious employment, the failure of the successive national and sectorial strikes undermined confrontational struggle and gradually eroded union legitimacy. The basis for the Left's presumption that the working class would inevitably be the leading class in a project to transform the whole of society became increasingly doubtful. This view of labor action conflicted with the daily practice of unions and the needs of the rank and file in the context of representative democracy.

All these factors weakened the CGTP. A dynamic and growing labor movement requires the reproduction of wage labor; in other words, the principal means of labor absorption must be employment in capitalist firms in which there is a clear separation between owners of labor and owners of capital. The crisis of the Peruvian import-substituting development model resulted in a massive increase in the informal sector. Fewer workers were incorporated into wage work through the productive process; as a result, the vitality of the labor movement was undermined.

Consider the pattern of wages and strikes between 1980 and 1991. Wages rose in the periods 1981–82 and 1985–87. These years were followed by periods of recession and declining salaries. The sharpest decline in wages occurred after 1988 (followed by a short period of relief) and between 1990 and 1992. Policies of stabilization were implemented in 1988 and 1990. The first "shock therapy" was implemented by the populist government of Alan García; the second one by the steadfastly neoliberal government of Alberto Fujimori.

During the twelve years between 1980 and 1992, the CGTP staged twelve national strikes. They were motivated by resistance to declining wages and faltering job security. By December 1992, real wages were scarcely one-third of the 1979 levels. The most successful strikes were those staged during periods of rising wages, and the least successful were those during recessionary periods. The latter were intended to counter the closing of factories and the decrease in wages, but the increasing ineffectiveness of these strikes accounts for the CGTP's decision not to call a general strike in 1989.

Unions at the Outset of the Fujimori Government

Contrary to expectations of increased radicalization under the Fujimori administration, a growing gap emerged between the direction provided by union leaders and the actual response of rank-and-file workers: workers became less likely to believe in the efficacy of union actions, while union leaders lost legitimacy and support within their organizations. Strikes had proven useless in resolving the most urgent problems facing workers. In the long run, in fact, they were perceived to have contributed to economic policies that led to further social deterioration.

Two divergent philosophies have developed out of the recessionary conditions of the 1980s. The first one is based on a growing pragmatism among stable unionized workers for whom moderate strategies have prevailed. These workers have placed greater priority on the preservation of the workplace than on that of wages. Implicit in this pragmatism is a rejection of confrontation and a willingness to negotiate and collaborate with the firm.

A second philosophy of union strategy has focused on the leadership and union vanguard. This more ideological posture has reaffirmed an insistence on radicalism, calling for national and sectoral stoppages and strikes, often against the will of the rank and file. This intensification of radicalism has led not only to a widening of the gap between the union leadership and their constituents, but also to the erosion of the legitimacy of the upper echelons of the union movement.

Many workers questioned the behavior of union leaders who became members of parliament. Labor representatives in parliament were incapable of putting forth anything but radical demands, and they did not appear to offer viable programs to solve the country's economic problems. Moreover, they were unable to institutionalize labor rights, which were usually achieved by way of union action. Thus, union leaders have not been exempt from the contempt that working-class Peruvians have for the entire political class.

Union leaders are widely seen as mired in bureaucratic practices with ever-weakening and superficial links to their social base. The weak base of unions was manifested in the 1990s, when, as a result of the elections for a new parliament, none of the top union leaders—among them the secretary general of the CGTP and the director of a powerful trade union—were reelected as members of parliament.

It is in this context that, soon after taking power in 1990, Alberto Fujimori put in place a neoliberal model involving drastic adjustments to the economy. These measures extend the number of temporary workers, whose aspirations, as we have seen, were not represented in the program of the CGTP. They had no voice through existing trade unions.

The neoliberal policies of Fujimori sharpened the ideological crisis of so-called class-struggle-oriented (*clasista*) trade unionism within the CGTP. The Communist Party of Peru continues to exercise enormous influence among the leaders of the CGTP, and the ideological crisis within the CGTP revolved around the inability of the proletariat—as a leading force for social change—to challenge the neoliberal ideological offensive of the Fujimori government.

Overnight, stabilization measures by Fujimori reduced the purchasing power of workers by 80 percent. Yet he retained very high approval ratings in public-opinion polls, and soon after the so-called Fujishock of 1990, the CGTP openly failed in its efforts to organize a national strike aimed at protesting the effects of the austerity program.

An abrupt change had taken place in the "common sense" of working-class people. The García government had attempted to improve conditions through policies of confrontation with the International Monetary Fund and refusing to service the foreign debt, but these heterodox policies, as Wise points out in chapter three of this book, resulted in dizzying inflation and left public finances and state companies in shambles. The final three years of the García administration witnessed an accelerated deterioration in the living conditions of the population after two years of encouraging reactivation (1985–87). This produced, in countless Peruvians, a belief in the need for more orthodox economic measures.

Although Alberto Fujimori was elected on a platform that rejected shock therapy, his turn toward orthodoxy did not drive away the support of the population. This support was based on the conviction of many that it was senseless to fight the IMF; it was also based on the prestige of the Japanese model. Many Peruvians thought that Japan viewed Peru sympathetically and would invest in the country if it had a president of Japanese descent seeking to reinsert Peru into the international financial community.

Fujimori projected an image of efficiency that contrasted with that of the "traditional" political class. He was seen as a pragmatic statesman able to provide solutions that the traditional political class would not. This, as Cameron notes in chapter two of this volume, in part explains the massive popular—and even labor—support for the 5 April autogolpe.

As far as one can tell by analyzing public-opinion polls, the approval of the new constitution in 1993 was mainly a vote of confidence and support for Fujimori's leadership and his appeal to the country for the need to alter the constitutional order. The president proposed to create the conditions for attracting foreign investment by eliminating social rights that had been enshrined in the 1979 constitution.

Calls for strike action by the CGTP to protest against Fujimori's tough austerity measures—among the most severe the world has ever seen—failed to generate working-class support. In the first month of the government of Fujimori, the rift between the leadership of the labor movement and its base was already evident. The CGTP called two strikes against labor-legislation reforms, but these also failed. In an attempt to appeal to sectors of the business community that were disenchanted with liberalizing policies, one sector of the CGTP issued a communiqué that questioned the implementation and social consequences of neoliberal reforms. Aside from that isolated effort, the hard-line leadership prevailed within the CGTP. The only strikes that occurred in the aftermath of the austerity measures announced by Fujimori were not in protest against the government's policies; rather, they were caused by firms failing to comply with contracts.

Privatization

By 1992, Fujimori was pursuing a policy of privatization of public enterprises that affected organized labor. It is important to note the enormous weight that this sector has had in the country's economy. State-owned enterprises (SOEs) grew during the government of General Velasco, accounting for a major share of national investment. This also gave rise to trade unions centered on public enterprises.

Privatization affects public-sector unions directly and other unions indirectly. Fujimori revoked the policy of wage and salary indexing that had been won by workers during the García administration. Fujimori's government skillfully exploited the gap between the higher salaries of public-sector workers and the lower salaries in the private sector. Indexing was proof of the privileges that public-sector unions enjoyed, and it went against the government's objectives of austerity and sacrifice from all social sectors.

The public sector had little prestige. It was widely perceived as excessively bureaucratic, inefficient, overstaffed, clientelistic, riddled with patronage, and unable to provide quality service. Two decades after the formation of SOEs, the well-respected public image that public management had achieved in the Velasco years, which had evolved around an efficient managerial echelon, underwent a spectacular process of erosion. Patronage worsened during the García years, and the case of Petro-Perú was widely considered one of the worst examples. Allowed to employ twelve thousand workers, the company was found to have hired twice as many. This created a widespread consensus on the need for privatizations.

The Rationalization of the Public Sector

A related aspect of the liberal offensive involved the so-called rationalization of the public sector. The state, according to this view, needed to be downsized. Once its enormous financial burden was reduced, the state could concentrate on activities outside of the market, such as education, health, and infrastructure. Public-sector unions, united behind the Central Intersectorial de Trabajadores Estatales (CITE),[4] failed to win public sympathy for their efforts to resist these changes. In the face of massive layoffs and early retirements, CITE promoted confrontation with the government and its economic policies, but the fight ended in failure after a one-month strike revealed the public-sector workers' isolation. Demonstrations and street violence plagued the CITE strike, largely due to the infiltration of the Shining Path. As a result, its image and credibility were damaged in the eyes of the rank and file and public opinion. Support for rationalization of the public sector was largely due to the anger of the public about corruption in the public sector. Thus, rationalization presented as part of a larger campaign against corruption in government was very popular.

Radical modification in labor legislation, attempted by the government in the first months of 1991 through a draconian strike law, prompted an attempt to unify unions representing public servants. A front representing the mining, petroleum, and electrical unions was formed, demanding that legislation nullifying rights such as salary indexation be repealed. Some rights were preserved, even though the principal objective of the initiative—the repeal of the legislation—was not achieved.

During the same period, a number of strikes began; the teachers' union went on a strike that lasted more than three months. Such actions re-

4. CITE emerged and was consolidated early in the decade and was strongly influenced by the ideas of the radical Left.

flected a tendency to anchor union action in a confrontational strategy, even though strikes by the mining, textile, and metal-bending unions proved unsuccessful. Nonetheless, the CGTP called for yet another general strike on 18 July 1991, which failed once again. This displayed more plainly the fissure between the union base and its leaders. It also revealed the support that president Fujimori enjoyed and the fear that the recession inspired among working people.

Unions released communiqués regarding the wage situation and the closing of plants, but they were not able to promote global or united proposals expressing the collective interests of the working class. The calls by the leadership to mobilize to counter neoliberal policies failed to find firm footing among workers, and the unpopularity of union leaders grew when some resorted to extreme measures such as striking at hospitals and shutting down emergency services.

A package of legislative decrees made public in November 1991, designed to increase the flexibility and productivity of labor, prompted rejection by the most important union leaders and federations. These measures were modified, but not rejected, by the parliament. Here again, the lack of support in public opinion for the union position and the absence of grassroots solidarity was clear. The minister of economy even proposed eliminating the minimum wage and the eight-hour workday with no apparent negative repercussions on President Fujimori's popularity rating.

Workers and the Coup of 5 April 1992

The analysis presented above sets a context for the events of 5 April 1992. The autogolpe received massive support from the public and, in particular, from the popular sectors. The labor movement was unable to articulate a coherent position: most workers supported the coup and the suspension of democracy, yet union leaders were opposed. Strong and emphatic pronouncements against the coup by the CGTP and other unions did not express the opinions of the rank and file, who continued to support Fujimori's neoliberal modernizing project.

The call for a third national strike at the end of July 1992, amid a fierce offensive by Sendero Luminoso, found no acceptance. The CGTP condemned a recently enacted new law that restricted important aspects of collective bargaining, unionization, and the right to strike. But this only gave the final proof of the dramatic rift between the union leaders and rank-and-file workers, because calls to mobilize against the law fell upon deaf ears. Almost half of Peru's wage earners demonstrated little concern with the measures.

Relations Between Stable and Contract Workers

What explains the deep rift between union leaders and the rank and file? A key source of the problem was that union leaders failed to understand the phenomenon of work flexibilization. They failed to see how the massive increase in the number of contract or temporary workers would decisively undermine trade unions in Peru.

Flexibilization and changes in the labor market led to conflict and discrimination between stable and temporary workers, a situation that was exacerbated by the attitude of temporary workers toward strikes and other measures involving the use of force. At the same time, the presence of temporary workers put pressure on the discipline and productivity of stable workers.

The fissure between the two is complex and goes beyond the obstacles to unionizing temporary workers. The two types of workers have different interests. Surveys and interviews conducted by the author suggest that temporary workers seek to defend their own interests outside of collective bargaining. As mobile workers, they negotiate their interests individually, based on performance criteria. Unionized workers, by contrast, are more prone to use strikes and aggressive collective bargaining, based on worker solidarity (Balbi 1993, 1989; Balbi and Gamero 1990).

Clasista workers tend to be hostile toward performance assessment in the workplace, an attitude that has its origin in the anti-management radicalism and egalitarianism of *clasismo* in the 1970s in Peru. Performance evaluation is seen as synonymous with greater exploitation, and its acceptance by workers is seen as selling out to management. At the same time, temporary workers feel discriminated against in the workplace and believe that union platforms fail to incorporate their grievances, while unions waver between denouncing programs of flexibilization and, during periods of recession, defending them. Not only have unions failed to develop policies and proposals to address unemployment, rarely have they taken up the interests and concerns of the 230,000 Peruvian youths who are incorporated into the labor market each year—most of them into casual, temporary, or precarious employment.

Modernization of the Labor Market?

Temporary workers tend to be young people between eighteen and twenty-five years of age, seeking to improve their chances of entering the job market by upgrading their technical qualifications. The strategies of new job entrants have given greater fluidity to the labor force, in that temporary workers constantly move from one company to the other. They are casualties of prolonged recession, which undermines their ability to establish a stable work contract. Once they have acquired skills and experience, temporary workers also move in search of better opportunities. Such workers are not prone to, nor are they sympathizers of, violent options or collective action though trade-union organization.

The growing number of precarious workers who do not unionize has critically weakened Peruvian organized labor. Union difficulties are further compounded by the problem of organizing collective action among wage workers in small businesses, where there are no unions. This has contributed to the fragmentation of workers as well as undermining union solidarity and leading to the trade unions' loss of representativeness, especially at the national level in the CGTP, where *clasismo* remains strong.

The once-powerful CGTP no longer has the certainty of a political project in which the proletariat is the historical agent of change. In the past, the Marxist leadership of organized labor gave unity to a range of social and political movements. In the current crisis, however, workers have a negative view of unions, which are seen as being associated with particular political interests.

Interviews of workers conducted by the author on the topic of labor discipline in the workplace show that the rank and file support legislation aimed at eliminating tolerance for tardiness, untimely strikes, decreased productivity, and theft. The new legislation permits employers to dismiss workers engaging in any of these offenses without taking the case to the proper authorities. Workers interviewed expressed agreement with this new legislation, acknowledging that in the past there was loosening in discipline, irresponsibility toward performance, and laxness with regard to theft and damage to company goods.

These interviews confirm that there is a willingness to accept the costs of adjustment implicit in neoliberal reforms, which are accepted as an inevitable necessity. In 1992, despite a deep recession, the productivity in industry increased by 12 percent. This was partly as a result of new measures in the workplace. Yet sharp tensions in the workplace also remain.

The Challenges of Trade Unionism in the Face of Modernization

Peruvian trade unionism faces the urgent need to renew not only its strategies, style, and fields of activity, but also its vision of society in general. Vertical formulas to restore discipline will not alone resolve the deep discord that exists in the country's factories.

The discord is fed by profound resentment and feelings of contempt by the workers toward managers whose racist behaviour is manifested in various ways. One indicator of the tensions in the workplace is the numerous assassinations of management staff in the factories at the hands of Sendero Luminoso. Conflicts in the workplace need to be resolved through a search for consensus between workers and management.

There is a fissure between a politicized and an intensely ideological trade-union vanguard that is unable to respond to the neoliberal project and to the rank-and-file union membership. Interviews illustrate that the rank and file are critical of the CGTP and supportive of the neoliberal project—even though that project implies crushing or dismantling the labor legislation that emerged during the Velasco government.

Conclusions

This chapter has argued that important changes in the labor market in Peru are occurring as a result of the process of flexibilization. This process does not imply technological restructuring; flexibilization is required by management as a result of the inability of firms to maintain stable workers within the context of an economy in protracted recession. In a continuing recession—in 1992 the GNP fell by 3.5 percent—the process of restructuring is driven more by the liberalization of markets than by technological factors. Therefore, flexibilization has a different meaning in Peru than it does in developed countries and in some industries in countries such as Brazil and Mexico.

Increasingly, however, with the modification or disappearance of the rigidities brought about by labor stability, we find a growing dynamism in the labor market. There is a new breed of more skilled workers who enter the market without the prospect of job stability, and it is on this basis that higher levels of competitiveness and increases in productivity are achieved. A temporary worker is always being tested and can always be fired. Temporary workers' strategies for improving their working conditions and wages do not lead them to collective action. This is due not only to management policies that obstruct their ability to organize, but also because once temporary workers are placed in the workplace with stable workers, the former experience discrimination that undermines any possibility of their seeing the union as the defender of their interests. For such workers, the best way to gain access to improvements in working conditions and remuneration is through better performance, not union demands. Therefore, the temporary worker places a premium on individual social mobility rather than on collective action.

Adjustment policies have achieved an increase in productivity and a greater desire for the acquisition of technical skills. Ernesto Kritz (1988) finds something similar in Argentina: "Contrary to what occurred in the late 1970s, when flexibilization was being expounded almost solely by neo-liberal theorists and by oligopolist businessmen who saw it as a way to increase profit margins, in the future it will become an instrument of accepted individual achievement and even acclaimed by growing sectors of wage earners, particularly those techno-bureaucrats in the modern bloc."

Even in the normative sphere of labor practices, the space for collective action by unions is becoming exhausted. Oddly, acceptance of individualistic competition in the labor market, until recently seen as a sign of weakness, is increasingly becoming an accepted value among those sectors that are upwardly mobile.

In Peru, the emphasis on technical training may create a worker with higher qualifications, a multifaceted worker who adapts to any number of different jobs. This marks a discontinuity with the mentality of workers during the 1970s, who preferred a rigid job definition. Such workers resisted changes in their job description and were suspicious that such changes would be used in a hostile way by employers.

But while recent labor legislation encourages the creation of a multifaceted worker, it also endorses hierarchy in the workplace. And a free hand for management in the workplace lends itself to illegal practices. Peruvian neoliberalism is producing an authoritarian modernization of the economy. Since the autogolpe of April 1992, the Fujimori government has dismantled nearly all of the labor rights that were enshrined in the constitution of 1979. Legislation is being passed that radically changes state-labor relations and modifies collective bargaining.

But despite its often drastic or brutal policies, the Fujimori government has also initiated a process of modernization of the job market in which technical qualification, individual achievement, productivity, and competitiveness have been given greater emphasis in the determination of wages. Some companies have benefited from the new policy of labor relations and have gained competitiveness through a more flexible workforce. Significant improvements in productivity were registered in the large and medium firms by 1995, even with the lower number of stable workers. New labor relations and transactions are emerging. At the same time, the indiscriminate use of unqualified temporary workers to bring down labor costs has resulted in inefficiencies and unexpected problems in the operation of industrial machinery.

The grave crisis facing trade unionism is sharpened by its own inability to renew itself and eschew ineffective practices. It needs to address the demands of workers who have been incorporated into the job market in temporary conditions; legislation dictates that a temporary worker has the same rights and salary as those who are stable, even if in many instances the unions do not demand that these rights be respected. This is yet another source of tension between temporary and stable workers. In the long term, the strengthening of a renewed labor movement—despite what many in the business community may believe—is of fundamental importance to building a country that is viable, productive, and efficient.

6

THE GROWTH AND LIMITATIONS OF THE PERUVIAN RIGHT

Francisco Durand

Throughout the twentieth century, Peru's political process was influenced by a fierce, often undemocratic struggle between well-organized and ideologically defined political forces. While conservatives defended free-market policies, deregulation, and an economy centered around the private sector, populists and socialists (at times both coalesced against the Right) fought for an interventionist state, a social-welfare system, and labor rights.

The century started with the predominance of the old Right under the leadership of the landed oligarchy. Its influence over the state remained unchallenged until the crisis of 1930, when socialist and populist parties made a determined attempt to introduce social change through revolutionary means. The old Right managed to retain its influence for four decades, despite its isolation from Peru's majorities. In 1968, however, it virtually ceased to exist as a political force. A revolutionary military government came to power and unleashed a series of sweeping and effective anti-oligarchic reforms. These drastic changes forced the Right to gradually renovate itself.

The crisis of the 1980s provided a historic opportunity for the old Right to again exercise ideological influence and place advocates of state interventionism on the defensive. When the military "revolutionaries" abandoned state politics and restored democracy at the beginning of the 1980s, socialists, populists, and the Right vied to redefine the orientation of the state. In the 1990s the stalemate ended, and the balance of forces shifted more definitely in favor of the external and internal forces that advocated economic liberalism.

In 1990 the Fujimori administration implemented a drastic stabilization plan, in an effort to bring inflation under control and resolve the fiscal crisis of the state. At the same time, as Carol Wise suggests in her chapter in this volume, the regime was more determined than previous administrations (under Presidents Francisco Morales Bermúdez and Fernando Belaúnde Terry) to establish a stable, working relationship with international financial institutions and to more fully embrace free-market policies. This orientation involved an immediate elimination of indiscriminate subsidies and the adoption of labor laws that were more hospitable to the demands of the private sector. In addition, the role of the state as an economic agent was significantly reduced through the introduction of a radical privatization program, massive layoffs, a privatization of state-run pension funds, and a reorganization of the tax-administration agency. In sum, the Peru of the 1990s is very different from what the country was only a decade ago. The changes recently introduced will make a return to earlier socialist and populist policies much more difficult.

The forces of the new Right have played a key role in these changes. Their different associations and organizations have successfully maintained the political initiative from the beginning of the crisis, despite momentary losses of influence, occasional electoral defeats, and the debacle of the new Right's leader, novelist Mario Vargas Llosa. Moreover, the Right's ideological influence was intensely felt both in the media and in the new pro-business orientation of the educational system. As neoliberal policies were institutionalized and the economy stabilized, the new Right seemed better positioned to exert a lasting influence on policy while keeping traditional rivals off balance.

The purpose of this chapter is to analyze the dramatic shift in the balance of forces provoked by the new Right. It provides a dynamic perspective, focusing on the formation of a political actor in a particular context, and then assessing the question of continuity and change within the conservative political forces in contemporary Peru. The Right is not seen as a single bloc; rather, this chapter differentiates between old and new elements, and between social and political components. This task is necessary if we are to understand the Right's internal composition and to identify those factors that are instrumental in provoking or blocking change.

For that purpose, the analysis of the Right is centered on the socioeconomic elites, the conservative movements of the Catholic church, the role of neoliberal intellectuals, and the political parties associated with the new Right. Finally, the chapter attempts to determine both the limits and the possibilities of the new Right's influence on Peruvian politics, ending with the assessment of two troubling questions: how strong is the new Right's commitment to democracy, and can economic liberalism be positively combined with political liberalism.

The Peruvian Right

Before defining the Right, it is important to establish the differences between the traditional elite and the one that emerged from the ashes of General Velasco's successful anti-oligarchic revolution of 1968–75. Prior to 1968, the conservative side of the political spectrum was largely made up of a closed circle of aristocratic families that controlled the nation's wealth in association with a small group of well-educated elites. Foreigners of European origin, and the companies they represented, were also part of this intimate elite at the turn of the century. They controlled large estates (haciendas) and plantations, mines and company towns. Natural resources (oil and minerals, wool and rubber, cotton and sugar) were exploited with the help of the cheap labor of Indian, African, and Chinese workers.

The oligarchy and its allies were at the center of Peruvian politics and society at a time when the boundaries between the private and public sectors were ill defined. Those who controlled the economy were also in charge of governmental affairs, and they openly used their influence to protect economic interests (Valderrama and Ludmann 1979; Bourricaud 1970). The reigning economic doctrine was Manchesterian liberalism, which emphasized comparative advantage, the exploitation of natural resources destined for the world market, and the opening of the Peruvian market to manufactured imports.[1] The most prominent advocates of economic liberalism, like Alejandro Garland of the Lima chamber of commerce in the 1920s and Pedro Beltrán of the National Agrarian Society in the 1950s and 1960s, promoted the expansion of the export sector at the expense of manufacturing industries (Beltrán 1994, 1974; Garland 1905). Such nascent activities were often described by Peruvian liberals as "artificial industries," thus undeserving of promotional policies (Revilla 1981).

Social problems received scant attention by the "sugar and cotton bar-

---

1. For an exhaustive analysis of the Peruvian export economy, see Thorp and Bertram (1978). For an analysis of early economic liberalism, see Gootenberg (1988, chap. 3).

ons" despite the organization of labor unions. In the 1920s, intellectuals associated with socialism (a concept articulated by José Carlos Mariátegui, founder of the Socialist Party) and proponents of radical versions of populism inspired by the Mexican revolution (led by Victor Raúl Haya de la Torre, founder of APRA) organized and mobilized the masses in urban areas.[2] The elites remained secluded in residential neighborhoods, summer towns, clubs, and casinos (Laos 1929), their social isolation as extreme as the concentration of their wealth. The elites were fearful of mass movements and radical parties and thus ready to call on the military guardians of "order and progress" whenever necessary. Although the elites were admired by those who avidly read the social pages of the most prestigious newspapers and magazines, that admiration was often combined with envy, and perhaps with veiled social hate. The presence of other cultural and ideological elements in Peru accentuated the elites' social isolation. The aristocracy was proud of its European origin and customs; at the same time, despite some remarkable exceptions, it showed an open disdain for the Indian and popular cultures. As José de la Riva Agüero, a leading intellectual of Lima's aristocracy, dramatically expressed it (cited in Bourricaud 1970, 53): "How slack and feeble was the patriotism of the creole bourgeoisie! In the souls of these newly-rich merchants, what ignorance of ancient Peruvian traditions, what stupid and suicidal contempt for the nation, what sordid Levantine egotism!"[3]

An especially important link existed between elites and the hierarchy of the Catholic church, whose conservative leanings coincided with their interests. Once the Aristocratic Republic and its main political expression, the Partido Civil, disappeared in the 1920s, the oligarchy's modes of political influence became more indirect, based increasingly on their ability to coopt and monitor a series of dictatorial regimes and, on occasion, even reformist political parties.[4] As François Bourricaud, one of the most astute observers of the old regime, remarked (1970, 52), "without governing directly, the oligarchy managed on the whole to inspire and impose poli-

2. For a history of the labor movement, see Sulmont (1977, 41–45). For a history of parties and ideologies, see Adrianzén (1990 and 1987).

3. His great grandson, José de la Riva Agüero (who bears the same name as his predecessor), correctly argues that the old families "only learned how to enrich themselves forgetting about their responsibilities as a ruling class." *Oiga*, 30 July 1991, 7.

4. On elite political parties in the first half of the century, see Miro Quesada Laos (1961). On the Aristocratic Republic (1895–29), the period of strongest conservative influence, see Planas (1994). On conservative ideas and leaders, including Riva Agüero, see Adrianzén (1987, chaps. 3, 5, and 6).

cies in accordance with its wishes and interests." The influence of the oligarchic Right lasted until the 1960s, when its ideas were openly challenged and its rivals—socialism and populism—gained increased support among peasants, urban dwellers, professionals, and military officers, as well as among a new generation of priests and nuns who wanted a church more closely identified with the poor.

The 1960s was the last decade of oligarchic influence. Its hegemony had already been threatened by the social and political forces that emerged in the process of urbanization and industrialization. The economic power of rural Peru was vanishing and the economy was demonstrating a dynamism based on the expansion of the manufacturing industry and financial services. The universities and the press were increasingly influenced by reformers and modernizers, who argued in favor of changes to "cancel the oligarchic past." New forces (the Christian Democrats, Acción Popular, and the new Left) emerged and rapidly developed, adding strength to the anti-oligarchic bloc initially led by the Peruvian Communist Party (or Partido Comunista del Perú) and APRA (Cotler 1978, 335).

Within the church, Liberation Theology found fertile ground.[5] Inspired by the Second Vatican Council (1962–65) and the second conference of Latin American bishops held in Medellín in 1968, radical Catholics questioned the church's traditional role of being "a privileged ally of the dominant sectors of the state," and advocated that the church be brought "closer to the oppressed and marginal groups of society" (Ghio 1992, 183). The radical church, the reformist intellectuals of Popular Action, and the Christian Democrats exerted a powerful influence over the military, particularly the army; they questioned its role, as described by General Velasco, as the "watch dog of the oligarchy" (Cotler 1978; Pease 1977).

Velasco, a humble soldier of Indian and Chinese origin who became general and president, led an assault against the elites on 3 October 1968. His government launched a series of reforms that not only expropriated the oligarchy's haciendas and banks, but also closed its newspapers and dissolved its key trade association, the National Agrarian Society.[6]

Velasco deposed President Belaúnde, whose mild populist policies had failed to limit the powers of the oligarchy during his first administration

---

5. For a history of the Catholic church in the twentieth century, see Klaiber (1977).

6. For an account of the oligarchy's point of view of these events, see Beltrán (1994, 455–72; and 1974, 147–55).

(1963–68). The military regime inaugurated a new era of intense governmental controls, radical social reforms, and widespread intervention of
the public sector in the economy. While Velasco fiercely attacked the oligarchy, he also sought the support of "modern business people" who were
organized around the banking sector and its financial holding companies.[7]

Supported by fragments of the Left and radical factions of the Christian
Democrats and Popular Action, the military shifted the intellectual debate to its own version of dependency theory and initially succeeded in
placing the discourse advocated by liberals on the defensive. It is in this
context that diverse elements of a renovated Right emerged and questioned the validity of dependency theory, Liberation Theology, and state
interventionism. After Velasco's ouster from power in 1975, the new Right
found a more hospitable environment for its ideas. Part of its strength
derived from international financial organizations that also advocated the
end of the populist and interventionist state in order to solve the fiscal
crisis of the state and overcome a prolonged recession aggravated by a
growing debt crisis.

The aftermath of the Velasco era was a period of growth and expansion
for the new Right. Intellectuals and political leaders who had privileged
access to the media played a key role in this process. Before explaining
the dynamics that led to the revival of the Right, a brief comparison between old and new elements is necessary.

The socioeconomic base of the new Right is centered around modern
economic conglomerates known in Spanish as *grupos de poder económico*
(economic power groups, in control of holding companies). The *grupos*
are the leading segment of national private capital, the heirs of the oligarchy.[8] This economic elite is more urban than rural, and more bourgeois
than aristocratic. Its economic interests are expressed through a new set
of trade associations organized around CONFIEP, formed in 1984. Associations of banks, manufacturing industries, and insurance companies are
now the leading economic interest groups in Peruvian politics.

7. Carlos Malpica (1990) has described the links between Velasco's government and the
new economic elites. According to this version, Velasco and his generals used to get together
during the weekends with the leaders of powerful conglomerates (*grupos de poder*) like Romero, Lanata Piaggio, Ferreyros, and others. The group was known as ALTECO, an acronym
formed by the first two letters of the Spanish words *almuerzo, té, comida* (lunch, tea, dinner).

8. For an interesting analysis of the formation and evolution of Peru's most dynamic and
influential conglomerate, the Romero group, see Reaño and Vásquez (1988). Carlos Malpica, the author of *Los dueños del Perú*, the most accurate source on the assets of the oligarchy, has also written a book on the "new owners." See Malpica (1990 and 1968).

The new elites, even if they are predominantly white (or *blanquiñoso*, "whitish"), are more open than were the old ones, partly because their older members were excluded from oligarchic circles. The education and success of this new elite has been based more on merit than on social background. In contrast to its pre-Velasco counterpart, the new elite in Peru is more one of money and entrepreneurial talent than of land, old names, and refined manners. Its conservative religious components are relatively new organizations such as Opus Dei, a movement that actively recruits business elites. New organizations have appeared, particularly think tanks organized by ideologues and technocrats educated abroad. These organizations are a crucial element of the modern Right, exerting intellectual influence over the mass media (particularly television) through their own specialized journals and newspapers. Political movements have also developed, attempting to build a more direct form of political influence, based on ideologies that incorporate segments of the poor as allies.

Despite these differences, the old and new Right share an important common trait. The Right continues to be based mostly on elite recruits of European origin, and as a result continues to suffer from social isolation.[9] During the last decade this problem has arguably worsened, given that poverty has increased at alarming rates while the middle class has shrunk. Although this point requires a more exhaustive analysis, a revealing indication concerning the social gap is highlighted in a poll conducted in 1991. The statistics suggest a difference between the facts surrounding poverty (approximately one out of two Peruvians is below the poverty line) and the actual perceptions of the populace. According to a study conducted by DESCO, 71 percent of Peruvians consider themselves part of the lower class, 27 percent part of the middle class, and only 0.5 percent part of the upper class.

There is, in addition, another element to consider. Even though the Right maintains a level of distrust of recent military regimes and advocates the need to combine economic with political liberalism, it nonetheless places a higher priority on order and stability than on popular participation and democracy. As O'Donnell (1992a) puts it, the national bourgeoisie in the Latin America of the 1980s "prefers a consensus of democracy that is contingent on one's perception of the consequences of changing contextual factors." In other words, if threats emerge and

---

9. For an analysis of envy and the danger posed by a wide income gap in Third World nations, an analysis related to powerful conglomerates, see Leff (1986).

challenges develop from populist and socialist coalitions, the upper class (together with the middle class), will again "look for its unreliable but indispensable military guardians" (O'Donnell 1992a, 46).

The Revival of the Right in Peru

The political evolution of the post-oligarchic Right can be divided into two clearly distinct phases. In the first phase (mid-1970s to mid-1980s), the forces of populism and socialism were still politically strong and ideologically influential. In this period, the emerging Right took the initiative in criticizing the limits and contradictions of populist policies and pointing out the dangers of state interventionism as well as the negative effects of nationalism on the economy. When the economic crisis worsened, the neoliberal discourse defended by the Right provided the most convincing diagnosis of its causes and the most appealing solutions for overcoming the recession.

The turning point for the Right came in 1975, when General Velasco was ousted from power. In the period that followed, the elites increased their influence over the government and actively engaged in a battle of ideas with socialism and populism. But despite the greater influence of the Right in the regime's economic management, the inability to revive a moribund economy provided an opportunity for socialist and populist groups to block and forestall many stabilization policies.

In her chapter in this book, Wise notes the interplay between economic stabilization and the political pressures that were brought to bear on the Morales Bermúdez and Belaúnde regimes. Political pressures, including labor strikes, demonstrations, and electoral gains by the Left, forced both regimes to back away from a more vigorous implementation of neoliberal policies, and in 1985, the election of APRA's Alan García to the presidency provoked an even more dramatic shift toward nationalist, populist, and interventionist policies.

The second phase began in 1987, when the different components of the new Right became more closely coordinated, more openly influential over society as a whole, and more willing to initiate the difficult road to organizing a conservative political party with mass appeal. On 28 July 1987, President García announced an attempt to nationalize the financial system. He unleashed an unprecedented barrage of opposition from liberal forces, which ultimately killed his proposal and helped mire his government in a near-continuous political crisis for the next two years.

García's measure awakened the fears that had originated during Velasco's statist revolution, and it forced the Right to emerge out of the shadows and openly defend its position in the political arena. At this critical juncture, the new Right momentarily became the leading political force in the country. It was the first time that, to the surprise of most analysts, the Right showed an ability to gain a degree of popular support.[10]

This success led to more ambitious projects for the Right. In 1988 Vargas Llosa, the leader of the anti-nationalization front, organized a political movement and launched a campaign for the presidency. Despite his initial organizational success, Vargas Llosa lost the 1990 election to an unknown university rector named Alberto Fujimori. Fujimori won the second round of elections, as Cameron points out in his chapter in this volume, largely with the support of socialist and populist voters who were fearful of a Vargas Llosa presidency. Rather than signaling a defeat for the Right's neoliberal macroeconomic agenda, the election simply shifted the responsibility for implementing this agenda to a different political group. The elections of 1995, won by the Fujimori coalition in a landslide, assured the continuity of neoliberalism and signaled the electoral demise of populist and socialist political parties.

Several factors, all tightly interconnected, led to the persistence of the Right's agenda. The trends in the world economy toward globalization, together with the lasting influence of international financial organizations over heavily indebted nations like Peru, limited macroeconomic choices to neoliberal policies. If Peru was to receive desperately needed financial assistance, then its macroeconomic choices would be heavily influenced by political and economic actors with links to institutions advocating neoliberal policies. Moreover, neoliberal policies were advocated by technocrats within the state apparatus who had backing from new Right think tanks. Religious movements within the church, stimulated by conservative trends in the Vatican, also helped to consolidate the shift to the Right. Together with the sense of urgency that came from the growing violence of the late 1980s, this combination of economic and non-economic factors created a powerful coalition of domestic and international forces in

---

10. Vargas Llosa organized a meeting in one of Lima's biggest plazas, Plaza San Martín, where a crowd of forty thousand people cheered the new leader. For an account of this momentous event and the political battles that followed, see Vargas Llosa, M. (1993, 42–46).

favor of the continuing rightward move in Peruvian politics. Each of these factors will now be examined in turn.

The International Right

The neoconservative revolution in developed countries, expressed ideologically in the counteroffensive of new conservative ideologues against the welfare state, originated in the 1970s. It gathered momentum in the 1980s, with the electoral victories of Margaret Thatcher and Ronald Reagan in 1979 and 1980 respectively (Crawford 1980; King 1993). During the course of the 1980s an increasingly complex network of foundations, universities, think tanks, governmental agencies, and international financial organizations crafted the conditions for multidimensional (political, cultural, economic) support of neoconservative movements worldwide. These events occurred at a time when nations such as Argentina and Chile were already developing policies of deregulation, privatization, and economic liberalization, although guided by military regimes that were imposing policy changes without seeking consensus (Schamis 1992).

Meanwhile, the political exhaustion of the import-substitution model of economic development was accelerated throughout the region. Trapped by decreasing international reserves and high levels of indebtedness, most Latin American nations had little choice but to turn to the International Monetary Fund and the World Bank for assistance. These institutions, in turn, used their influence to promote a neoliberal agenda that reinforced the pivotal role played by the new Right. In Peru, and throughout Latin America, stabilization plans were adopted under the sponsorship of these twin organizations, who conditioned continued financial support on the maintenance of an approved economic program.[11] The arguments against state interventionism and in favor of economic liberalization were greatly reinforced with the sudden collapse of Soviet communism in Europe (Fukuyama 1992). The international Right focused more clearly on democracy and the combination of economic and political liberalism as a model to be disseminated in Latin America, a region that was moving toward democracy faster than any other in the Third World (Warnock 1988). The international Right coincided with the emergence of a domestic Right, and both forces mutually reinforced the changes sponsored by

---

11. For a critical approach on international financial organizations, see Strange (1974). For a debate on the issue of conditionality, first defended by the International Monetary Fund and soon after used also by the World Bank, see Williamson (1983).

their respective agendas. Although the specific connections between the Latin American and the international Right have not been sufficiently studied, most scholars concur on the critical importance played by the international Right in stimulating its Latin American counterparts (Cueva 1987; Hinkelanmert 1989; Bromley 1990; Borón 1990).

Conservatism in the Vatican

Another external influence was the role played by an increasingly conservative church. The election of Pope John Paul II in 1978 rapidly reoriented the Catholic church toward a theologically conservative and politically anti-socialist direction. This shift from the radicalism of previous decades animated conservative Catholic organizations throughout the region. Since the Catholic church was highly centralized, the influence of the Vatican was felt immediately (Ghio 1992, 186–87).

In 1979, the Latin American Bishop's Conference (CELAM) met in Puebla, Mexico, under the initiative of conservative clerics. The conference signaled the end of Liberation Theology as the most influential doctrine within the Latin American church, and its replacement by a more conservative, less critical vision of capitalism known as the Theology of Culture. While Theology of Liberation had centered its analysis on oppressive socioeconomic and political structures that needed to be changed, Theology of Culture emphasized the contribution of Catholicism to Latin America's culture, ideas, and values, while emphasizing reconciliation.[12] The conservative trends in CELAM were consolidated in the Santo Domingo conference of 1992.

Aside from doctrinal changes, conservatism was also felt in the church's hierarchy when the Vatican appointed more conservative bishops, displacing the radicals. The fact that the Jesuits lost their privileged position in the Vatican and a new order, Opus Dei (highly elitist and closely connected to business elites), became closer to the pope and the Roman Curia, also indicated conservative empowerment in the church.

The growing strength of Opus Dei and Sodalitium Vitae (a church movement led by Luis Figari) were the clearest indications of the new conservative tide in the church. Father Gustavo Gutiérrez, the author of the book *Teología de la liberación* that popularized Liberation Theology, was increasingly criticized in the church and in Catholic universities. The

---

12. According to the Catholic militant Juan Carlos Cortázar, Theology of Culture was the most sophisticated and successful attempt to counteract the intellectual influence of Theology of Liberation in Peru. Interview, Lima, 28 June 1994.

pope's two visits to Peru, in 1985 and 1987, with their general attacks on progressive positions within the church, helped conservatives isolate Gutiérrez and his followers (Ghio 1992).

Symbolic of the shift to the Right in the church was the election of a group of conservative Catholic students to the student government of the Catholic University of Peru, the nation's leading educational institution. Within the hierarchy of the church, a new generation of bishops appointed by the Vatican altered the balance of forces between liberation theologians and conservatives in favor of the latter. Moreover, the Opus Dei increased its influence in Cañete, Ayacucho (led by Luis Cipriani, leader of Opus Dei), Chiclayo, Piura, and Huancavelica, while Sodalitium Vitae became closely connected to the bishop of Arequipa. One of the most important events in this changing balance of forces was the elevation in 1990 of Vargas Alzamora, a pro-Sodalitium Vitae advocate, to archbishop of Lima.[13] By the early 1990s, conservative authorities had gained significant ground within the Catholic church and controlled the hierarchy in Peru's most important cities.[14] In 1995, Archbishop Vargas Alzamora became cardinal of Peru.

The Great Peruvian Depression

The recession that Peru experienced almost continuously from 1976 to 1992 helped promote closer ties between the international Right and the Peruvian Right, as well as increasing the attractiveness of the radical break that the Right promised. As Wise, Carmen Rosa Balbi, and others point out in this book, Peru's economy was wracked by high levels of inflation and growing unemployment and foreign debt. The precipitous decline of government revenues contributed to a deterioration of the country's institutions and infrastructure.

State institutions became underfunded, highly corrupt, and constantly under attack by particularly destructive guerrilla movements. The authority of the state was gradually eroded by both the fiscal crisis and the antistatist offensive of the new Right. The growing rates of participation in the informal economy, as well as contraband and drug trafficking, served as

13. On Vargas Alzamora and his links to the new Right, see Klaiber (1990). On the connections between Opus Dei, AMA-GI, and Libertad, see *Sí*, 16 May 1990, 16–16A. On Bishop Cipriani's role during the Fujimori administration and its links to the Vatican, see *Caretas*, 19 January 1995, 12–13; and *Expreso*, 1 July 1995, 2.

14. For a history of changes in the church, see Klaiber (1977, 182). For information on the conservatives' influence on the church, see *Marka*, 13 November 1975, 11–13; and *Caretas*, 4 March 1993, 18–20.

indications of how a weak and ineffective state created opportunities for actors to operate outside of the country's legal and institutional framework.[15] Even more alarming was the declining ability of the state to provide services such as health care, education, and security. It was not uncommon in the late 1980s to find hospitals that lacked needles. Schools and public offices closed for weeks because teachers and bureaucrats were on strike, and, even more alarming, police officers were engaged in criminal activities such as armed robbery, drug trafficking, and kidnappings.[16]

In this context, it was particularly difficult for advocates of socialism and populism to praise a model centered around a strong, interventionist state. At the same time, this deterioration became the strongest evidence in the new Right's argument that the state was not a tool but an obstacle for economic development. The fact that this deterioration of the state structure occurred during Alan García's administration, a president who was as incompetent as he was corrupt, helped define populism and socialism more clearly with the failures of his government. A "liberal" economic order seemed for the first time the preferred option for most Peruvians, who were in the midst of a desperate economic situation and the rise of political violence. Few seemed to care that the specific policies advocated by liberals might actually worsen their situation (Husain et al. 1992, 3).

Neoliberal Intellectuals and Think Tanks

Two Peruvian neoconservative intellectuals with strong international recognition and connections, Mario Vargas Llosa and Hernando de Soto, led the battle of ideas against populism and socialism in the period following

15. Institutional deterioration is not limited to the state. In fact, local governments, political parties, and interest groups of all kinds also suffered institutional decay during the Great Depression. The 1980s were, thus, a regressive period for society as a whole. On the negative impact of the recession on political parties, see Crabtree (1994).

16. Testimonies of several people who had firsthand experiences of this kind were taken in July 1994. A doctor interviewed stated that in a public hospital where he worked, nurses, lacking adequate supplies, had to sharpen the needles on the walls and used them until patients found it unbearable to support a shot. A municipal law-enforcement officer from Magdalena del Mar stated that every time he caught a criminal offender, he was immediately threatened with a lawsuit. This is an indication that the judicial system is an obstacle for law enforcement, because criminals can bribe judges. The author of this chapter was assaulted and pistol-whipped by a joint band of criminals and policemen in 1988; part of the band was later captured, including an officer of the Guardia Republicana. Most Peruvians tell anecdotes like the ones referred to above.

the late 1970s. Vargas Llosa, a famous novelist deeply interested in ideological matters, had ties with conservative writers and scholars in Europe
and the United States. He participated with the Mexican neoconservative
writer Octavio Paz, in journals and fora that disseminated their opinions.
De Soto, in turn, was well connected within the European banking community, international financial organizations, and conservative think tanks
linked to the Republican Party in the United States.[17]

A new diagnosis of the causes and consequences of underdevelopment
from a neoconservative point of view signaled the most important moment in the ideological offensive against the Left and the center of the
political spectrum. The book *The Other Path,* written by De Soto and policy
experts of his think tank, Instituto Libertad y Democracia, with a forward
by Vargas Llosa, criticized the role of the state in the economy as the
center of rent-seeking practices that prevented development. Informal entrepreneurs were portrayed as the new economic force capable of developing market forces outside the legal and institutional framework (Pásara
1991). The poor, in this version, were seen as agents of economic development who were marginalized by the formal sector. De Soto's core ideas
caught the imagination of a new generation of followers who, tired of the
populist and socialist discourse (including Liberation Theology), disseminated their ideas through the media, in news magazines, newspapers,
journals, and on television.[18]

Together with Instituto Libertad y Democracia, formed in 1978, and
Apoyo S. A., an influential consulting and polling firm, new Right organizations competed with leftist nongovernmental organizations in the
dissemination of ideas. Two of these organizations deserve to be mentioned, both formed by former technocrats identified with economic liberalism. The Instituto de Economia de Mercado, led by former minister
of economy (1992–93) Carlos Boloña, was formed in 1994. One of its
first publications was a selection of articles by Pedro Beltrán, a tribute to
the father of the old Right. The Instituto de Politica Económica was
formed in 1995 by Roberto Abusada, former vice minister of commerce
(1980–83), with the support of the World Bank and leading business
people.

17. For a detailed study of De Soto's international connections, see Bromley (1990).
18. Pedro Cateriano and Federico Salazar (Channel 4), Jaime Baily (Channel 5), Jorge
Morelli (*Expreso*), and Pedro Planas (*Oiga*), among others, are worth mentioning. In some
cases, former leftist militants like Fernando Rospigliosi also became converted to the Right
(*Caretas*).

The Threat Factor

One final factor that accelerated the formation and consolidation of the new Right as a social and political movement was the social threat against the elites. Everyday Peruvian life and politics in the 1980s became unusually violent as a result of rising street crime and the emergence of the guerrilla movements Sendero Luminoso (Shining Path) and the Tupac Amaru Revolutionary Movement (MRTA). The threat factor, however, became a far more serious problem when the government proved unable to control it. In fact, although the armed forces and the police tried to violently repress the revolutionary challenge, they did not even ameliorate the rate of violence for more than ten years, as Roberts and Peceny point out in their chapter in this book.

The expansion of these movements and their attacks against the elites and the business sector, including assaults and destruction of companies, kidnapping of business people, and demands to pay "revolutionary taxes," created a rising sense of chaos. In the same period, an intense acceleration of street crimes served to increase tensions and fears.[19]

The new Right successfully mobilized supporters by tapping into the feelings of anger, uncertainty, and fear that gripped elites and the middle class. In this context, the need for political action for the elites became urgent, in order to do something before it was too late. The title of De Soto's book is, in that sense, quite revealing. It offers another path (economic liberalism) besides that of the Shining Path (revolutionary socialism). De Soto reinforced the idea of urgent political action to destroy the old state and generate a new one, open and democratic in terms of economic opportunities for all economic agents, including the informal sector.

Perhaps his most important ideological innovation was to create a popular version of liberalism. This version departed from the oligarchic one in that it saw the informal entrepreneurs as the champions of market forces and opened the possibility for the elites to join forces with the masses to defend the principle of private property. The modernity of the new version of liberalism was based upon an ideological formula of embracing the informals as entrepreneurs. It was a way of ending social isola-

---

19. The two sources of violence were analyzed by a congressional committee led by Senator Enrique Bernales in 1988 (Senado de la República 1988). Abundant statistical information about political violence and street crime for the 1980–90 period is found in Webb and Fernández Baca (1991, 327–58).

tion, the most serious problem encountered by the Right. To put this idea into practice, it was necessary to create a political party.

The Formation of a Political Organization

Before the process of intense politicization was ignited by the nationalization of the banks, the new Right was characterized by a core constituency of entrepreneurs (managers and owners), technocrats, and neoconservative intellectuals. In contrast to their oligarchic predecessors, the new Right was far more modern and open.[20] Yet in many ways it was still a closed elitist circle of European origin that preferred to influence public opinion indirectly through the media it controlled rather than through mass political activity.

In the aftermath of the bank nationalization, the new Right developed forms of political organization beyond interest groups (economic or religious), in order to extend their societal influence in a more effective and integrated manner. Advocates of liberalism sought to broaden their appeal to the lower-class majority in order to effectively compete in the struggle for political power as an organized political force. In the view of many, the old parties (Popular Action and the Partido Popular Cristiano, or Christian Popular Party) were too linked to the past to serve as a vehicle of interest aggregation. Thus, a new alternative was needed.

The nationalization of the banks on 28 July 1987 provided an opportunity to consolidate the new Right's unity, to legitimize its leaders, and to further mobilize young recruits in the defense of their ideological agenda.[21] In this context of rapid politicization, the idea of creating a political movement suddenly emerged. Vargas Llosa became the leading figure and eventually the founder of a new movement (Movimiento Libertad,

20. Even if the new liberal discourse criticized rent seeking, it also had an important appeal in the private sector, one of its main practitioners. Since the center of the attack was the state and policies of interventionism, the business elites felt attracted to the liberal discourse. It is worth mentioning that the Confederation of Private Entrepreneurial Institutions (CONFIEP), the "peak" business association, adopted the neoconservative discourse and had close links to both De Soto and Vargas Llosa. Interview with CONFIEP's manager, Lima, May 1995.

21. For an extensive account of the causes and consequences of the nationalization, and of how the elites reacted to it, see Durand (1994, 157–77).

hereafter Libertad) that formed part of a political front (Frente Demo-crático) in the 1990 general elections.

The lessons learned in this process, initiated in mid-1987, were to be bitter ones. Vargas Llosa's front won significant victories in the municipal elections of 1989 (56 out of 178 municipalities) and did fairly well in the first round of the general elections in 1990, obtaining 27.61 percent of the votes (Cameron 1994, 119). However, his own personal dream of ob-taining an overwhelming "liberal mandate" was not achieved (Vargas Llosa, M. 1991). Since the leading candidate did not obtain 50 percent of the votes, the two top contenders in the runoff elections, Vargas Llosa and Fujimori, had to compete again.

The results were an "electoral earthquake" for the new Right (Schmidt 1991). As Cameron notes in his chapter in this book, populist- and social-ist-leaning voters saw an opportunity to side against Vargas Llosa, who was portrayed as an elitist, "white" candidate, by voting for Fujimori, an inde-pendent non-white popular candidate. After the election, the front was dissolved and Vargas Llosa retired from politics and abandoned Peru. Thus Libertad lost its leader and saw its platform coopted by the new Fujimori administration, leaving the movement splintered. In 1992 youn-ger followers of Libertad, led by Rafael Rey, a Catholic openly identified with Opus Dei, formed Renovación, a new conservative political move-ment that supported the Fujimori administration.

The presidential coup of 5 April 1992, which witnessed Fujimori closing the Congress and the judicial system in the midst of a political crisis, created a new source of tension within the new Right. The different com-ponents of the Right and their organizations divided over the issue of whether to support Fujimori (Renovación) or defend constitutional de-mocracy, as Vargas Llosa advocated.[22] In the aftermath of the "Fujigolpe," Libertad found itself divided and without a leading figure and did poorly in the 1993 municipal and congressional elections. The possibilities of developing a new Right political party were thus lost. Only Renovación remained as a significant political force, although it was still unable to cross class boundaries and create a neoconservative movement with mass support.

One of the main characteristics of the political and social organizations

---

22. Both Mario Vargas Llosa and his press secretary, his son Alvaro, have written exten-sively on the campaign and the political events that followed the 1990 election. See Vargas Llosa, A. (1991) and Vargas Llosa, M. (1991). One of Mario Vargas Llosa's latest novels, *Pez en el agua*, is a bitter but honest account of his political frustrations (1993).

of the new Right has been their elitist nature. The electoral results demonstrate that their political support has been restricted to the upper class and the upper middle class, with only occasional and limited influence over the poorer majorities. Elitism has continued to be an important source of the new Right's political problems and social isolation. There are several key components to the new Right's elitism, to which we will now turn.

Public Opinion

Several polls taken in the late 1980s indicated that the Democratic Front of Vargas Llosa was perceived by public opinion to be an elitist organization. Even if the struggle to oppose the nationalization of the banks and Vargas Llosa himself initially had significant popular support, most Peruvians still saw the Democratic Front as an organization of the rich. In June 1989, when asked "which of the following groups is represented in the Democratic Front," 52 percent responded "the business sector" and 38 percent "the bankers"; only 16 percent stated that Vargas Llosa's organization represented "blue collar workers, peasants and labor unions" (*Caretas*, 19 June 1989, 16).

The elitist image limited the new Right's political appeal in the elections as Alvaro Vargas Llosa, the press secretary of the Democratic Front, openly recognized in his personal account of his father's defeat (1991). During the electoral campaign, Vargas Llosa's major challenge was to get in touch with and mobilize the poor. He did not succeed, however, even among the so-called informal sector, who, at least in theory and according to De Soto, had an affinity with Libertad.[23]

Leadership of Right-Wing Movements

The composition of Libertad was, without question, elitist. The founders of its first public manifesto were technocrats, university professors, intellectuals, business people, investors, conservative journalists, well-known artists, and writers who belonged to Lima's exclusive circles (*El Comercio*, 5 August 1987, 2). The senators and deputies who represented Libertad in the 1990–92 Congress had similar features. Out of six senators, three were former presidents of the peak business association, CONFIEP (Vega

---

23. De Soto himself attempted without success to create a formal- informal union in 1987, to defend the banks.

Alvear, Vega Llona, and Villegas). Another was a university professor at the Universidad del Pacífico, Peru's reputable business-oriented university. The two others were a lawyer in a prestigious firm (Ferrero) and a well-known architect (Cruchaga).

All nine Libertad deputies elected in 1990 belonged to the upper class or the upper-middle class. Three of them (Rey, Ghersi, and Cateriano) were conservative Catholics linked to Opus Dei and AMA-GI, another conservative Catholic organization.[24] In 1992, as explained above, they formed Renovación, whose elitist trait was even sharper than that of Libertad. Libertad's most enthusiastic followers and core leadership had distinct upper-class backgrounds. One of its young supporters openly admitted during an interview that "we all lived in the same exclusive neighborhoods; none of us have ever been in the shantytowns."[25]

Electoral Behavior

In the 1989 municipal elections, when the Democratic Front was the leading political force, there was a strong correlation between voting behavior and social class: the higher the social class, the stronger the percentage of votes obtained by the Democratic Front. For example, in five upper-class districts of Lima (San Isidro, Miraflores, Jesús María, San Borja, and Magdalena), the vote for the Democratic Front averaged 68.8 percent, while in Lima as a whole it averaged only 51.67 percent.[26]

Elite electoral behavior in Lima changed after the 1990 elections, gradually shifting from Libertad and the Christian Popular Party to Fujimori and, to a lesser extent, to Renovación. Elite districts voted massively for Vargas Llosa in 1990 (70.2 percent). In the 1992 congressional elections, held after Fujimori closed Congress, the elites supported Fujimori with 49.2 percent of the vote; they also supported two conservative parties (the Christian Popular Party and Renovación, which attracted 9.8 and 7.1 percent of elite votes respectively). In 1993, a referendum was held to support or oppose the new constitution sponsored by Fujimori after the coup. Yes won in the same six elite districts with an average of 64.7 per-

---

24. See Movimiento Libertad (1988).
25. Confidential interview in San Antonio, Texas, 2 May 1994.
26. Data based on an author's study of elite voting behavior. See paper presented to the XIX Latin American Studies Association, Washington D.C., September 1995: "Fujimorismo y comportamiento electoral de las elites." For the 1989 municipal elections, see Roncagliolo (1990, 16).

cent of the votes. At the same time, yes only obtained 52.33 percent of the votes at the national level. This time, the new Right's core constituents supported even more enthusiastically Fujimori, the new leader who was putting into practice part of their agenda (economic liberalization, order), even though they had voted overwhelmingly against him in 1990.[27] In the 1995 general elections, which Fujimori won by 64 percent the votes, Lima's elites maintained its allegiance to the new leader (who attracted 59.1 percent of their votes).

The Two Rights and the Question of Democracy

The first half of the 1990s was a period of contradictory trends for the new Right. While it extended its intellectual, policy-making and cultural influences (Guadalupe 1992), it did not develop its political organizations or even maintain the cohesiveness of its various constituent groups. Some of its organizational problems resulted from divisions provoked by the Fujimori administration in general, and the 1992 coup in particular. Those who closely identified themselves with Vargas Llosa viewed Fujimori as a rival who had to be stopped. This camp largely consisted of the majority of Libertad's political leaders. Part of the Right, thus, tended to oppose Fujimori, a position that was even more evident after the coup. Some manifested a racist rejection of "El Chino" Fujimori, a feeling that was also expressed in conservative news magazines that criticized Fujimori with unusual ferocity. This position, however, was limited to the political Right.

Most of the business sector consistently supported Fujimori after he announced his support of economic liberalism. This support proved critical, particularly in the immediate aftermath of the coup, by providing Fujimori with a solid base of support (Pásara 1992, 53).[28] However, the fact that one important trade associations (Organización Nacional Agraria) had withdrawn from CONFIEP after the coup is a clear indication of disagreements within business over its support for the regime. The best

27. Although Fujimori closed Congress, he soon went back to democracy in 1993. Several elections were held after the 5 April 1992 coup (municipal, congressional, and the referendum). For that reason, his government has been described as an intermediate regime, a "democradura" rather than a dictatorship. See López (1993).

28. Interview with a former vice minister of industry who held this position during the autogolpe, Lima, 8 June 1994.

indicator of the closeness of the regime and business was the number of business leaders serving in the Fujimori cabinet. In 1993–94, the minister of economy and finance (Camet), the minister of industry (Bustamante), and the prime minister and minister of foreign relations (Goldenberg) were all well-known leaders of the business community. A close relationship also existed between the regime and other new-Right organizations, such as the Instituto Libertad y Democracia and conservative religious organizations. For example, the bishop of Ayacucho, Luis Cipriani, head of Opus Dei, maintained close relations with Fujimori and had been a member of the National and Social Development Compensation Fund (FONCODES) since its formation in 1991. In 1995, Fujimori replaced a businessman as minister of foreign relations by a member of Renovación (Tudela).

The political behavior of the elites in the 1993 referendum, mentioned above, is also quite clear. Most members of Lima's elites supported Fujimori's new constitution and voted against the anti-Fujimori position of Libertad and other parties. The percentage of votes (56 percent in the 1992, 1993, and 1995 elections) in five upper-income areas of Lima was high enough to dispel doubt about elite support for Fujimori. The explanation of this rupture between the pro-Fujimori and the anti-Fujimori new Right is based on the ability of Fujimori to enact the major parts of the new Right's agenda. To this end, the application of a stabilization plan and the continuation of orthodox economic policies during the first six months were critical.

In addition, Fujimori demonstrated a calculated determination to create conditions of governability at a moment when society seemed on the brink of collapse. The fact that Fujimori had a systematic plan to defeat terrorism, a strategy that proved its worth soon after the 1992 coup, when Guzmán and most of the Shining Path's Central Committee were captured, reinforced the elite's support of his administration. Moreover, it must be taken into account that other social groups shared similar opinions, since Fujimori's approval rate was consistently above 55 percent (Panfichi 1994). But even if the autogolpe was broadly supported, elite support has been more consistent and enthusiastic, especially in the business community.[29]

---

29. In a number of interviews with business leaders of IPAE and CONFIEP, the leading business organizations all coincided in voicing open support to Fujimori. For the first time in decades, according to one, a governmental succession had not generated uncertainty. One, however, showed some fear that Fujimori was concentrating too much political power. Lima, June and July 1995.

The particularly difficult circumstances Peru faced in the late 1980s created a consensus among elites on the need for order, even if democratic procedures had to be sacrificed. Fujimori's charismatic leadership provided a sense of governability in a time of crisis, which was seen as indispensable in reinforcing the continuation of the kind of economic order advocated by the Right. In this context democracy suffered, but its torment was considered inevitable by many Peruvians and by a majority of the upper classes. When threatened by violence, conservatives have shown a stronger preference for order and stability. If democracy accompanies it and the degree of uncertainty is manageable, most of the new Right's components will support it. If democracy seems unable to stop chaos, social disintegration, and institutional deterioration, the elites preferred option is some form of authoritarian order. The case of Peru thus confirms the well-established notion that elite support for democratic institutions is conditioned by their perception of threats to their social, economic, and political positions.

Conclusion

The new Right in Peru emerged from the ashes of Velasco's anti-oligarchic revolution. In 1968, General Velasco eliminated the oligarchy as a social, economic, and political class, paving the way, ironically, for the formation of a more modern Right. The old Right was aristocratic in nature, closed to newcomers, and clearly antidemocratic. It also was a stoic believer in a type of economic liberalism open to the world and favorable to the exploitation of natural resources, even if progress only benefited a handful of wealthy families and foreign corporations. Its social isolation was extreme. The oligarchy, since the 1920s, had been operating without an official political party and was ready to align itself with military regimes or compromise with parties that showed a willingness to forge pacts with it. Influence over civil society was exerted through the media and the hierarchy of the Catholic church, while economic interests were defended by the National Agrarian Society, the core trade association.

After Velasco, the Right emerged with new faces, different organizations, leaders, and cadres. It remained elitist in nature and still suffered from social isolation, but it was now more bourgeois and open to new members from the professional middle class. The modern Right is convinced that development creates opportunities for all Peruvians. Economic interests are defended through a peak business association (CONFIEP), a confederation of trade associations. Influence over the modern media is strong. Public opinion is influenced by a variety of well-financed think tanks and the support of intellectuals such as Vargas Llosa and De Soto. In the church, conservative movements such as Opus Dei and Sodalitium Vitae have been able to gain ground. In terms of political organizations, through Libertad and Renovación, the new Right has attempted without much success to build a political party capable of connecting the elites with the masses. Social isolation, thus, remains a serious problem, although it is somehow counteracted by the elites' influence over the media and by the recent emergence of the common-sense notion that liberalism offers the solution to Peru's contemporary problems.

The revival of the Right, its newfound ability to fight successfully against well-organized rivals such as the forces of populism and socialism, is a result of a combination of factors. It has clearly been stimulated by the neoconservative revolutions in developed nations and by changes in the Vatican, trends reinforced by the collapse of communism. Peruvian intellectuals and technocrats have linked the nation with the international Right, forming a powerful coalition to change economic policies and redefine the role of the state.

As a result of this combination of factors, the particularly intense clash between populist and socialist forces and liberalism seems to be finally shifting in favor of the latter. The stalemate has been broken. The Right and the business sector have become better organized and more influential, while the political organization and interest groups of its rivals have clearly lost ground.

Circumstances have also favored conservative actors. The economic recession and international economic trends have created positive conditions for advocates of liberalism. The threat factor and the deterioration of the state apparatus have also forced the elites to become politically mobilized and organized. The event that accelerated the new Right's political formation and internal unity was the nationalization of the banks in 1987. It was at this critical juncture that the new Right's constituents, organizations, and parties finally emerged from the shadows.

However, the Right's political consolidation has not been complete. The electoral results since the new Right's emergence indicate difficulties in the extension of its influence over the masses. Vargas Llosa's defeat in 1990 and the subsequent division of the new Right into two camps, one in favor of Fujimori (Renovación) and the other in the opposition, are factors that delineate internal tensions. Most of the rightist groups that support Fujimori emphasize the importance of order and economic progress, rather than of democracy. In the view of the new rightists, the threat factor, particularly social and political violence, undermines their personal interests, creates political uncertainty, and weakens the chances of consolidating the process of economic liberalization. Fujimori's ability to sustain the economic model after a successful stabilization program and to weaken terrorism is at the heart of the new Right's support for his administration and the autogolpe. Opposition to Fujimori came from the political expressions of the Right and some of the elites.

The new Right's support for economic liberalism is, in other words, more consistent than its support for democracy. Its political strategy, conditioned by its elitist nature, reinforces the need for order as a precondition for economic progress. That, combined with its isolation from the masses, a limitation that is offset by the spread of economic liberalism, generates a distrust for democracy and a reliance on strong leaders.

PART III

VIOLENCE AND HUMAN RIGHTS

7

AFTER THE FALL OF ABIMAEL GUZMÁN
THE LIMITS OF SENDERO LUMINOSO

Carlos Iván Degregori

If man, as Shakespeare wrote, is made from the material of his dreams, there is no doubt that in Abimael Guzmán we confront the product of a grotesque nightmare.[1] On 12 September 1992, Guzmán, known to his followers in the Shining Path as President Gonzalo, was captured in a safe house in Lima. In the aftermath of the "capture of the century," much was said about the leader's personality, his psychology, and even his neurology.[2] This chapter emphasizes the manner in which the political personality of the recently captured prisoner marked the history of Sendero Luminoso from the outset and came to be projected throughout the country in twelve years of armed warfare, from 1980 to 1992; the chapter also considers the effects that his capture has had on his followers.

The Shining Path Experience

The emergence of Sendero Luminoso marks a radical point of rupture with the model of Latin American armed struggle that began with the Cuban Revolution and ended, simplifying of course, with the electoral defeat of the Sandinista government and the negotiated resolution of the

1. This chapter was translated by Carlos Rosales. It is part of a larger work edited by David Apter, entitled *Violence and Democracy*, which is forthcoming.
2. For a review of the literature on the Shining Path, see Palmer (1992c), Starn (1992), and Poole and Rénique (1992, chap. 2). Detailed studies of the Shining Path are provided by Degregori (1990) and Gorriti (1990).

civil war in El Salvador.[3] This is a rupture with all the romanticism that characterized this period of Latin American history. Out of the Cuban Revolution emerged the image of the heroic guerrilla fighter rising up in arms against oligarchs and dictators, and through almost sheer willpower sweeping away systems of oppression that had existed for centuries. But in the aftermath of the heroic guerrilla, there emerged the image of the bureaucratic revolutionary.

The classic guerrilla movement clearly underestimated the role of bureaucratic organization in the making of a revolutionary movement and society.[4] Guzmán was the culmination of this shift from romanticism to calculation. He built an authoritative organization and converted it, by its own definition, into a "war machine." He was a cold planner of mass death: "the triumph of the revolution will cost one million deaths," he said in a televised appearance on 24 September 1992.

That very bureaucratic essence was what allowed his capture, along with that of his meticulously organized party files, to take place. Unlike Ché Guevara, for example, who was captured in combat and later assassinated, or President Allende, who took his life before falling into the hands of General Pinochet, Abimael Guzmán merely declared, when captured, "it was my turn to lose."[5] His revolutionary project was more associated with lawyers, teachers, and priests, who for centuries had formed the bureaucratic nexus of traditional power, whereas the protagonists of previous models of armed struggle had more frequently been writers, artists, bohemians, and other members of a counterculture that stemmed from the big cities of peripheral capitalism.

Teachers, lawyers, and priests are more associated with pre-capitalist cities, or with medium and small towns at the margins of (if not forgotten by) capitalist development. By contrast, the guerrillas of the 1960s were the "children of progress." They were the rebellious children of a continent in expansion, enveloped in a period when developmentalists, *dependentistas,* and orthodox Marxists shared unlimited faith in progress. Sendero Luminoso, however, made inroads in society during Latin America's so-called lost decade, among the "children of the crisis," for whom Guzmán's proposal of "war communism" seemed appealing. War communism

3. I do not wish to idealize the previous cycle, I share the "critique of armed struggle" that different authors have made and I only point out the tendencies.
4. See Régis Debray's digressions about the party in his 1967 essay, *Revolution in the Revolution?*
5. *Resúmen Semanal* 15 (9–15 September 1992): 2.

implied total collectivism and top-down equalization; it also suggested the possibility of finding an order in which the anger of the excluded and the hopeless would be channeled into a violent struggle. Guzmán's was an order in which everything "is born from the barrel of a gun."

There are other contrasts that can be made between these two models of revolutionary politics. Where the leaders of the previous models of warfare were nomadic guerrillas operating in open spaces, Guzmán's trajectory was sedentary and almost claustrophobic. Never during the 1970s did he make a speech in a public plaza. He moved between the cell, his studies, his classroom, and the auditorium. During the 1980s, while underground, he moved about in the trunks of cars, from hiding place to hiding place, from room to room, from desk to desk, reading and writing tirelessly, but never appearing publicly.

Perhaps one of the most interesting differences with models inspired in the Cuban Revolution is that the Sendero experience always favored theory over pragmatism. Sendero's project was more an ideological and pedagogical project than a military and political one. Hence its emphasis on the preparation of a "guiding thought," while classical guerrilla movements in the Americas were willing to subordinate theory to practice and action.

This contrast even takes on a physical dimension in the bodies of the protagonists. Guzmán as prisoner conveyed a sedentary image. His fat naked torso displayed to the television cameras stands in sharp contrast with the photos of the young corpse of Ché in Nancahuazu. But in the end, bodies did not matter. Neither did feelings. That is why Laura Zambrano, comrade Meche, one of the leaders who was caught alongside Guzmán, could assert in an interview some years ago that love has a class character.

Guzmán's adventure, regardless of how bloody its results, was fundamentally intellectual; it aspired to be scientific, indeed doctoral. Never in the revolutionary tradition—maybe because there never was a guerrilla with the soul of a lawyer and bureaucrat—has there been so much insistence on the doctoral character of the leader. On the Shining Path's posters Guzmán occupies the center, dressed in a suit, wearing glasses, book in hand, surrounded by masses carrying rifles and flags. His lawyer and his "ambassador" (so-called by the press) to London, Adolfo Olaechea, insisted that he be addressed as Doctor Abimael Guzmán and that his status as an intellectual be recognized (Olaechea cited in *La República*, 17 September 1992, 2): "That man [Fujimori] is not in the least ashamed nor embarrassed to humiliate Peru in trying to humiliate an intellectual, a true university professor like Doctor Abimael Guzmán."

That insistence had to do with the need for recognition and legitimation of mestizo provincial intellectuals in a centralized and racist country. It was also due to the very personality of the future cosmocrat. In a book written by a friend and admirer of Guzmán, the following depiction is found, which was possibly agreed to by the Sendero leader, for it corresponds to his self-image (Gutiérrez 1988, 256–57): "Abimael Guzmán would be a unique case among revolutionary intellectuals who yield to Marxism not for ethical reasons like an existential inquiry, or a cathartic therapy to exorcise certain obsessions, but rather by way of reason, only after waging a scorching debate in his soul between idealism and materialism."

Earlier in the book, the same author suggests: "Abimael Guzmán's adolescence and youth was a secret, tenacious, unyielding and arduous adventure of the mind" (Gutiérrez, 1988).

The Fundamentalism of Sendero Luminoso

Guzmán is certainly a fascinating character. No one could have imagined that inside that rather plump professor of extremely calm appearance, with his traditional suit and thick glasses, who strolled daily by Ayacucho's parade grounds, burned such scalding fires. His was an "adventure of the mind" whose first great chapter took place in the decade of the 1970s. It was then that Guzmán turned the University of Huamanga in Ayacucho into a kind of Andean Yenan where, in Maoist fashion, a "primitive accumulation of symbolic capital" was produced. This allowed him to transform the Sendero Luminoso into a "discourse community," and his cadres into a "people of the book."

Such a community made it possible for certain marginal sectors—not the poorest, but rather those functionally superfluous—to collectivize risk and display a willingness to die and kill in the name of an "overcoming project." This was done within an organization that, according to its own definition, was turned into a war machine, an apparatus able to effectively channel the pain of Guzmán's followers and transform it into rage.

For this discourse community, Guzmán was a cosmocrat in a mythological plan capable of converting the myth into a logical discourse that would open the minds of young students to the possibilities that until then had been far from reach. In that process, the cosmocrat turned into a figure more like a spiritual leader or ayatollah than like other leaders of the Marxist tradition.[6] "Gonzalo thought" was more like a Tibetan version of Marxism in which the revolutionary idea is embodied in certain individuals or "swords"—Marx, Lenin, Mao, Gonzalo—somewhat in the way that the Buddha's spirit is embodied in each new Dalai Lama.

Sendero Luminoso represents a rupture not only with the Latin American guerrilla tradition, with which Guzmán broke early on at the 1964 Fifth Congress of the Peruvian Communist Party–Red Flag, but also with Maoism itself. The point of rupture begins even before the start of the armed struggle. Only by turning into a fundamentalist movement would it be possible for Sendero to initiate the armed struggle in such adverse conditions, shielding itself against a reality so overwhelmingly divergent from its own interpretation.

It should be remembered that the Shining Path was intent on initiating its adventure at a crucial moment in Peruvian history as well as in that of international communism. On both fronts its chances were limited. In the late 1970s, Peru was going through an intense period of social mobilization, as Mauceri pointed out in chapter one of this book. This was the period of the massive national strikes of 1977 and 1978, which contributed to the transition to civilian rule. Sendero played no part in this process, refusing to join the coalition of leftist parties that participated in elections and remaining marginal to the negotiations occurring in Lima. In Sendero's view, the parties of the Left were little more than pro-Soviet revisionists. The entire electoral process that occurred and the transition itself were described as unimportant in changing what for Sendero was essentially a fascist regime.

Sendero in this period was just as isolated from international trends as it was from national currents. On the international level, Mao Tse-tung had died in 1976; the Gang of Four, headed by his widow, Jiang Qing, had been defeated; and the cultural revolution, which fed the imagination of a good part of the Peruvian Left, had come to an end. Maoism had begun a rapid decline, and in the wake of the Pol Pot regime in Cambodia would no longer seem as attractive a model for building a new society as it had been in previous decades.

The dimension of Sendero's rupture with previous revolutionary models

6. A possible exception is Kim Il Sung.

is gauged in three crucial texts that Guzmán wrote between 1979 and 1980. They are, to my mind, his most striking works, or at least the texts most full of meaning, passion, and persuasive power. His objective was to unite his "handful of communists," and he utilized to that effect a rhetorical recourse that could be called "flash forward." The text goes forward in time and envisages a distant future when the revolutionary project has finally succeeded. It attempts to erase time and instill certainty into the future. The goddess of history is on Guzmán's side, as is the goddess of matter, which is the other name for the same divinity.

The first text is called "For the New Flag." It was written in September 1979, eight months prior to the beginning of the armed struggle. It starts with a biblical phrase: "Many are called but few are the ones chosen." The occasion was the pledging of allegiance to the party's flag—which, incidentally, is red. But what is most impressive is the text's emphasis on the need for a personal, internal rupture. "Two flags [struggle] in the soul, one black and one red. We are the Left, let us sacrifice the black one." To do this, it is necessary to "wash our souls, wash them thoroughly. . . . Enough of individual putrid waters, godforsaken manure." In fact, the entire book is filled with biblical phrases, some even copied literally, for instance: "The party is the salt of the earth, the living tree, the others are parasites."

Everyone, according to Guzmán, should have to experience the scorching intellectual battles of the cosmocrat, so as to finally end up washed and born again, like the born-again Christians. Many analysts of Sendero have emphasized the Indian or Andean character of the organization and its ideology. These interpretations suggest that Sendero is somehow alien to the westernized elites of Peru and that it is an expression of characteristics largely indigenous in origin.[7] Yet it is not possible to understand the party apart from western traditions, both religious and ideological.

The second text that needs to be examined is entitled "On Three Chapters of Our History." It was written in December 1979, five months before armed actions began. In it Guzmán argues that once purified, the true communists should know how to construe their history so that they can transcend their current circumstances and be projected into the future.

This is when the flash-forward technique is utilized extensively. Before presenting the history of Peru, the narrator urges his listeners to free

---

7. For a debate on the Andean character of the Shining Path, see Mayer (1991) and Starn (1991a).

their minds "to the revolutionary imagination" and place themselves in the second half of the twenty-first century. From there, one may envisage history as written by future communists, the readers' heirs. What would the heirs of the revolution say? At that point in the text, the cosmocrat begins the narration as if he were a historian from the twenty-first century: "There was a time when shadows prevailed . . ."

Thousands of years of Peruvian history are then condensed in three grand chapters that take us from darkness into light. The first one, "On How Shadows Prevailed," covers the period from the arrival of humans in the Andes up to the early stages of the twentieth century, when, alongside the new imperialist order, "a new class originates; it is the proletariat, and a new chapter emerges."

If anything catches the reader's attention, it is the fact that scant regard is really given to the past. Guzmán does not attempt to recover a lost paradise. It is striking to find little mention or regard for the Inca empire, particularly when that period has held such fascination for historians and romantics alike and has formed the basis for utopian movements throughout Peruvian history. In the text's absolutely classist vision, ethnicity remains unmentioned; what matters is the emergence of the state—and of classes—during the time of the Wari, a pre-Inca civilization centered near modern-day Ayacucho. All of history revolves around the further elaboration of these two fundamental concepts, and everything else is marginal to this centrality. The conquest of the Wari by the Incas, who are subsequently conquered themselves by the Spanish, is little more than a substitution of exploiters. Paradise lies in the future and not in the past. In this, Sendero remained a thoroughly modern organization. There are no attempts anywhere in Sendero's literature to romanticize or hark back to pre-Columbian times.

The title of the second chapter is "On How Light Originated and Steel Was Forged." In it, Mariátegui and the young Peruvian proletariat play the leading role until, as in a cosmology, from the darkness "A purer, more resplendent light started to emerge, we carried that light in our chest, in our soul. That light fused with the earth and that clay turned into lead. Light, clay, lead, the PARTY emerges in 1928 . . ."

This is no longer the language of the Bible. This is a new Bible with a proletarian genesis. History is accelerated to the point of dizziness until ecstasy is reached. In effect, the second chapter of this text culminates in the decade of the 1970s, when "Our people were enlightened by a brighter light [than] Marxist-Leninist thought, or Mao Tse-tung; we were at first dazzled, the breaking of interminable light, light and nothing more; little by little our eyes began to understand that light, we lowered our vision and began to see our country, Mariátegui as well as our reality, and found our perspective: the Reconstruction of the Party."

Mount Tabor, Christmas, and Pentecost are condensed in a single phrase. The disciples, those marginals who are functionally superfluous, are ready to speak in tongues and to become the leading characters in the third chapter, which begins the same day the cosmocrat delivers his speech. Its title: "On How the Walls Crumbled and Dawn Broke."

The last and most important text is entitled "We Are the Initiators." This was a speech delivered at the closing ceremony of Sendero Luminoso's First Military School on 19 April 1980, less than a month away from the start of military actions. Guzmán's followers having been purified and enabled to interpret the past, present, and future, it was now possible for them to move to action. In doing so, they would shake the world. According to Guzmán, the inception of the armed struggle in the remote Peruvian Andes meant that "we began the strategic offensive of the world revolution."

The cosmocrat plots a line that goes from the oldest mass struggles, including the Paris Commune, the October Revolution, the Chinese Revolution, and the Cultural Revolution, until the day when "all those magnificent, centuries-old actions are concentrated here. The promise is unlocked, the future unfolds: ILA 80" (*inicio de la lucha armada,* "beginning of the armed struggle"). According to Guzmán, ILA 80 is possible because he has made it possible and because there is strategic equilibrium at the world level. In equilibrium "The people are angry, they arm themselves and rising up in rebellion put a hangman's rope to the necks of imperialism and the reactionaries, they grab them by their throats and grip them; and necessarily strangle them, necessarily. They will shred the reactionary flesh and the black scraps will be submerged in the mud. What is left over will be burned and the ashes will be scattered by the winds of the earth so that only the sinister memory remains of what will never be again because it can not and must not be again."

The hate in the language is a foreshadowing of the violence that is to come. What is important to comprehend is how so much pain and anger could have been accumulated. How could an army of "head hunters" have been generated in Peru in 1980, after which nothing would ever be the same? In the next section we will examine how this fundamentalism developed along three intertwined lines: a death cult, the abolition of the ego, and the consecration of the leader.

Death Cult, Abolition of the Ego, and Consecration of the Leader

The death cult is exacerbated at every stage of the "popular struggle." As noted by Gustavo Gorriti (1990), in 1982 Guzmán pointed to the need to pay "the quota" of blood necessary for the revolution to triumph. From 1989 onward, when Sendero Luminoso was intent on reaching "strategic equilibrium," Guzmán's followers began to speak of a million deaths and of the convenience of "genocide" in order to reach that equilibrium. The emergence of the cult was made easier by the rejection of individuality. The militants had to "carry their lives at the tip of their fingers" and be willing to pay "the quota" and "cross the river of blood" necessary for the triumph of the revolution.

In the three aforementioned texts one can already observe an angry willingness to obliterate individuality. This is linked to the teleological, predetermined vision of history that is held. In "The Two Flags," this willingness leads to the need to be yoked onto the carriage of history, which is also that of Guzmán. It is expressed in phrases from the biblical tradition: "The proletariat is the bonfire, a fraction of one of its spark are we. . . . Can a spark rise against the bonfire? The sparks cannot contain the flames. . . . Silly it is to want to destroy matter. How could grains stop the wheels of a mill? They would be pulverized."

In the "Three Chapters of Our History," the futurist imagery acquires an almost science-fiction aspect: "Let's place ourselves in the second half of the next century, history will have been written by us and those that follow us, the future communists, because we are inexhaustible; others will come and still others, and those that come will be us."

The future is a total "us." Guzmán's vision approximates Gaia, the planet on which the Second Foundation of Isaac Asimov's novels take place, more than the Catholic church's image of the mystical body of Christ. At the same time, in that great "us" some are "more equal" than others. The *caudillo*'s ego is exalted through a personality cult unlike no other in history.[8] Let us provide one example: since early 1980, militants have had to sign a "letter of subjection," not to the party nor to the "revolutionary line," but rather to President Gonzalo. In "The Two Flags," Guzmán had already explained this development by resorting to one of Beethoven's compositions, banned in China during the Cultural Revolution: "The Ninth Symphony has a distinct characteristic: it features a low sound that increases gradually and forges a light until it bursts into musical explosion. Human voices come in, the voices of the choral, it is the earth that has converted into a voice; over the background of the choral four individuals sing, voices that sing louder are generated, but there is one voice that would sing even louder. Never before had it been possible, but after many attempts, it was achieved in this century and what was once seen as impossible has now been accomplished."

It is clear that Guzmán identifies himself with that voice which succeeds in "reaching the top." In the obsessive pursuit of that dream, in the midst of a rising river of blood, the *caudillo*-master is being transformed into a master-messiah. The references to Mariátegui disappear. President Gonzalo is turned into "the greatest Marxist-Leninist-Maoist alive" and "the fourth sword of Marxism" after Marx, Lenin, and Mao, the soloist of the Ninth Symphony, who takes the baton right where Mao left off and was defeated and is capable of releasing the roar that will transform the world.

This is the character who fell prisoner in September 1992. Individuals like this do not spring up like weeds or mushrooms after the rain. In this case, clichés like "A tough act to follow" or "He leaves a vacuum hard to fill" must be taken literally. And yet that was precisely the dilemma that faced Sendero after the capture of the "fourth sword."

The Fall of the Leader, the Collapse of the Movement

The year 1992 was something of a low point in Peruvian history. Along with the economic crisis, political violence appeared to increase exponentially. Many observers from abroad began to suggest the possibility of a Sendero victory. The Rand Corporation, for example, published a report

8. Looking back at Stalin and Mao, their cults only originated after they had taken power.

painting a bleak picture, warning that Sendero could surround and strangle the capital of Lima. In July of that year, an armed strike paralyzed the capital. Luis Arce Borja, Sendero's spokesman in Europe, declared that Sendero would negotiate nothing except the government's surrender. In the wake of the announcement of Sendero's VI Gran Plan Militar in August, which declared the "consolidation of strategic equilibrium," most Peruvians were awaiting a new offensive projected to coincide with the October election of a new Congress.

But then, unexpectedly, on 12 September 1992, agents of the special antiterrorist police unit DINCOTE captured Guzmán and two of the three Political Bureau members, along with party archives. By the end of the year, nineteen of the twenty-two members of Sendero's Central Committee had been captured. Within twelve days after that, Guzmán and other party members were tried and sentenced by a special military tribunal. Shortly thereafter, Guzmán took advantage of the regime's clumsy attempt to display him publicly in a cage, by calling on his supporters to carry out the VI Gran Plan. It appeared by December that Sendero's high command had reorganized and that they were beginning to carry out his call for action. The country was rocked by a series of attacks, fewer than in previous years but enough to demonstrate that Guzmán still enjoyed primacy in the organization's schemes. Committees were formed in Peru and abroad to "Protect the Life of President Gonzalo."

On the first anniversary of Guzmán's capture, Sendero launched a series of attacks throughout the country and issued a statement proclaiming, "What has the puppet Fujimori, that evil Oriental serpent, gained by imprisoning the greatest living Marxist-Leninist-Maoist? Nothing, because the popular war continues unstoppably!"[9] But on 1 October 1993, a new surprise developed: at the United Nations, President Fujimori read a letter supposedly from Gonzalo, asking to open peace talks with the regime. Shortly thereafter another letter was released reiterating the call for peace talks and telling Guzmán's followers that negotiations were needed to "preserve strengths."

While both letters were greeted with incredulity, they were quickly followed by a well-groomed Abimael Guzmán appearing on television from prison, dressed in a new Mao-style suit and reiterating what was contained in the letters. Sendero responded to these events by suggesting that the television images showed an imposter and the letters from Guzmán were

9. *El Diario,* September 1993.

forgeries.[10] Nonetheless, just days before the 28 October referendum on a new constitution, Guzmán appeared once again on television. This time he called on his followers to avoid "provocations" and to "struggle for a peace agreement."

Over the next several months, the reality of Guzmán's newfound stance began to sink into his followers as well as outside observers. From within the prison walls where he was confined, Guzmán began to organize the party's II Congress, which argued that a new "political stage" had been reached in the war, whose priority should now be peace negotiations with the regime. In the early part of 1994, the majority of Sendero militants in prison seemed to back Guzmán's position. However, Sendero militants outside of prison began to oppose the almost daily stream of reports coming from Guzmán and carried by the media. Led by comrade "Feliciano," leader of the Popular Army and the only member of the Political Bureau not to be captured, Sendero began to reaffirm "*pensamiento Gonzalo*" while separating itself from the persona of Abimael Guzmán. Actions continued to be carried out throughout the country, but, according to most sources, the level of terrorist actions in 1994 was the lowest since 1981.

Conclusion: The Last Temptation of President Gonzalo

For most Sendero members, Guzmán appeared to have accurately interpreted the laws of history for the twelve years between 1980 and 1992. During this long period, Guzmán also seemed able to direct the military and political struggle against the "old and corrupt state" in a way that maintained his almost mythic proportions. It was said that he was nowhere and everywhere and that he could never be found. Because of this mythic dimension surrounding his persona, his capture represented a stunning blow to the movement. Both the letters and his television appearances broke the mythical aura. In the wake of his capture, hundreds of Senderistas have taken advantage of the various amnesty laws passed by the Fujimori regime to surrender themselves, turn in their weapons, and tell all they know about the organization.

This movement toward dialogue and negotiations, which has taken

10. *El Diario*, October 1993.

place among other guerrilla groups in Latin America with only minimal effect on their internal dynamics, has proved so devastating to Sendero because it has broken one of the most important pillars on which Sendero constructed its identity after the 1977–80 period. What was an intellectual construction for Guzmán was a religious and mystical identity for his militant followers during the 1980s. This was the faith that fueled the Sendero war machine for thirteen years. The imprisonment of the great leader did not necessarily challenge that faith. Many historical and mythical figures passed through a period in hell, and prison was not seen as an irreversible condition—particularly if the historical tide made revolution inevitable. Even the death of Guzmán would not have been devastating, given that his mythical presence and leadership had been far more important to Sendero combatants during the 1980s than was his actual physical presence.

What proved more devastating than the fact of imprisonment or the possibility of death was Guzmán's dramatic change in persona and tactics. Guzmán's actions after his imprisonment represented a coming down from the cross in which the mythic godlike figure became not only human but just an ordinary politician interested in negotiating and deal making. His descent was the result of an ability to shift roles from prophet to politician. It also suggests that behind the mythic prophet there always lay the politician. His discourse had changed, as he readily admitted, because he wished to preserve Sendero Luminoso and his own role in the party into the next century. For Abimael Guzmán, his own personal history had been confused with the history of the party for some time.

While Guzmán managed to maintain the loyalty of his followers who accompanied him in prison, those outside of the prison's walls decided to break with the great leader. Calling themselves Sendero Rojo, they vowed to continue a war through the violence that had now become their only possible basis of identity and life.

But Sendero Rojo continues its war in the worst possible conditions. It faces a much more confident and capable security apparatus, desertions among its ranks, and the possibility of betrayals from those in prison. Above all, Feliciano and other leaders are cadres but not cosmocrats. They cannot accumulate the type of symbolic capital that Guzmán had and used, especially not within a short period. Sendero Rojo may continue its war for some time at a reduced level, but it will be impossible for the militants to find a "fifth sword of Marxism" in Peru, or, for that matter, anywhere else in the world.

8

HUMAN RIGHTS AND UNITED STATES POLICY TOWARD PERU

Kenneth Roberts and Mark Peceny

Over the course of the 1980s, Peruvian society was plunged into a maelstrom of violence unlike anything the nation had experienced in modern times (Instituto de Defensa Legal 1990; Comisión Especial del Senado 1989). The spiral of political violence—which had claimed over 27,000 lives by the end of 1995—had multiple sources and diverse actors, all in a complex web of insurgent movements, state security forces, drug traffickers, death squads, and civilian paramilitary patrols. While Sendero Luminoso gained notoriety for its violent attacks on the civilian population, the Peruvian armed forces became known for their repressive response as the state's counterinsurgency campaign led to forced disappearances, Andean massacres, and the systematic use of torture (Amnesty International 1989; Americas Watch 1988). Despite rhetorical commitments to human rights by elected officials, the pattern of violations continued through the Belaúnde, García, and Fujimori administrations, none of which proved capable of devising a counterinsurgency strategy that was compatible with minimum standards of human rights, democratic accountability, or the rule of law.

Prior to the suspension of the constitutional order by President Alberto Fujimori in April 1992, the Peruvian political system had an almost schizophrenic character. On the one hand, executive and legislative officials were chosen in highly competitive elections that were contested by parties spanning the political spectrum. Political debate in the printed press was vigorous and pluralistic; even the newspaper of Sendero Luminoso, *El Diario,* was allowed to publish until November 1989, after which it was banned for advocating political assassinations. Labor unions, peasant associations, and shantytown organizations were active in civil society, articulating political and economic claims despite periodic police harassment.

On the other hand, army units on counterinsurgency patrols were accused of mass killings, beatings, detentions, and rape in highland communities, while police and military troops routinely tortured political prisoners and common criminals in all parts of the country. From 1987 to 1990, the United Nations Working Group on Enforced or Involuntary Disappearances named Peru as the nation with the largest number of disappearances in the world; even Peru's attorney general acknowledged over four thousand cases of unresolved disappearances through 1990 (Amnesty International 1991, 5).

The Peruvian case thus presents a number of unusual features for the study of human rights in Latin America. First, the most severe violations of human rights have not occurred under a military regime but under a civilian, constitutional regime with formal democratic arrangements. Although human-rights violations were not unknown under the 1968–80 military regime in Peru, the number and severity of violations increased dramatically after 1982, when the elected Belaúnde government initiated military counterinsurgency practices against Sendero Luminoso in the southern Andean highlands.

Second, violence deliberately aimed at civilian noncombatants has been unusually two-sided in Peru, as Sendero Luminoso has far surpassed other leftist guerrilla movements in Latin America in its systematic and often indiscriminate attacks on civilian targets. Both Sendero and state security forces have engaged in political assassinations, and both have retaliated against indigenous communities suspected of aiding the other. Sendero Luminoso has also made widespread use of car bombs and has frequently targeted leaders of grassroots community organizations for assassination, as they are viewed as competitors for the political loyalty of the popular sectors.[1]

1. Although this analysis will generally follow international legal conventions, under which human-rights violations are understood to be abuses committed by governing authorities against their citizens or subjects, a good case could be made for the application of human-rights standards to the Shining Path as well, given the group's systematic violation of international rules of war and humanitarian norms (Shifter 1990). In recent years human-rights organizations have attributed the majority of political killings in Peru to the Shining Path, not to state security forces. According to the Coordinadora Nacional de Derechos Humanos, a coalition of more than forty independent Peruvian human-rights organizations, the Shining Path was responsible for 842 political assassinations in 1991 and for 946 in 1992. In comparison, although military control of information from the emergency zones compli-

It is clear, then, that Peru's civilian institutions and democratic procedures failed systematically both to uphold constitutional guarantees for
human rights and to defend the population from the violent activities of
insurgent groups. Perhaps more fundamental, as Philip Mauceri suggests
in chapter one of this volume, they failed to translate the democratic
norms of citizenship, representation, participation, and accountability
into effective levers to legitimate and empower the state in its conflict
with a guerrilla movement whose principal weapons were terror and intimidation. These two failures were mutually reinforcing: the state's sporadic presence and uncertain legitimacy in Peru's indigenous Andean
heartland encouraged a repressive response to Sendero's initial gains,
while its arbitrary use of violence undermined the political and institutional foundations for legitimate authority. The erosion of fiscal, judicial,
and administrative capabilities vitiated any attempt to develop a less-mil-
itarized and more integral political and economic response to the challenge of Sendero Luminoso.

Indeed, this erosion exacerbated the state's dependence upon its coercive apparatus, while leaving security forces as the only visible and opera-
tive state institutions in ever-larger stretches of Peruvian territory. By fighting terror with terror, the state was stripped of any consensual basis and
reduced to its essential core as a coercive instrument. As such, Fujimori's
autogolpe in April 1992 did not so much initiate as formalize the authoritarian character of state power in Peru; subsequent efforts to provide his
new regime with a constitutional veneer have done little to change this
underlying reality.

The coercive response to the challenge of Sendero Luminoso should
thus be understood as a reflection of the state's inherent weakness in
Peru, rather than of its strength. In fact, the repressive and arbitrary exercise of coercive power was one of the clearest indicators of the deinstitutionalization and disintegration of Peru's democratic regime. Progres-
sively weakened in its capacity to integrate society, extract resources,

---

cates accurate investigation of abuses, the Coordinadora was able to document 99 extrajudicial executions by state agents in 1991 and 114 in 1992 (testimony of Coletta Youngers
before the Subcommittee on Western Hemisphere Affairs, U.S. House of Representatives, 10
March 1993).

The Shining Path makes no pretense of adhering to conventional human-rights standards; as stated in the movement's newspaper *El Diario* in July 1991, "Human rights are
based on the bourgeois conception of the world, which centers on the individual and con-
ceives humanity as a family in order to deny the class struggle" (cited in "Testimonios de la
Guerra" 1991, 52).

provide collective goods, and administer public affairs, the state not only relied upon coercive power but granted its coercive instruments considerable autonomy from civilian institutions and governmental authorities. This deinstitutionalization had three critical dimensions that rendered inoperative the constitutional guarantees of human rights: (1) the abdication of civilian political authority to military command structures in emergency zones; (2) the breakdown of juridical mechanisms designed to enforce constitutional safeguards; and (3) the marginalization or political neutralization of representative institutions that could have held state security forces accountable to legal and democratic norms.

The analysis that follows explores two sides of the human-rights issue in Peru. First, on the domestic front, it explains how these institutional failures engendered an autonomization of the state's coercive apparatus in the pursuit of counterinsurgency objectives in Peru, enabling the armed forces to operate militarily with virtually unfettered political and legal impunity. Second, on the international front, it explores the impact of human-rights issues on U.S. policy toward Peru, as the U.S. government moved to support Peruvian police and military forces in the struggle against drug trafficking and Sendero Luminoso in the late 1980s and early 1990s. In particular, this section tries to explain how U.S. policy makers, in their search for a coherent response to Peru's multifaceted crisis, have balanced domestic political concerns with conflicting, post–Cold War foreign-policy objectives.

Abdicating Civilian Authority: Emergency Zones and Counterinsurgency Strategy

Perhaps the most visible manifestation of political deinstitutionalization in Peru has been the abdication of civilian political authority in zones that have been placed under a state of emergency. Peru's 1980 constitution empowered the president to declare and renew a state of emergency unilaterally, requiring only that Congress be notified. In territories placed under a state of emergency, constitutional freedoms of movement and assembly were suspended, along with freedoms from arbitrary arrest and unwarranted searches and seizures (International Commission of Jurists 1983, 272–73). Security forces were thus able to enter private homes and arrest individuals without warrants. A state of emergency also allowed the president to transfer responsibility for maintaining public order to the armed forces. In practice, the latter provision granted political and administrative authority to military commanders in all emergency zones outside of Lima, effectively displacing elected local officials. Operating under the authority of the Armed Forces Joint Command, political-military commands in the emergency zones controlled all military, police, and paramilitary civil-defense forces, while assuming responsibility for the coordination and implementation of executive policies (García-Sayán 1987a).

A state of emergency was first declared by the Belaúnde administration in December 1982, creating a political-military command structure for five provinces in Ayacucho, the remote southern Andean department where Sendero Luminoso began its armed struggle in May 1980, as well as for two provinces in the neighboring departments of Huancavelica and Apurímac. Initially, Belaúnde had responded to the insurgency by decreeing a sweeping antiterrorist law that enabled the police to arrest and detain suspects for up to fifteen days without court interference. However, Sendero's rapid expansion in Ayacucho demonstrated the inefficacy of such police measures and convinced Belaúnde to send military forces to the southern highlands. The first state of emergency thus signaled the beginning of military counterinsurgency, as well as the first critical step in the erosion of civilian political authority.

States of emergency were declared in new zones as the military conflict spread, leading to dramatic upsurges in human-rights violations. With basic liberties formally suspended and civilian officials superseded by military commanders, judicial institutions for the most part ceased to function in emergency zones. The armed forces denied civilian courts access to detention centers, making it impossible to pursue writs of habeus corpus, while blocking the Public Ministry from conducting effective investigations of alleged abuses.[2] As such, there were no institutionalized political or legal constraints on the armed forces in their development and pursuit of counterinsurgency objectives (Mauceri 1989, 40). Counterinsurgency strategy became a basic prerogative of the armed forces (Stepan 1988, 92–127), which not only formulated policies independent of civilian institutions, but also enjoyed complete operational autonomy.

---

2. The Public Ministry, like its sister institution, the Defensoría del Pueblo, is an independent monitoring institution designed to protect individual rights and liberties. In theory, the Public Ministry was intended to receive complaints of human-rights abuses, conduct investigations, and even initiate prosecution against police or military officials. As will be seen, this institution has systematically failed to perform (or, in some cases, has been blocked from performing) such critical functions.

Not surprisingly, the military initiated a scorched-earth campaign in the southern highlands in 1983 and 1984, when military sweeps through indigenous communities resulted in a wave of forced disappearances and mass killings, along with massive dislocation of the local population.[3] By December 1983, one year after the initial declaration of a state of emergency, the attorney general's office acknowledged receiving over 1,200 allegations of forced disappearances (Americas Watch 1984, 102).[4] The military's strategy was perhaps best summed up by the minister of war, General Luis Cisneros, who stated that "We are professional soldiers and we are trained to kill. . . . To be successful [in Ayacucho] we have to begin to kill Senderistas and civilians. . . . We may kill sixty people, and at best, there are three Senderistas among them . . . and the police will say that all sixty were Senderistas" (Americas Watch 1984, 87).

The tolerance of such widespread human-rights violations by the Belaúnde administration generated controversy in Peru and subjected the country to international criticism. Even within the armed forces, there were commanders who favored a less-militaristic counterinsurgency strategy, believing that an effective response to Sendero Luminoso required forms of social, political, and economic development as well as repressive action (Mauceri 1989, 45–49). The election of Alan García in 1985 brought to office a new president who advocated such an "integral," developmentalist approach to the problem of insurgency. García also pledged to reassert civilian political authority and redesign counterinsurgency strategy to ensure that human-rights standards were upheld. In his inaugural address, García declared that "the use of death as a means to an end is unacceptable under a democratic system. . . . The law will be strictly applied to those who violate human rights by assassinations, extrajudicial executions and torture. . . . It is not necessary to fall into barbarism to fight barbarism" (Washington Office on Latin America 1987, 23). García publicly condemned several massacres perpetrated by the armed forces in Ayacucho and promised to remove the responsible officials.

The early years of the García administration brought a temporary, if modest, improvement in the human-rights situation, at least with respect to

3. By the early 1990s, estimates placed the number of displaced persons in Peru at more than two hundred thousand, with most coming from the southern highlands. For an analysis of their plight, see Kirk (1992).

4. This preliminary figure is higher than the final number of disappearances reported for 1983 in Table 8.1. In part this is due to the subsequent clarification of cases where individuals reappeared or were confirmed as deceased.

the number of disappearances (see Table 8.1). However, the situation dete-
riorated again in the late 1980s, as Peru plunged into an economic crisis and
Sendero expanded its base of military operations to the central and northern Andes, the Upper Huallaga Valley coca-growing region, and the Lima
metropolitan area. As the fighting spread, so did the emergency zones; by
June 1989, all or part of nine departments were in a state of emergency. By
July 1991 the state of emergency covered eighty-five provinces in sixteen of
Peru's twenty-four departments, including over half the national population
and 40 percent of the territory (Amnesty International 1991, 13).

Table 8.1. Forced Disappearances in Peru, 1983–1994

Year	Disappearances
1983	696
1984	574
1985	253
1986	99*
1987	69
1988	293
1989	306
1990	204
1991	279
1992	282
1993	168
1994	67

Sources: 1983–90: Comisión de Derechos Humanos, *Informe Estadístico*, and
the Coordinadora Nacional de Derechos Humanos, both cited in Americas
Watch 1992, 19.
1991–92: Public Ministry of Peru.
1993: U.S. Department of State, *Country Reports on
Human Rights Practices for 1994* (Washington, D.C.:
U.S. Government Printing Office, 1995), 483.
1994: Amnesty International, cited in *Resúmen Semanal*
(5–11 July 1995): 4.
*The figure for 1986 refers to the number of disappearances in the emergency
zones, as do the figures for the preceding years. If we include the 115 inmates
from the El Frontón prison who remained unaccounted for after the June
1986 prison uprising and massacre, the number of disappearances for 1986
totals 214.

Note: The data from the Comisión de Derechos Humanos provide the best annual breakdown of the number of disappearances and are useful for following general trends, but
figures vary considerably from one investigative organization to the next. Both Amnesty
International and the attorney general's office in Peru provide aggregate figures through
1990 that are higher than those in Table 8.1, with Amnesty listing over 3,700 disappearances
between 1983 and 1990 and the attorney general's office over 4,000. See Amnesty International (1991, 5).

As the crisis deepened, the García administration's initial concern for human rights virtually evaporated. Like Belaúnde before him, García came to rely increasingly upon a strategy of military repression to contain Sendero and a second guerrilla movement that emerged in 1984, the Movimiento Revolucionario Tupac Amaru (MRTA). The early, ambitious rhetoric about Andean development schemes never materialized into an integrated strategy for combating the insurgency, as development projects were undermined by the absence of bureaucratic coordination, a burgeoning fiscal crisis, and the lack of security for government personnel in the highlands (Obando 1991).

Human-rights violations proliferated as García added new territories to the emergency zones, and departments such as Huánuco, Junín, San Martín, and Lima rivaled and at times surpassed the southern Andean departments of Ayacucho, Apurímac, and Huancavelica in the number of reported disappearances. The total number of disappearances rose again after 1988, although remaining below the exceptionally high levels of 1983 and 1984. Also in 1988, disappearances were reported for the first time outside the emergency zones, and a shadowy death squad known as the Comando Rodrigo Franco began a campaign of threats, bombings, and assassinations. Widely linked to sectors of the National Police and García's APRA party, including then-interior minister Agustín Mantilla, the Comando was named for an APRA leader killed by Sendero Luminoso.

García also proposed new legislation to broaden the scope of activities identified as "terrorist," and he moved to repeal Law 24,700. This law had been designed to provide detainees with legal counsel and to ensure that criminal investigations would be conducted by public prosecutors rather than by police forces, who routinely relied upon torture as a method of extracting information in interrogations (Americas Watch 1988).

The election of Fujimori in 1990 brought little substantive change either in counterinsurgency practices or in the protection of human rights. Fujimori quickly dismissed some 250 police officers—most with political ties to APRA—who had been charged with corruption or with having links to paramilitary groups. He also pledged to create a National Human Rights Commission, clean up the prison system, and vigorously enforce human-rights standards. The commission, however, was never established, and although Fujimori increased penalties for police officers accused of human-rights violations, he took more significant steps to erode civilian institutions, empower the armed forces, and shield military activities from oversight and control.

Lacking a congressional majority and a solid party organization to sustain his government, Fujimori ruled from the outset through a de facto alliance with sectors of the armed forces. The new president named active-duty military officers to head the Ministries of Defense and Interior, thus establishing military control over police forces. Early in his administration, Fujimori clashed with Congress by proposing a constitutional amendment to try terrorist cases in closed military courts, and by issuing a controversial decree that effectively granted military personnel immunity from prosecution. This decree declared military personnel to be on duty twenty-four hours a day in the emergency zones, thus bringing them under the jurisdiction of military courts, and also allowed them to hide their identity through the use of false names (Americas Watch 1992, 27–28). Ominously, both Fujimori and his justice minister condemned human-rights organizations for criticizing military abuses; as stated by the president in a naval ceremony in 1991, "In spite of being organizations set up to defend human rights, they only defend the subversives and ignore the rights of many innocent people who are murdered by them. . . . They play the game of subversion and are a machinery set up by narco-terrorism."[5]

Although promising, like García, to incorporate development objectives into the counterinsurgency strategy, Fujimori faced similar impediments. An emergency-assistance plan to cushion the effects of the economic "shock" program imposed by Fujimori when he assumed the presidency in August 1990 was long delayed and underfunded, resulting in a further reduction of already precarious living standards.[6] In the Upper Huallaga Valley, where police and military forces confronted drug traffickers, Sendero, and the MRTA, an alternative development project designed to woo *campesinos* away from coca production and the guerrilla insurgencies was neutralized by government corruption and violence, leading to the resignation of top presidential adviser Hernando de Soto (González 1991).

Consequently, the Fujimori administration's primary initial contribution to the counterinsurgency strategy was a vigorous promotion and arming of paramilitary civil-defense patrols under the supervision of local military forces. Although voluntary in some locales, in others these patrols were forced on the population.[7] They became frequent targets of attacks

5. *Latin America Weekly Report*, 24 October 1991, 11.
6. See the section on social policy by Carol Wise in Chapter 3 of this volume.
7. Autonomous peasant patrols known as *rondas campesinas* have long provided a form of grass-roots security from cattle thieves and other threats to highlands communities, but the paramilitary patrols established under military command to confront the Shining Path are

by Sendero and have been accused of exacerbating local conflicts and committing human-rights violations in a number of communities (Amnesty International 1991, 21–22). Although civil patrols have successfully resisted Sendero advances in some areas, they represent a militarization of civil society that provides graphic evidence of the state's own incapacity to provide basic forms of protection. Not surprisingly, sectors of the armed forces have been reluctant to create such "parallel" security structures, while popular organizations have expressed concern that civil autonomy will be exchanged for military control (Democracia y Socialismo 1990, 70–71).

Without any fundamental change in counterinsurgency doctrine or practice, the patterns of disappearances, torture, and extrajudicial executions continued into the Fujimori administration. The human-rights situation remained especially severe in the emergency zones. After Fujimori's first year in office, Amnesty International (1991, 17) claimed that:

> The detention procedures followed by the armed forces in areas of emergency and military administration have been largely unchanged since December 1982. Detentions are carried out without warrant and military zone commanders systematically deny that they have occurred. In most cases, the armed forces have failed to notify any civilian authority of arrests and have routinely denied that the arrests occurred to judges and prosecutors attached to the Public Ministry who have sought to locate detainees. The armed forces have generally prevented all access by civilian authorities to detainees in military establishments and refused to give any information about those in custody.

When Peru's human-rights violations sparked U.S. congressional opposition to economic and military assistance in 1991, the Fujimori administration pledged to establish a registry of detainees, have the attorney general's office publish monthly reports on human-rights violations, and grant the Public Ministry access to all detention centers and the authority to investigate alleged disappearances. While acknowledging "credible re-

---

characterized by less autonomy and community accountability. Military commands established civil patrols in Ayacucho as early as 1982, but their number increased dramatically in the late 1980s and early 1990s when presidents García and Fujimori encouraged their formation and the distribution of firearms. Recent estimates suggest that there were over 4,600 rural patrols and several hundred urban patrols in Peru by 1992, with some one hundred thousand members (Starn 1992, 65–67).

ports" of ongoing abuses, the U.S. State Department commended Peru for making "a concerted effort to improve respect for human rights." It claimed a significant improvement in the overall human-rights situation during the second half of 1991, including a reduction in the number of disappearances and progress in establishing mechanisms for civilian oversight of detention facilities (Department of State 1992, 709).

However, Fujimori's suspension of the constitutional order in April 1992 represented a severe reversal of efforts to establish institutionalized protections for human rights. The military-backed autogolpe led to the dissolution of Congress, which had challenged Fujimori's efforts to shield the armed forces from civilian oversight. It also brought a purging of the judiciary, including several judges who had been notable for accepting writs of habeus corpus and other human-rights petitions, and a temporary abrogation of the chapter in the penal code that criminalized enforced disappearances.

New antiterrorist decrees allowed for summary prosecution in military courts or secretive civilian tribunals by anonymous or "faceless" judges. The decrees were so broadly conceived that they allowed individuals to be tried who were apologists for terrorism, who provoked anxiety, or who affected international relations. A treason law was also decreed that gave secret military courts jurisdiction over treason cases, facilitated procedures for preventive detention, allowed suspects to be held incommunicado for extended periods, and suspended the right to habeus corpus and other forms of legal petition for individuals accused of terrorism or treason (Human Rights Watch 1992, 134–38; *Andean Newsletter,* 24 August 1992, 6). After years of accusing human-rights organizations of protecting or apologizing for Sendero Luminoso, the Fujimori administration used the new antiterrorist legislation to detain and initiate criminal proceedings against several Peruvian human-rights activists.

Fujimori's legislative decrees placed the entire country on a legal standing comparable to that which existed in the emergency zones after 1982. The civilian court system and representative institutions were seriously weakened, the autonomy and impunity of the military's counterinsurgency strategy were reinforced, and constitutional rights and protections were emasculated. In short, Fujimori—with widespread popular approval—attacked the only political institutions that theoretically had the ability to check executive and military power.

Under international political and economic pressure, Fujimori moved quickly to hold elections for a Constituent Assembly, followed by a plebiscite to ratify the new constitution. The redesigned legal and constitutional framework concentrated power in the executive branch, while enhancing the political prerogatives and operational autonomy of the armed forces in the counterinsurgency campaign (Mercado Jarrín 1993–94). Institutional checks on presidential power were limited by political changes as well as by constitutional provisions; the autonomy of the judiciary was undermined by extensive purging and by Fujimori's provisional appointment of hundreds of new judges. At the same time, legislative compliance was assured by a pro-Fujimori majority in the new Congress.

These institutional changes did not translate directly into higher levels of human-rights abuses, at least with respect to disappearances and extrajudicial executions. In fact, as shown in Table 8.1 above, the number of reported disappearances decreased in the mid-1990s as the military threat of Sendero receded, as did the number of extrajudicial executions. However, any hope that this improvement reflected a fundamental change in counterinsurgency strategy was dashed by new reports from Peruvian human-rights organizations of widespread summary executions and helicopter rocket attacks on villages in a military campaign against Sendero in the Huallaga Valley in April 1994 (Washington Office on Latin America 1994, 12–15).

Furthermore, although deaths attributed to political violence fell from 3,101 in 1992 to 1,692 in 1993, the number of provinces under a state of emergency increased from fifty-two to sixty-six. At the end of 1994, nearly half the population continued to live in emergency zones. Human-rights groups have found it impossible to gather information in many of these zones, and the intermittent operation of the Public Ministry's special prosecutors for human rights has further eroded civilian oversight of counterinsurgency practices (Youngers 1994, 6–7).

In short, Fujimori's restructuring of the political regime undermined institutional checks and balances that were already notoriously inadequate for the protection of human rights. As such, it left the basic structure of military impunity intact. This impunity reflects the persistent failure of the judicial and legislative branches to exercise oversight responsibilities and enforce legal norms in counterinsurgency operations. As shown below, the breakdown of the judicial system was an integral component of the generalized erosion of political institutions and the abdication of civilian political authority in Peru. This breakdown was a critical factor in the failure of Peru's democratic regime to uphold even the most minimal standards of human rights.

The Breakdown of the Judiciary and Military Impunity

When Fujimori suspended the constitutional order in 1992, he condemned the judicial system for its corruption, incompetence, and inability to apply legal sanctions against suspected subversives or drug traffickers.[8] Assuming dictatorial powers, he quickly purged 13 members of the Supreme Court and fired over 100 judges and prosecutors. But if the judiciary had failed to play an effective role in the struggle against Sendero Luminoso, it was even less effective as a guardian of human rights.

From the beginning of the counterinsurgency war, the judicial system broke down in two critical areas. First, the courts and the Public Ministry did not consistently investigate alleged human-rights violations or enforce basic constitutional protections. Second, the judiciary not only failed to prosecute military officials who were responsible for violations, but failed even to assert jurisdiction over crimes committed against the civilian population. Taken together, these two institutional failures assured that the armed forces enjoyed legal impunity in their conduct of the counterinsurgency war, much as the abdication of civilian administrative authority assured them of political autonomy.

The failure to investigate violations and enforce legal safeguards was attributable to several factors. Security threats (from both Sendero and the armed forces) elicited a widespread withdrawal of judges and prosecutors from emergency zones. Where judicial authorities remained in the emergency zones, they were generally denied access to military detention facilities as well as information about detainees. Investigations were further impeded by a lack of resources, erratic political support, and military intimidation. Consequently, only a fraction of the reported cases of human-rights violations were ever investigated by civilian courts or the Public Ministry. The judicial system was so ineffectual that few individuals even tried to take advantage of streamlined procedures to file writs of habeus corpus, the most important constitutional safeguard provided to individuals and one of the few basic rights that was not legally derogable in a

---

8. For example, in 1992 civilian courts tried over 1,100 cases for terrorism but convicted and sentenced only thirty-seven individuals, in part due to the lack of security provided by the state to members of the judiciary. In contrast, the military tribunals established after August 1992 by Fujimori's legislative decrees passed out 131 prison sentences in their first 154 cases, including 104 life sentences. See *Latin America Weekly Report*, 25 February 1993, 95.

state of emergency. For example, despite over two thousand denunciations of detentions and disappearances in Ayacucho in 1983 and 1984, only fourteen writs of habeus corpus were filed (García-Sayan 1987b, 131). When they were filed, these writs were routinely rejected by civilian judges on grounds of insufficient evidence; in a 1990 case involving the police detention and disappearance of a student in Lima, the Supreme Court annulled one of the few writs that had ever been upheld by the lower courts (Amnesty International 1991, 60–61).

On the rare occasions when independent investigations led to formal legal charges, the Supreme Court usually upheld military impunity by transferring jurisdiction from civilian to military courts. Although the 1980 constitution conceded military jurisdiction only in cases where both the victim and defendant were members of the armed forces, the Supreme Court ruled that alleged human-rights violations occurred in the line of duty, and it consistently granted jurisdiction to military courts even when the victims were civilians.[9] To date, military tribunals have handed down convictions against members of the armed forces only in a handful of cases.

In one case, a military court in January 1992 sentenced a retired army major to fifteen years in prison for ordering subordinates to murder a civilian and hide his body. In another revealing case, involving the trial of five army officers for the 1985 massacre of sixty-nine villagers in Accomarca, a tribunal acquitted the four senior officials but convicted Sub-Lieutenant Telmo Hurtado for "abuse of authority with disobedience." Hurtado was sentenced to four years of prison and immediate dismissal from the army, but he was neither confined nor discharged. A new army investigation found that all five officers had "engaged in rape, the burning alive of captured peasants, on-the-spot executions, the murder of witnesses and the wanton destruction of homes" (Human Rights Watch 1992, 135). However, a retrial confirmed the initial acquittals (on the grounds that the senior officers had been following higher orders) and resentenced Hurtado in 1992. His sentence was subsequently suspended; he never served time in prison, and he was promoted to the rank of captain rather than discharged from the army.

---

9. A rare exception occurred in 1986, when the Supreme Court granted civilian jurisdiction in a case involving a journalist, Jaime Ayala, who disappeared after entering a marine barracks to investigate the discovery of a clandestine grave in Calqui, Ayacucho. Charges were filed against the marine base commander, who then "disappeared" in a staged kidnapping and successfully filed a petition of annulment that transfered jurisdiction to a military tribunal, effectively closing the case (Americas Watch 1988, 41).

The multiple impediments to effective investigation and prosecution of human-rights violations are perhaps best manifested in the aftermath of the Cayara massacre in the department of Ayacucho in May 1988. A day after Sendero guerrillas ambushed an army patrol in a neighboring village, army soldiers entered Cayara and killed between twenty-eight and thirty-one people. They returned four days later and detained more villagers, dozens of whom disappeared. An investigation was begun by Dr. Carlos Escobar, who had been named by the Public Ministry the year before as special prosecutor for the investigation of disappearances in Ayacucho. Escobar's courageous work had already led to the reappearance of several individuals who had been secretly detained, and he had been credited with helping produce a temporary improvement in the human-rights situation in Ayacucho in 1987. However, his efforts to establish public accountability for military actions had earned him the enmity of the armed forces, which became evident during the Cayara investigation.

Escobar was able to gather physical evidence of the massacre in Cayara, and he identified General José Valdivia Dueñas, the political-military commander of the Ayacucho emergency zone, as the responsible official. Escobar recommended that charges be filed against Valdivia, but the provincial prosecutor ruled that it was not possible to individualize responsibility. The case was closed in January 1990, when the provincial prosecutor filed a resolution that denied a massacre had occurred at Cayara, claimed the alleged victims had fled the village due to their involvement with the insurgency, and asserted that the witness testimonies gathered by Escobar had been falsified under terrorist threats.[10] In the meantime, nine witnesses of the massacre from Cayara were killed or disappeared in various incidents involving the security forces (Department of State 1990, 710–11), and the attorney general closed Escobar's office. Lacking police protection and political support, Escobar was forced to flee the country in November 1989 after a series of death threats. In January 1992 General Valdivia was promoted, with President Fujimori's support, to the position of chief of the General Staff of the Armed Forces Joint Command.

Controversy over the Cayara massacre also precipitated a congressional investigation. The pitfalls and political impediments that obstructed this investigation are analyzed below, as they are representative of another institutional failure that has plagued Peru's democratic regime: the politi-

10. Resolución No. Uno-Noventa," Ministerio Público, Fiscalía Provincial Mixta de Victor Fajardo, Ayacucho, 23 January 1990.

cal marginalization and inefficacy of the legislature in monitoring counterinsurgency policies and containing abuses of authority. Although the
Peruvian Congress was left standing on the sidelines during the initial
stages of the war against Sendero Luminoso, it struggled against considerable political obstacles to assert a measure of civilian control and democratic accountability over the counterinsurgency effort. The development
of such accountability was arrested by Fujimori's autogolpe, which came at
a time when Congress had checked presidential efforts to enhance military and executive powers in the counterinsurgency campaign.

Obstacles to Congressional Oversight and Control

The Peruvian Congress played a limited role in the initial design and
implementation of counterinsurgency policy. With the president empowered by the constitution to declare states of emergency unilaterally,
Congress had no control over the suspension of basic civil rights and liberties. Once in place, states of emergency shielded the political power
and operational autonomy of the armed forces, while diminishing local
civilian institutions that might have helped Congress perform a monitoring function. Indeed, crucial decisions to broaden the scope of military
activities in the emergency zones were made by executive decree in consultation with defense advisers; such decrees were not always officially
published, creating a veil of ignorance that inhibited congressional scrutiny. The veil of ignorance even carried over to military spending, as Congress received only a budget with aggregate defense figures that did not
identify specific programs or operations (Mauceri 1989, 61–62). A mil-
itaristic strategy that was sanctioned by the executive branch and shielded
by high levels of military autonomy thus provided few opportunities for a
congressional role in policy formulation.

Nevertheless, the 1983–84 scorched-earth campaign placed human
rights on the political agenda in Peru and encouraged individual members of Congress to adopt a more activist stance. Under the 1980 constitution, the Congress had wide-ranging investigative powers that enabled special commissions to visit the sites of alleged human-rights abuses, take
testimony from witnesses, and solicit evidence from military officials. In
theory, these commissions could not only monitor and clarify alleged

abuses of power, but also issue reports that would serve as the basis for judicial investigations and subsequent criminal proceedings.

The effective exercise of these powers, however, was politically problematic. For example, following the Cayara massacre, investigative commissions were established in both houses of Congress, headed by representatives of the majority party, APRA. Enrique Melgar, who headed the Senate commission, was widely criticized for obstructing the investigation of the massacre and protecting the responsible military officials. According to Americas Watch, Melgar slowed the pace of inquiry, refused to cooperate with prosecutor Escobar's investigation, and declined to meet with witnesses to the massacre. When the APRA majority on the Melgar Commission filed its official report in May 1989, it concluded "categorically that there was no abuse on the part of military personnel in Cayara" (Americas Watch 1992, 48). The report attributed the allegations against General Validivia to a subversive campaign, recommending that charges be filed against Escobar for usurping the investigative authority of the provincial public prosecutor (Amnesty International 1989, 32–33). The investigative commission also produced minority reports from United Left senators Gustavo Mohme and Javier Diez Canseco that blamed General Valdivia's political-military command for both the Cayara massacre and its subsequent cover-up.

However, the Cayara investigation was indicative of the partisan political considerations that consistently eroded the effectiveness of congressional human-rights monitoring in the 1980s. Special congressional commissions were established to investigate the 1986 prison massacres that suppressed a rebellion by Sendero Luminoso inmates,[11] as well as the paramilitary activities of the Comando Rodrigo Franco in 1989, particularly its alleged role in the assassination of two United Left congressional deputies. The investigation of the prison massacres produced a majority, APRA-led report that absolved President García and other political officials of any responsibility for the massacre.

In contrast, a minority report recommended that impeachment-type proceedings be initiated in Congress against García, vice minister of the interior Augustín Mantilla, the attorney general, and other officials. The Senate rejected the minority report, ensuring immunity for top APRA government officials; military courts were granted jurisdiction in the trials

---

11. The June 1986 uprising culminated in the massacre of between 200 and 250 inmates in three separate prisons, many of whom were summarily executed after surrendering.

that followed, leading to the conviction of two low-ranking police officers but the acquittal of all higher-ranking police and military officials (Americas Watch 1988, 61–65).

Likewise, the investigation of the Comando Rodrigo Franco produced a preliminary report that thoroughly documented paramilitary activities and implied complicity on the part of governmental and police authorities. However, the Aprista head of the investigative commission backed away from such assertions and tried to link paramilitary activities to the political Left. Once again, the commission concluded by issuing separate majority and minority reports, which precluded effective congressional action. While the majority report downplayed evidence of paramilitary activities, the minority report linked them explicitly to APRA officials and state security forces (Americas Watch 1992, 49–51).

In these cases, then, investigative commissions were neutralized by partisan splits between the APRA majority, which routinely sought to shield the García government and military officials from culpability, and opposition members who found evidence of high-level responsibility or complicity. Although the investigations and minority reports of opposition congressional representatives had great value for the clarification of events and the public exposure of responsible individuals,[12] APRA's legislative majority blocked effective congressional action or judicial proceedings based upon the findings of investigative commissions. In the previously mentioned case of the massacre at Accomarca, political divisions were overcome sufficiently for an investigative commission to recommend prosecution and convince the Senate to relay its findings to the Public Ministry for further investigation. However, the Supreme Court awarded jurisdiction in the case to military courts, which did not follow up on prosecution (Amnesty International 1991, 57–58).

If political divisions undermined the impact of congressional investigative commissions, they also blocked the passage of legislation that could have reduced military impunity and reinforced civilian political and legal authority. For example, the lower house blocked legislation that had been approved by the Senate in 1986 to establish legal sanctions for specific human-rights violations and grant legal jurisdiction for such cases to civil-

12. Likewise, the Senate's Special Commission for the study of violence, better known as the Bernales Commission, played a vital role in investigating the sources and patterns of violence in Peru. Although the commission encouraged government investigation of individual cases, its annual reports were designed to identify general trends in political violence rather than to attribute responsibility for specific violations of human rights.

ian courts. Similarly, legislative proposals to augment civilian authority in the emergency zones were blocked by congressional opponents.

With APRA's fall from power in 1990, there no longer existed an automatic legislative majority to shield the executive branch and block congressional action on human rights. Indeed, Congress emerged as an important counterweight to Fujimori's efforts to buttress executive and military control of counterinsurgency practices. Congress resisted an early proposal to give military courts jurisdiction over terrorist cases, and it repealed a presidential decree that ensured military jurisdiction over human-rights violations committed in emergency zones. In May 1991, a Senate commission investigating a 1990 massacre in Chumbivilcas detailed a pattern of egregious abuses by an army patrol, demanding that legal action be taken against the commander of the local army base and the military commanders of Ayacucho and Apurímac. The commission boldly charged successive defense ministers, both army generals, with complicity and cover-up in the case, and it recommended that the Chamber of Deputies consider prosecution of defense minister General Jorge Torres Aciego for his alleged role (Americas Watch 1992, 51–56).

In the final months before the April 1992 autogolpe, the usually fractious Congress demonstrated greater unity of action in blocking or forcing the revision of a series of "pacification" decrees issued by Fujimori in November 1991. Congress blocked a decree that would have clarified the political authority of military commanders over civilian officials in the emergency zones, proposing instead the creation of unified command structures with joint civilian-military participation at the regional and national levels. Likewise, Congress objected to a decree establishing an executive-controlled National Intelligence Service with the authority to oblige individuals to provide information, services, or personal assets deemed essential to the counterinsurgency effort (Adrianzén 1992a). Congress also proposed laws to strengthen and facilitate habeus corpus procedures, and, after repealing a decree that established civil-defense patrols in urban areas under military supervision, forced Fujimori to accept the registry of urban *rondas* with local civilian authorities.[13]

What role this more assertive congressional stance might have played in Fujimori's decision to suspend the constitutional order is open to debate. What seems clear is that the unrestrained authority that Fujimori sought and that Congress obstructed was finally acquired via an autogolpe. With

---

13. *Andean Newsletter,* 9 March 1992, 5.

a pro-Fujimori majority and a much weaker Left-wing contingent, the new Congress formed in the aftermath of the autogolpe was considerably more compliant on human-rights issues.

The best example of this is the notorious La Cantuta case, named for the university where a professor and nine students were abducted and "disappeared" by security forces in July 1992. The Ministry of Defense denied that security forces had detained the missing persons, and writs of habeas corpus were not recognized. However, dissident military officers leaked information to Left-wing congressman Henry Pease that the ten individuals had been abducted and killed by a special detachment of the army's intelligence service. The Congress began a special investigation of the case, which prompted the army commander to send tanks into the streets of Lima in April 1993 as a show of force. In response to the intimidation tactics, the Congress scaled back its investigation, agreeing to interview only high-ranking military officers rather than the personnel directly involved. Meanwhile, the third-ranking officer in the army hierarchy, General Rodolfo Robles Espinoza, publicly declared that the assassinations had been conducted by special forces with the direct knowledge of the army and intelligence chiefs; fearing for his life, Robles left immediately for exile in Argentina.

The congressional investigation produced a majority report backing Robles's charges and a minority report denying any military involvement. Although the Congress voted to adopt the minority report and exculpate the military, the case was rejuvenated when journalists acting on dissident-military tips discovered clandestine graves with the remains of some of the missing students. The Public Ministry ordered the excavation of the grave sites and compiled evidence for the prosecution of the responsible military officers before civilian courts. However, the military court system had initiated its own investigation and claimed exclusive jurisdiction over the case. When the Supreme Court came to a deadlock in its initial attempt to define jurisdiction in the case, Fujimori's supporters in Congress rushed through a patently unconstitutional bill in February 1994, enabling a narrow Supreme Court majority to assign jurisdiction to the military court system. A military tribunal subsequently tried and sentenced nine army officers to jail terms for their role in the massacre, but investigations into the involvement of higher-ranking officers were blocked. The officers were then set free, and they reportedly returned to active military duty when Congress passed a general-amnesty law in June 1995. This episode clearly demonstrated the supine position of Peru's reconstituted legislative and judicial branches vis-à-vis the executive and the armed forces, and the extent to which they helped the military to institutionalize the norm of impunity.

Fujimori's political reconstruction, therefore, represented far more than a solution to executive-legislative gridlock; more fundamentally, it signaled the failure of repeated efforts to devise a set of democratic institutions and policies that could meet the challenge of Sendero Luminoso. Having failed to resolve the inherent tensions between democracy and counterinsurgency (Cornell and Roberts 1990), Peru's leaders opted for a thinly veiled authoritarian alternative. Rather than harness democratic rights and principles in the struggle against a ruthless insurgency, successive administrations negated or suspended them. Democratic practices were not treated as levers to link the state to civil society and mobilize society for its own defense; instead, elected officials perceived them as weaknesses that undermined national security.

Ironically, while Fujimori's autogolpe swept away institutional constraints on his power in the domestic arena, it exposed his regime to new international constraints. In the months preceding the autogolpe, the Fujimori government had completed Peru's reinsertion in the international financial community by resuming payments on the national debt and reaching agreements to open new lines of credit with the IMF, the Inter-American Development Bank, and the Paris Club. It had also reached an agreement with the Bush administration on a new program of military and economic assistance, completing Peru's rapprochement with the United States. The autogolpe interrupted both of these processes, leading to a temporary withdrawal of international political and economic support as the United States and the Organization of American States (OAS) pressured Fujimori to restore constitutional normalcy. It also renewed U.S. congressional criticism of human-rights conditions in Peru, which had delayed Bush administration plans to involve the United States more fully in the struggle against drug trafficking and Sendero Luminoso.

The autogolpe thus exacerbated the contradictory interests and objectives of U.S. policy toward Peru, and it raised two important questions regarding human rights and U.S. policies. First, to what extent have human-rights concerns influenced U.S. policies toward Peru? Second, are there means by which the United States and the international community can improve the human-rights performance of the Peruvian government, especially given the ineffectiveness of Peru's domestic institutions in achieving this goal? These issues are addressed below through an analysis of the competing objectives of U.S. foreign policy toward Peru.

Balancing Competing Interests: U.S. Policy and Human Rights

Although the United States became more deeply involved in Peru in the late 1980s and early 1990s, the suspension of U.S. military assistance and some forms of economic aid following the April 1992 autogolpe highlights a central puzzle of U.S.-Peruvian relations. Despite the fact that Peru faced a strong Maoist insurgency and is the world's largest producer of coca, the United States provided the Peruvian government with limited and sporadic support during the 1980s and early 1990s, in contrast to the extensive U.S. role in El Salvador during the same period.

This limited U.S. role was, in part, a legacy of the economic nationalism and independent defense policies pursued by the Peruvian military regime of 1968–80, which expropriated several U.S. multinational corporations and terminated the U.S. military mission. The Velasco government reached agreements with the Soviet Union for arms sales and military training, and the Soviets remained a major provider of military equipment and assistance through most of the 1980s. Furthermore, President García's defiant pledge to limit debt-service payments, and his subsequent decision to suspend payments altogether, strained relations with the Reagan administration and resulted in Peru's marginalization from U.S.-backed international financial institutions (Palmer 1992b).

The only significant area in which the United States was able to cooperate with the García government was in drug enforcement. The Drug Enforcement Administration (DEA) initiated Operation Snowcap in 1987, under which U.S. agents supported local police forces in crop eradication and drug interdiction in Peru, Bolivia, and Ecuador. The program also involved U.S. Army Special Forces (Green Berets) in the training of local police forces and the construction of a counter-narcotics operations base at Santa Lucía in the Upper Huallaga Valley. This cooperation was somewhat tentative, however, as the U.S. and Peruvian governments had different priorities in the drug war.[14] Consequently, the level of U.S. counter-narcotics aid grew slowly from $4 million to $10 million per year between 1985 and 1989 (Palmer 1992a, 68).

14. While the United States emphasized "supply-side" control of the drug trade, Peru often gave priority to the war against Sendero Luminoso, fearing that crop-eradication programs would alienate peasant producers of coca leaves and create fertile terrain for Sendero's advance in the Upper Huallaga Valley. For an analysis of the complex linkages between the guerrilla movement, peasant producers, and drug traffickers, see Gonzales (1992).

However, as the Cold War thawed and the Central American conflicts moved toward the negotiating table, the Bush administration made the war on drugs the centerpiece of its security policy in Latin America. In September 1989, the administration announced its "Andean strategy" to suppress the cocaine trade at its source points. The strategy entailed a sharp increase in U.S. economic and military assistance to the Andean region, along with a major new role for both U.S. and Latin American military forces in the war on drugs. The program took effect in February 1990, when President Bush signed the Declaration of Cartagena with the presidents of Peru, Colombia, and Bolivia. The strategy called for a $2.2 billion, five-year aid program to cut the supply of cocaine from the Andean region. It also entailed a significant increase in U.S. involvement in Peru, from total aid of $18.7 million in fiscal year (FY) 1989 to $66.6 million in FY 1990, $128.8 million in FY 1991, and $168.8 million in FY 1992 and the years beyond (Washington Office on Latin America 1991, 10).

Of the $701.8 million in aid projected over the five-year period, roughly half ($376.7 million) was to consist of economic assistance, while the other half was earmarked for military and police aid. Even the economic assistance, however, was conditioned on Peruvian acceptance of a largely military strategy for fighting the drug war. While the military assistance was officially appropriated solely for the purpose of fighting drug trafficking, in practice a substantial portion of this money was spent on military counterinsurgency units that were fighting the Shining Path. The linkage between counter-narcotics and counterinsurgency was justified on the grounds that Sendero Luminoso was inextricably involved in the drug trade in the Upper Huallaga Valley (Washington Office on Latin America 1991, 43–66)

Despite the commitment of the Bush administration to play a more active role in Peru, U.S. military and economic assistance lagged well behind the original targets throughout the 1990–92 period. To the surprise of the Bush administration, the first barrier to the implementation of its strategy was the Peruvian government. President García accepted $19 million in U.S. assistance for anti-narcotics police forces, but he rejected $35.9 million in military assistance, along with $4 million in economic-support funds and $6.8 million to assist DEA liaison with the Peruvian military. The Peruvian military, in fact, had long been wary of involvement in the drug war, in part due to its fear that counter-narcotics operations would drive peasant farmers to the side of Sendero Luminoso. Then in

September 1990, President Fujimori reiterated Peru's rejection of the initial U.S. aid package because of its emphasis on the military components of the drug war. Fujimori insisted that the U.S. aid program should prioritize development assistance for the encouragement of long-range alternatives to coca production for farmers in the Upper Huallaga. The consequence of this disagreement was that the large majority of funds slated to go to Peru in FY 1990 went instead to Colombia (Palmer 1992a, 71–72).

This impasse was overcome on 14 May 1991, when the Fujimori government and the Bush administration signed an agreement signifying a general commitment by the United States to place more emphasis on economic assistance. The United States made no specific commitment, however, to support the "alternative development program" or the crop-substitution plan outlined by President Fujimori in his counterproposal of January 1991 (Soberón 1992, 2–3; Youngers and Call 1991). The most important outcome of these negotiations was that the Fujimori government agreed to accept a substantial amount of U.S. military assistance to "feed, equip, train, provide with uniforms, and adequately support the armed and police forces who will be fighting against narcotrafficking and those who support and encourage it" (Department of State 1991, 7). By including "those who support and encourage" narcotrafficking, the agreement implicitly brought the U.S. aid mission into the war against Sendero Luminoso, which routinely served as an intermediary between narcotraffickers and peasant producers of coca in the Upper Huallaga Valley.

At this point, however, a second important obstacle to the original strategy of the Bush administration emerged. Concern over human-rights violations in Peru and Colombia led to mounting U.S. congressional opposition to military assistance, spawning legislative efforts to limit and condition U.S. military aid under the Andean Initiative. Although Defense Department personnel assured the U.S. Congress that U.S. trainers were "required to teach respect for human rights in both formal classroom lectures/discussions and in practical hands-on instruction" (U.S. Congress 1991a), a substantial increase in military assistance was likely to reinforce the strength and autonomy of military institutions that had demonstrated a consistent pattern of human-rights abuses. Consequently, in October 1990 the U.S. Congress passed the International Narcotics Control Act, which stipulated that U.S. aid could be disbursed only after presidential certification that the recipient nation had cooperated in narcotics control, demonstrated respect for human rights, and exercised government control over security forces.[15]

This legislation became an important constraint on U.S. policy once an agreement had been reached with the Fujimori government regarding the content of the U.S. aid package in May 1991. The Bush administration certified on 30 July 1991 that the Peruvian government met the congressional requirements necessary for the release of $34.9 million in military assistance and $60 million in economic assistance earmarked for FY 1992. However, all four congressional committees with jurisdiction over this certification—the House Foreign Affairs Committee, the House Foreign Operations Subcommittee, the Senate Foreign Relations Committee, and the Senate Foreign Operations Subcommittee—claimed that Peru had not met the conditions established by Congress, and they mandated a temporary suspension of aid.[16]

In September 1991, Congress agreed to release most of the aid, with the exception of $10.05 million in counterinsurgency training and weaponry designated for the Peruvian army. However, Congress attached more stringent conditions on military aid than had been applied previously. The Bush administration was instructed to withhold military aid until: (1) mechanisms were established to ensure that aid would be provided through civilian authorities; (2) a central public registry of individuals detained by Peruvian security forces had been created; (3) the International Committee of the Red Cross and the Peruvian judiciary had been granted access to all detention centers; and (4) the administration had informed Congress about the measures taken by the Peruvian government to discipline and prosecute individuals responsible for a series of specified human-rights violations.[17]

Ironically, Congress was in the process of debating whether to increase military aid to Peru in March and April 1992 when Fujimori launched his autogolpe. Assistant Secretary of State Bernard Aronson immediately announced the suspension of military aid and most economic assistance, although the United States continued humanitarian aid and part of its counter-narcotics program. Simultaneously, Robert Torricelli, a Democratic Representative from New Jersey and chair of the House Western

15. For an analysis of this human-rights conditionality, see the Washington Office on Latin America's *Andean Initiative Legislative Update*, December 1990, 2–3.

16. For transcripts of parts of the congressional debate over Peru, see U.S. Congress (1991b). For an analysis, see *Andean Initiative Legislative Update*, October 1991, 4–12.

17. *Andean Initiative Legislative Update*, October 1991, 8.

Hemisphere Subcommittee, sent a letter to the Bush administration demanding such an aid suspension.[18] The United States coordinated policy with the OAS to put multilateral pressure on Fujimori to negotiate a return to constitutional rule. Direct U.S. military and economic assistance remained suspended for the remainder of the Bush administration, although the United States relaxed its pressure and approved World Bank and Inter-American Development Bank loans to Peru as Fujimori made plans to hold elections for a new Congress in November 1992. The U.S. Congress decided not to appropriate military-assistance funds for Peru in FY 1993 in order to pressure Fujimori into restoring democracy.

Therefore, even though the Bush administration fought hard to increase U.S. involvement in Peru, its policy was constrained by considerations of human rights and democracy. If human-rights concerns made it hard to get aid from Congress without strings attached before April 1992, it became even more difficult after Fujimori's dissolution of the democratic regime. In an era of fiscal austerity in the United States, human rights and democratic standards became important benchmarks in congressional debates over the allocation of diminishing foreign-aid dollars.

The Peruvian case provides a classic example of the dilemmas and trade-offs that confront policy makers when their basic objectives become incongruent. Although theoretically compatible, in practice policies that were designed to promote human rights and democracy came into conflict with the U.S. goal of strengthening the Peruvian government and security forces in their counterinsurgency and counter-narcotics wars. Why, then, did the U.S. condition and limit its support for these wars in the name of democracy and human rights, when historically it has so often subordinated human-rights considerations to security concerns in Latin America (Schoultz 1987)?

Clearly, the constraints of dealing with a Democratic-led Congress forced the Bush administration to give a higher priority to considerations of human rights and democracy. The important role of domestic political dynamics in these changing foreign-policy priorities can be seen in two areas. First, with the end of the Cold War, anticommunism was no longer a compelling ideological tool for forging a political consensus behind an interventionist foreign policy. Indeed, even before the end of the Cold War, domestic political constraints forced the Reagan administration to

18. For the responses of Aronson and Torricelli to the constitutional breakdown in Peru, see U.S. Congress (1992).

justify its counterinsurgency objectives in El Salvador in terms of promoting democracy, despite initial realpolitik protestations to the contrary (Arnson 1989). In short, liberal internationalist objectives such as the promotion of democracy and human rights may become essential tools for the construction of a bipartisan policy consensus, even if they are intermingled with traditional realist concerns. Cases as diverse as those of Peru and Panama suggest that if U.S. presidents want to pursue interventionist policies, they are likely to have to justify them to the U.S. Congress and public as efforts to promote democracy and human rights, in addition to tangible U.S. national-security interests.

On the other hand, there are also significant domestic political forces pushing the United States to take a less-active role in Third World crises. The foreign-aid bill has always been among the most unpopular spending bills to come before Congress, and it has become even less popular with the end of the Cold War and the fixation of the American public on domestic social and economic issues. Furthermore, billions of dollars of aid for Russia and the republics of the former Soviet Union must be extracted from a declining foreign-aid budget. With U.S. aid to Latin America cut by more than 50 percent between 1990 and 1994, liberal members of Congress, who have generally supported the concept of foreign aid but objected to assistance for undemocratic regimes with poor human-rights records, have played a crucial role in deciding how to divide shrinking foreign-aid allocations. Given its poor human-rights record and the dismantling of democratic institutions by President Fujimori, Peru was particularly vulnerable to an aid cutoff because of these congressional dynamics.

The contradictory tendencies toward liberal activism, domestic retrenchment, and realpolitik continued to produce ambiguous and inconsistent U.S. policies toward Peru under the Clinton administration. The new administration attempted to build consensus around a foreign policy of "democratic enlargement."[19] Accordingly, its first foreign-policy decision toward Peru was to withhold U.S. support for a $2.1 billion IMF bridge loan until the Fujimori government promised to facilitate the oversight functions of domestic and international human-rights groups. Subsequently, the U.S. government helped to organize and finance a Commission of International Jurists, which issued a critical report on the

19. See Anthony Lake, "A Call to Enlarge Democracy's Reach," *New York Times*, 26 September 1993, sec. 4.

administration of justice in Peru. This commission expressed particular concern over the use of "faceless" judges and other violations of due process in trials for treason and terrorism. The new administration also supported the work of Peru's independent Coordinadora Nacional de Derechos Humanos, and the State Department relied heavily upon information provided by the Coordinadora in preparing its 1993 review of human rights in Peru. When assistant secretary of state for Inter-American Affairs Alexander Watson and the Latin Americanist on the staff of the National Security Council, Richard Feinberg, visited Peru in January 1994, their first meeting was with representatives of the Coordinadora (Youngers 1994).

However, the Clinton administration also pushed an early normalization of relations with Peru, while accepting verbal promises from Fujimori to lift constraints on human-rights organizations and welcoming very partial steps toward redemocratization. In the summer of 1993, encouraged by Fujimori's economic liberalization and counterinsurgency victories, the Clinton administration tried to release some of the nearly $110 million in U.S. aid that had been suspended since the 1992 autogolpe. This effort was blocked, however, by congressional opponents who advocated more stringent human-rights conditionality. By the end of the year, a new consensus was building within the administration that the November constitutional plebiscite and the reduction in the most severe types of human-rights violations had created the minimal "democratic" conditions necessary to restore this aid,[20] despite Fujimori's failure to follow through completely on earlier promises.[21] However, a new State Department effort to release some of the frozen funds in early 1994 was derailed by the outcry over the granting of military jurisdiction in the case of La Cantuta. The Clinton administration tried once again in 1995 to restore military-aid funds for counternarcotics purposes, but congressional opposition spearheaded by Esteban Torres, a Democratic representative from California, blocked their release.

Although high-profile cases such as La Cantuta galvanized congressional human-rights concerns, they did not lead to a complete termination of U.S. aid. Indeed, the political impact of suspending military assistance and economic-support funds was diminished by the continuation of fund-

20. See Nathaniel Nash, "No Longer a Pariah, Peru Is Being Recast As Business Magnet," *New York Times*, 2 November 1993, A1.

21. The plebiscite narrowly ratified the new constitution drawn up by the reconstituted Congress, thus providing a legal, if not entirely legitimate, foundation for Fujimori's regime.

ing for development assistance, the Food for Peace program, and police counternarcotics efforts. Funding for these programs totaled $137 million in 1994, making Peru the largest recipient of U.S. aid in Latin America, and the Clinton administration's 1995 request for $150.5 million was also the largest in the region.[22] Furthermore, although the administration proclaimed a desire to redirect the focus of counternarcotics strategy to demand-side educational and treatment programs in the United States,[23] it proposed that cutbacks in spending on border interdiction and transit countries be translated into increased spending in the source countries of the Andean region. Congressional resistance continued to block the military component of Peru's counternarcotics assistance, but the Clinton administration ratified much of the supply-side emphasis of earlier policies.

Conclusion

It is not clear how much leverage human-rights conditionality has on events inside Peru. The demonstration that the United States is capable of cutting aid to a country facing a leftist insurgency in the post–Cold War era increases the pressure to uphold human rights and democratic standards. However, the Peruvian case suggests that the United States remains reluctant to pull out completely under such conditions, and that a combination of verbal promises and relatively cosmetic reforms may be sufficient to maintain significant, if not wholehearted, support from the United States and, perhaps more important, from the international financial community. The maintenance of this support in Peru has been facilitated by the absence of a large network of activist groups in the United States working in solidarity with Sendero or in opposition to U.S. involvement. In contrast to El Salvador, where government security forces were responsible for the vast majority of civilian deaths and where U.S. churches and solidarity groups were outspoken opponents of U.S. policies,[24] there has been no significant domestic political constituency that has become activated over the U.S. role in Peru. Likewise, U.S. involvement there has not become an issue of controversy or even significant

22. *Latin America Weekly Report*, 17 March 1994, 114.
23. Joseph Treaster, "U.S. Altering Tactics in Drug War," *New York Times*, 17 September 1993, A7.
24. See *From Madness to Hope: The 12-Year War in El Salvador*, Report of the Commission on the Truth for El Salvador. New York: United Nations, 1993.

attention in the U.S. media, allowing policy debates to be largely contained within the foreign-policy community. Indeed, it is unlikely that
public opposition to U.S. policies will emerge as long as Sendero Luminoso's reputation for brutality continues to exceed—and justifiably so—
that of the Peruvian government.

It is not surprising, then, that the mixed signals sent by the United
States have had but a modest and sporadic effect on the behavior of the
Peruvian government. Fujimori has been quick to make promises in response to explicit congressional demands, but follow-through has been
notably lacking (Younger 1994). Although there was a temporary decline
in the number of disappearances over the second half of 1991, when the
U.S. Congress was debating human-rights conditionality, the number increased again in 1992, even though the Peruvian government had clear
incentives to improve its human-rights record if it wished to gain future
commitments of U.S. aid. Furthermore, the fact that Fujimori launched
his autogolpe only months after the 1991 congressional debate over aid to
Peru—and at a time when portions of military aid were still pending—
suggests that he is willing to forego U.S. assistance, if necessary, to achieve
domestic political objectives. Under such conditions, even a fully consistent, pro-democratic U.S. policy would have limited effect.

Where policies are less than fully consistent—as they have been in this
case—U.S. leverage is likely to be even more constrained. In the medium
term, Fujimori was able to exploit the ambiguous and contradictory nature of the U.S. response to his autogolpe. Even if Fujimori underestimated the strength of the initial U.S. and international reaction to his
constitutional suspension, he was able to contain its most serious effects
fairly quickly; the Bush administration clearly did not want to destabilize
Peru, and it accepted a gradual normalization of relations in response to
Fujimori's promises of a limited and controlled process of "redemocratization" (Youngers 1992). The pattern has not been notably different under
the Clinton administration, even if it has spoken more forcefully on behalf of human rights and adopted a more activist stance in some areas.

Nevertheless, in a context where domestic political institutions in Peru
are seriously underequipped to defend basic human rights, the role of the
international community is likely to be magnified. If Peru's former democratic regime proved incapable of enforcing human-rights safeguards,
there is every reason to question the efficacy of the new regime spawned
by Fujimori's political engineering. The judiciary has seen its jurisdiction
narrowed and its always-suspect autonomy vitiated by an autocratic presi-

dent. Likewise, the new Congress boasts a solid majority for Fujimori, and it has been considerably more amenable to executive demands than was its more independent predecessor. The decay of traditional political parties merely reinforces the process of deinstitutionalization, as it magnifies the role of individual personalities and weakens the mediating mechanisms that can represent and defend the interests of civil society vis-à-vis the state.[25]

For these enfeebled institutions to be able to overcome the birth defects of Peru's new political regime and effectively safeguard human rights, international support is likely to be necessary. More fundamentally, however, these institutions will have to succeed where those of Peru's previous democratic regime failed, namely, in demonstrating that democratic procedures and human-rights standards, far from being a liability in the struggle against Sendero Luminoso, are in fact the most efficacious means of mobilizing society for its own defense.

25. On the deinstitutionalization of the Peruvian party system, see Adrianzén (1992b) and chap. 2 in this volume, by Maxwell A. Cameron.

CONCLUSION

THREADS IN THE PERUVIAN LABYRINTH

Maxwell A. Cameron and Philip Mauceri

In recent years, Peru has undergone a dramatic transformation. President Alan García was elected in 1985 in an atmosphere of high expectations, yet he left a legacy of economic decline, hyperinflation, declining wages, shrinking tax revenues, isolation from the international financial community, and rampant insurgencies by the Shining Path and the Tupac Amaru Revolutionary Movement. President Alberto Fujimori was elected in 1990 amid doubt and uncertainty, but his initial successes in fighting inflation, renewing growth, and combating terrorism were rewarded with reelection in 1995.

Under Fujimori, Peru's virtual isolation from the international financial community was reversed and a process of debt renegotiation began with the support of a group of industrialized nations and international financial institutions. What was once considered among the world's riskiest countries for business began to experience a boom in foreign investment, rising stock prices, and growing exports. Within a few short years Peru had achieved the highest rate of economic growth in the world—with the country's GDP expanding by 12.5 percent in 1994. Nonetheless, it remains to be seen whether Fujimori's neoliberal economic model can produce endogenously sustainable economic growth.

Much of the renewed confidence in Peru has been the result of a climate of greater macroeconomic stability brought about by a less-erratic approach to policy making and a change in policy orientation to favor business. After a stabilization program was implemented in 1990, inflation declined from 139 percent in 1991 to 63 percent in 1992, 46 percent in 1993, and 15 percent in 1994. The successful fight against inflation provided the basis for a more predictable macroeconomic environment and, as a result, gross domestic investment increased from 15.5 percent of GDP in 1990 to 22.2 percent in 1994 (World Bank 1995, 433). The capture of Abimael Guzmán and the disarticulation of much of the Central Committee of the Shining Path helped to reassure local as well as foreign investors.

Progress on the economic front during the early 1990s, however, was combined with a reversal in democratic development. President Alberto Fujimori, elected in 1990 in spite of his lack of a solid coalition base or organized political party, demonstrated such a penchant for centralized, personal rule that Peruvians dubbed him Chinochet. The 5 April autogolpe was one event, albeit the decisive one, in a series of democratic setbacks that demonstrated that the president intended to rule by decree, subordinate the Congress to presidential authority, increase the powers of the armed forces, expand the intelligence service, purge the courts, meddle in military promotions, attack the church and political parties, offer amnesty to soldiers convicted of human-rights violations, and turn a blind eye to corruption among his civilian and military advisers.

Peru's flirtation with authoritarian rule contains disturbing lessons for the Latin American region. In the 1980s, repressive military rulers were replaced with elected civilians in the Southern Cone, the Andes, and Central America. However, the fragility of democracy was demonstrated by the widespread support for an attempted coup by Lieutenant Colonel Hugo Chávez Frías in Venezuela in February 1992, and by President Jorge Serrano Elías's copycat autogolpe in Guatemala in May–June 1993. The autocratic style of presidents in Latin America—from Mexico's Carlos Salinas de Gortari to Argentina's Carlos Saúl Menem and Venezuela's Rafael Caldera—provided conspicuous examples of how democratic institutions can be routinely flouted or abused. The impeachments of Presidents Carlos Andrés Pérez in Venezuela and Fernando Collor de Mello in Brazil revealed shocking levels of corruption that contributed to public disenchantment with democracy.

Peru's challenges differ from those of the rest of Latin America less in nature than in degree. David Scott Palmer (1995, 75) argues that "Peru's significant progress since 1990 . . . rests on a delicate political foundation that is personalistic and uncomfortable with political institutions—a combination that tends to be unstable over time. The main challenge Peru faces is converting significant progress into stable institutional development."

We tend to agree with this assessment. We hope that by examining the remarkable turnaround in Peru and assessing its sustainability, as well as by exploring the linkages between political and economic forces, we may provide insight into the broader prospects for democracy and development in Latin America.

In the introduction to this volume, we identified the following three themes as problems that unify the contributions of each of the chapters: institutional change, state-society relations, and democratization. By institutions, we mean the rules and enforcement mechanisms in society that structure incentives and provide a framework of certainty for individuals and groups (North 1991). State-society relations concern the interaction between the state—defined as a set of public institutions that monopolize the legitimate use of force—and societal associations such as interest groups, political parties, business firms, and other popular or elite organizations. Democracy, in minimalist, procedural terms, concerns whether the rules of the game provide an opportunity for representation and broad participation in decision making. Each of these "threads" is taken up in this review of our findings.

Institutional Reform or Decay?

Political Economy of State Building

In a perceptive essay on the state, Peter Evans (1992, 141) suggests that there is a "third wave of thinking about the state and development" that transcends the dichotomy between the unrealistically optimistic view of the state as an agent of structural change and the more pessimistic view that suggests the state should have no role beyond the enforcement of private-property rights and reduction of transaction costs. In this third view, the strength and effectiveness of the state as an institutional structure is a crucial determinant of development and structural transformation.

Building on the work of Max Weber, Alexander Gerschenkron, and Albert Hirschman, Evans argues that the state's ability to support markets depends on its having a bureaucracy that is a corporately coherent entity with meritocratic criteria for recruitment and promotion. Moreover, "late, late" industrializing nations require a more developmental state; rather than limiting themselves to providing a framework for markets, such states must organize markets, encourage risk taking, and foster long-term, socially productive forms of entrepreneurship. Although the requirements of a Weberian-style bureaucracy imply insulation from societal pressures, the tasks of "late, late" development require close connections with private capital. Evans captures this balance with an oxymoron: "embedded autonomy." In broad comparative terms, most Latin American states are intermediate cases between the successful East Asian states, which implemented programs of industrial transformation and adjustment with positive results, and the rent-seeking and predatory African states, which failed to achieve industrial transformation.

An intriguing implication of Evans's analysis is that neoliberal governments tend to fail to achieve transformation because they cannot balance autonomy with embeddedness. Neoliberal governments regard with suspicion connections between the state and society that constrain the rational and efficient decision-making capacity of technocrats and threaten to degenerate into clientelism and corruption. "Stress on insulation implies that in the absence of political pressure technically trained incumbents will make and implement economically correct policy decisions" (Evans 1992, 178). However, Latin American technocrats often have to operate in "patrimonial organizations" that "masquerade as Weberian bureaucracies" (Evans 1992, 177), and they are thus forced to fall back on clientelistic and corrupt exchanges to implement their policies.

Mexico provides a painful example of the potential problems associated with the strategy of insulating an effective technocratic team in charge of a weak and predatory state apparatus. The government of Carlos Salinas de Gortari (1988–94) made progress toward the institutionalization of connections with the private sector in the context of the North American Free Trade Agreement negotiations, but the legacy of centralized decision making and the capture of parts of the state apparatus by corrupt officials linked to powerful private economic conglomerates remained a problem.

On the one hand, the government ignored growing social pressures and demands (especially in the rural sector), and, on the other hand, it allowed corruption and nepotism to flourish unchecked in other sectors (banking, in the privatization process, in the relations between the ruling party and business). These problems were viewed as necessary evils on the road to reform, but the inability to sustain a balance between embeddedness and autonomy ultimately destabilized the political system.

Peru's problems are akin to those of Mexico. Carol Wise's chapter points to an unfinished agenda in the process of strengthening the country's institutions. She dates Peru's problems in the late 1980s and early 1990s to the demise of the primary-exporting, liberal economic model in the 1950s, at a time when state-business relations began to turn sour and the popular sectors emerged as a more powerful political force. In response, a shift occurred toward a more state-sponsored economic model. Wise identifies four key elements in this new model: dependence on external financing and lax management of key macroeconomic policies; reliance on public enterprises against a backdrop of a weak public administration; ambiguous and tense relations between the state and the private sector (which benefited from state policies but lacked confidence in the public sector's managerial abilities); and a chronic inability to coordinate social policy and distributive measures with the economic model.

Wise notes the sharp contrast between the Peruvian development model and the East Asian experience. Contrary to the view that East Asian countries pursued market-friendly policies while Latin America fostered protected industries, Wise's chapter contributes to a more nuanced understanding. The crucial difference between Latin America and East Asia concerns the nature and timing of state intervention, not whether the state intervened in the economy (Gereffi and Wyman 1990).

The Peruvian case is somewhat atypical in the Latin American context in the decades between the 1950s and the 1980s. The Peruvian state shifted between playing a minimal role in development to taking on too many tasks, always leaving a legacy of unfulfilled structural transformations. When a military government led by General Juan Velasco Alvarado (1968–75) finally attempted to implement long-overdue structural reforms, it was hindered by internal incoherence and the failure of efforts to build lasting connections with society (see McClintock and Lowenthal 1983, especially chapters by Cleaves, Pease García, and McClintock).

It is tempting to blame the problems associated with import-substitution industrialization (ISI) for the failure of military rule to implement a sustainable model of equitable development. Wise's chapter, and a more careful reading of the East Asian experience, point to a deeper lesson. The success or failure of a particular model of development depends on the external linkages; the quality of public administration; relations between the state and the private sector; and the ability to coordinate social and distributive goals with other economic objectives (Evans 1992, 178). The lack of bureaucracy, rather than its excess, is often an obstacle to the implementation of policies by governments of different economic orientations.

The record of the Fujimori government in terms of creating a more effective, developmental state is at best mixed. Fujimori inherited a state that had virtually collapsed. Having shrunk to one quarter of its previous size, the state's extractive and managerial capacities were almost negligible. By further reducing state employment and spending, Fujimori helped to create a very small state, but one that, as Wise notes in her chapter, is "still a far cry from the . . . efficient, market-supporting state" that exists in East Asian countries.

Efforts to reconstruct the extractive capacity of the state by overhauling and professionalizing tax (SUNAT) and customs (SUNAD) administrations, and the successful reinsertion into the international financial system through sustained debt renegotiation, have enabled Peru to improve its image and attract a significant inflow of foreign capital. The Peruvian state is less predatory and there are developmental "islands of efficiency" in an otherwise weak and ineffective public sector, but the lack of regulatory, distributive, and managerial capacity has led to a pattern of extremely unequal and unsustainable growth. As Wise notes, social-emergency programs have failed to ameliorate problems of distribution and equity. Moreover, the tightly knit and highly insulated character of the executive, where much power is concentrated and little is delegated, conflicts with the isolated and often beleaguered technocrats in other ministries. The combination of lack of attention to pressing social demands and the centralization of decision-making power is similar to the Mexican case.

Lack of dialogue has been a problem both in the regime's external relations and in its domestic actions. On the external front, Peru often unnecessarily alienated external actors through policies—such as the 1992 autogolpe and the 1995 amnesty law—that were adopted with scant attention to the likely reception abroad. The tendency of Fujimori to govern by the polls did not encourage the creation of reliable intermediaries. Wise notes the lack of linkages with society, the deterioration of representative institutions, and the marginalization of civil society, all of which represented serious future liabilities for the Peruvian government.

Christine Hunefeldt's chronicle of the evolving role of the state in the rural sector provides an example of Evans's "third wave" of theorizing about the developmental role of the state. She notes a shift in policy circles from technocratic optimism about the capacity of the state to uncertainty and pessimism, but she also stresses the emergence of patterns of self-help and grassroots development that transcend dichotomies be-

CONCLUSION 229

tween public and private, traditional and modern. Hunefeldt traces the heterogeneous patterns of association and ownership in the rural sector to the ambiguous legacy of the Velasco government.

The military regime under Velasco embarked on more encompassing developmental tasks than it could successfully accomplish, given the limited capacity of the public sector and the tension and contradictions between the state and society. With what seems in retrospect extraordinary naïveté, the military rulers believed that they could implement from above a development model that would, as Hunefeldt notes, "gain popular support, destroy oligarchic domination, control conflict and rural discontent, improve income distribution, stop massive migration to the cities, and create a stable agrarian sector for an expanding internal market."

The reforms resulted in a process of political mobilization, in response to which the military regime backed away from its own agenda. Subsequent policy oscillations between collectivism, market-oriented solutions, and heterodoxy accentuated the distrust and alienation between agriculturalists and the state, resulting in conflicts over property and management of cooperatives that were exploited by the Shining Path. Although ideological conflicts in the rural sector have been intense, peasant producers have pragmatically combined Andean forms of association and ownership with the exigencies of modernization.

While the Peruvian case provides an example of shifts in the role of the state as a developmental agent, there are also underlying continuities that are very typical of the Latin American development path, and that contrast sharply with the East Asian cases. Peru, like most of Latin America, never placed agriculture at the center of its development agenda. Whether part of ISI or export-led growth, the role of agriculture has been consistently reduced to providing a subsidy to industry, and the pattern of rural development promoted by the state has tended to emphasize large-scale enterprises (whether through the creation of large cooperatives or concentration of assets through privatization) rather than actively promoting small producers, as, for example, in South Korea's more equitable and dynamic rural-development model (Cameron and North 1996).

Crafting Political Institutions

Political institutions reflect the specific choices and preferences of social actors. What contributes to those preferences and choices has been the subject of a long and lively debate among comparativists. While some (Wiarda 1982) suggest the persistence of an Iberian cultural influence, others have stressed international economic structures (Cardoso and Faletto 1979) or domestic political choices (Collier and Collier 1991). The debate has taken on renewed importance in light of two major events in the region during the 1980s and 1990s: the transition to democracy and the adoption of neoliberal economic policies. Both events promised the development and consolidation of efficient and durable political institutions.

Transitions to democracy provide an opportunity to negotiate the rules of the game in the political system (O'Donnell and Schmitter 1986) and thus establish the basis for institutionalized relationships among political actors. Although the process tends to be elite driven, negotiations among political actors require consensus regarding basic rules for the transition to be a success. Democratic consolidation is often considered to be the continuous reiteration of the procedures established during the transition (see discussion of transitions below). Institutionalization is therefore a product of repeating the democratic game. But what happens when the original rules of the game come under renewed scrutiny and criticism, particularly for being less than democratic, representative, or simply for being inefficient?

Peru offers a good example of how the promise of newly crafted political institutions was slowly eroded. Many people simply stopped paying attention to old institutions. As Mauceri makes clear in Chapter 1, the transition process in Peru produced institutional arrangements that left many actors dissatisfied and that within a short period were viewed as obstacles. Unexpected changes often resulted from the failure of norms, strategies, and procedures, created by increasingly disconnected institutions to adapt to new circumstances.

As political institutions became inefficient, corrupt, unresponsive, and distant from the daily concerns of average citizens, their ability to shape behavior or structure social incentives declined. One common reaction during the 1980s was to turn away from traditional institutional channels and organizations. The emergence of strong grassroots movements, especially among the urban poor, may be understood in this context. The *comedores populares* in the pueblos jóvenes of Lima and the *rondas campesinas* in the highlands often represented new forms of association and organization in the face of institutional inertia and inefficiency. The uneasy relationship between these new organizations and traditional institutions—the party system, the state, the church—created both new possibilities and tensions in Peruvian society.

This dynamic was also found among the elite sectors of society. Durand's analysis of the emergence of the new Right during the 1980s offers a compelling example of how significant changes in the goals and makeup of key social actors created new pressures on institutional structures. A greater degree of organization in the business sector, combined with a revival in liberal economic ideals and a shift to the Right both in the Catholic church and in the United States and Europe, laid the basis for a reinvigorated Right in Peru. By the mid-1980s, conservative sectors of society felt an urgent need to reform existing institutions, which were hampering Peru's development. The sense of urgency, as Durand notes, was accompanied by the feelings of "anger, uncertainty, and threat that gripped elites and the middle class" in the 1980s. Among these sectors there was a clear sense that existing institutions and the political relations they had fostered were not only ineffective, they could not protect and advance their interests.

An additional problem that also flows directly out of issues of institutional capacity and integrity concerns human rights. The persistent violation of human rights during the 1980s and 1990s by government security forces must be set against the backdrop of the lack of sufficient oversight by the legislature of the military, military autonomy, and a court system that had failed by any standard of judicial practice. In their chapter, Roberts and Pecency effectively argue that human-rights violations are a direct result of institutional weaknesses, involving both the failure to enforce constitutional guarantees for the population and the inability of the state to defeat insurgents within the rule of law. These inabilities also helped to increasingly internationalize the struggle to ensure respect for human rights. Human-rights organizers and others turned to the world community when Peruvian institutions failed to protect human rights. As a result, international pressure, whether against abuses by the military during the 1980s or against the autogolpe of 1992, took on an unprecedented importance in Peruvian politics. However, the results of these pressures were not always clear, particularly when competing interests, such as the need to combat drug trafficking, were involved. As Roberts and Pecency suggest, "The Peruvian case provides a classic example of the dilemmas and trade-offs that confront policy makers when their basic objectives become incongruent."

Another notable example of the turn to noninstitutional channels is found in the electoral arena, where Peruvian voters starting in the late 1980s turned away from political parties and to independent candidates, including Alberto Fujimori. The informal economic sector reflects a flight from formality and is evidence of the failure of formal institutions (De

Soto 1989). The informal sector is defined as small firms operating in competitive markets with low barriers to entry, little start-up capital, and adapted technology. Likewise, independent candidates like Fujimori and ex-mayor of Lima Ricardo Belmont ran small, inexpensive campaigns, relied heavily on local radio and television, and seized entry opportunities to challenge the way parties "monopolize the electoral process" (Fujimori, cited in Cameron 1994, 151).

Given the declining legitimacy of Peru's political institutions, it is not surprising that the general reaction in the country was favorable to Fujimori's 1992 autogolpe. The erosion of institutional legitimacy by declining efficacy has been a major factor in previous breakdowns of democratic regimes (Linz 1978). Polls done both before and after the autogolpe consistently showed that although the majority of Peruvians supported democracy, they nonetheless supported Fujimori's actions against what were perceived as corrupt or inefficient institutions (Conaghan 1992). Support for Fujimori's authoritarian actions did not translate into support for a permanent break with the democratic order, but just with institutions that were seen as not meeting democratic expectations.

Similar problems of institutional weakening have affected other countries throughout Latin America, but with varying outcomes. In the case of Chile, the legacy of a very conservative transition was tempered by the fear of an authoritarian relapse as well as by slow but steady policy and institutional adaptations. A significant improvement of the economy, longstanding party loyalties, and an expectation of future institutional changes upon the retirement of General Augusto Pinochet provided a basis for consolidation during the mid-1990s. Argentina and Brazil during the 1980s appeared to suffer from some of the same institutional decay as did Peru, but in both cases economic and political reforms by the early 1990s reversed previous trends. In Argentina, four military rebellions between 1987 and 1990 and the recent memory of harsh military rule led to a reluctance on the part of most political actors to question the legitimacy of newly inaugurated political institutions.

Perhaps the closest parallel to Peru's institutional disintegration of the 1980s can be found in the 1990s in Venezuela. The fragmentation of what had been a stable party system, a confrontation between the president and the judiciary that led to the president's trial on corruption charges, and a severe economic crisis led to a dramatic decline in the efficacy and legitimacy of Venezuela's political institutions (Tulchin 1995).

Another trend that held out the promise of greater institutionalization during the 1990s has been neoliberalism. According to neoliberal theories, increased market competition and fiscal discipline require rational, stable, and reliable political institutions. In one of the oldest and most persistent forms of this argument, a direct link is made between the consolidation of democratic institutions and the discipline imposed by the market (Fukuyama 1992). This is most often contrasted with populism, where expansionary economic policies promote personalist and clientelistic behaviors on the part of governing officials (Dornbusch and Edwards 1991). One need look no further than Peru under Alan García for a stunning example of the classic affinity between populist economic policies and political practices that devalue institutions.

As numerous observers of neoliberalism in the 1990s have been pointing out, the supposed link between neoliberalism and strong institutional politics has not been apparent in Latin America (Roberts 1995; O'Donnell 1994). Rather, politicians from Menem to Collor de Mello have combined personalist political practices while pursuing neoliberal economics. As with Fujimori in Peru, these neoliberal caudillos eschewed institutional channels of participation, such as parties, labor unions, and business associations, in favor of "direct" communication with unorganized and unmobilized masses, either through the media or through the personal distribution of goods and favors by the executive. The new neoliberal caudillos disdain autonomous institutions in civil society as well as independence in the legislative and judicial branches of government. Confirming what Kahler (1990) termed the "paradox" between neoliberalism's anti-state rhetoric and its actions, Fujimori and other neoliberal leaders rely upon a strong executive and technocrats in the state bureaucracy to design and implement their policies. With a preference for personalism, centralization of power in the executive, and technocratic decision making, the neoliberal caudillos have seriously weakened the institutional basis for democracy.

State-Society Relations

Support for Market Reforms

One of the major puzzles confronting analysts of Latin America, as well as those of Eastern Europe and Russia, is why democratically elected governments implement radical and harsh austerity measures that burden the majority of the electorate, rather than choosing more gradual and less socially costly measures. Democratically elected presidents in Brazil, Russia, Poland, Bolivia, Argentina, Venezuela, and Peru have all implemented stabilization policies that have drastically reduced the income large sectors of the population. In some instances, these measures have been accompanied by protests—such as the Caracazo in Venezuela—but after over a decade and a half of such policies, what is more notable is the successful reelection of presidents in Peru and Argentina. The Peruvian case is especially puzzling given the minimal attention to providing a social-emergency program in the first years of the Fujimori government.

Fujimori's radical economic program makes considerably more sense in the light of a counterintuitive claim by Przeworski (1991, 174): "The strategy most likely to succeed is not the one that minimizes social costs. Radical programs are more likely to advance reforms farther under democratic conditions even if voters would have preferred to start with a gradual strategy. Hence, if politicians are concerned about the progress of reforms, they have an incentive to impose a radical strategy even against popular preferences and even when they know that this strategy will have to be moderated under popular pressure. Their optimal strategy is inconsistent."

Fujimori feared that opposition to reform would increase over time; by imposing a higher social cost at the outset of his mandate, he hoped to minimize opposition and restore growth before the end of his term. Paradoxically, "once the costs of reform set in, people do not want to go back" (Przeworski 1991, 170): sunk costs create a commitment to reform because the public wants to benefit in the future from transitional sacrifices.

The dynamics of reform analyzed by Przeworski are reinforced when considering the impact of neoliberal reforms on their most important potential opponent: the organized-labor movement. Balbi shows in her chapter how the growing divorce between labor leaders and the rank and file undermined the ability of the labor movement to counter neoliberal policies. Peru's central labor union, the General Confederation of Peruvian Workers (CGTP), was weakened by global and domestic forces leading to a more flexible labor market.

Strong labor legislation dating to the 1970s was undermined by the shift toward a more flexible workforce during the 1980s. The García government relaxed job-security rules, but more draconian changes were implemented by Fujimori. At the beginning of his mandate, he virtually eliminated job security. He increased employer discretion in firing workers, altering shifts, and changing contracts; he deregulated industrial relations and withdrew the Ministry of Labor from collective bargaining. At the same time, he tightened the conditions for unionization. Changes in the global economy have reduced the number of wage earners and the number of unionized workers, while the informal sector has expanded tremendously. General strikes, which were commonplace in the late 1970s and early 1980s, became all but impossible in the 1990s.

The chapter by Balbi focuses not only on these structural changes but also on the attitudinal shifts that have taken place among workers as they confront a changing reality in the workplace, the barrio, and in politics. What she found is astonishing. The alliance between unions and the barrios has been severed, and there has been a shift from confrontation to conciliation in the labor movement; the Left's ideology of *clasismo* was no longer appropriate. Thus, pragmatism in the rank and file contrasted with ideological extremism in the leadership. Workers placed more value on securing the workplace and keeping their jobs. They were willing to make compromises and negotiate concessions and were afraid of confrontation, and their linkages with the leadership became more bureaucratic and less intense.

Incredibly, labor leaders were unable to organize a general strike in the face of stabilization measures that reduced the acquisitive power of workers by as much as 80 percent and placed as much as 50 percent of the country below the poverty line overnight. Yet workers supported Fujimori, whom they associated with the positive characteristics of Japanese immigrants. Indeed, they even supported the privatization policies, since many state-owned enterprises were seen as corrupt, inefficient, and inviable. The public-sector union (CITE), which had been infiltrated by leaders with connections to clandestine groups, was broken with little union opposition. Even after the 1992 autogolpe, when Fujimori undertook his draconian reform of the collective-bargaining system, the efforts of the CGTP to organize a general strike were met with indifference from workers. Balbi's research suggests that analysts have failed to appreciate subtle differences in interests and values—like those dividing casual and permanent employees—that account for sharply different reactions to neoliberal reforms.

One might argue that the support of casual workers and the informal sector for Fujimori provides a refutation of the thesis that democracy is strengthened by the growing of power of organized labor in the process of capitalist development (Rueschemeyer, Stephens, and Stephens 1992). We would argue the reverse.

It is the organized-labor movement as a collective actor that has an interest in preserving an open political system. Isolated individual workers without collective-bargaining rights, who have weak unions or no unions, who are unprotected by state regulations and who are not covered by social-security benefits, are likely to share the heterogeneous political beliefs and values of the majority of the public. They will define interests in ways that are likely to be individualistic rather than in terms of the collective interests of the union movement. Thus the support for Fujimori among the rank and file, and particularly among casual or temporary workers and workers in the informal sector, is perfectly consistent with comparative research that demonstrates the link between the power of organized labor and democratic development. Indeed, the erosion of organized labor undermined a pillar of opposition to Fujimori's authoritarian measures—the CGTP.

State Power and State-Society Relations

The implications for state-society relations found in this collection are consistent with recent theoretical conceptualizations of state power and state-society dynamics. That relation is neither zero-sum nor constant across historical time (Migdal, Kohli, and Shue 1994). In the period covered by this book, state influence in society was extraordinarily high in the early 1970s, when the state bureaucracy was charged with reshaping social organization and economic activity. But by the end of the decade it had declined considerably, as unions, peasant organizations, and other social movements challenged state prerogatives. The economic crisis and political violence of the 1980s further weakened state influence. Yet after more than a decade of an erosion in state influence and capabilities, the Fujimori administration in the early 1990s successfully embarked on an effort to reassert state influence in society.

State capacities, understood as the ability to efficiently carry out the basic functions and goals of the state organization, increase or decrease as a result of both endogenous and exogenous factors. Wise points out in her chapter how state-led development adopted in the 1960s created significant inefficiencies in the state sector and led to external financial vulnerabilities during the 1980s. The declining value of Peru's traditional exports and the debt crisis of the 1980s cut into the state's resource base and thus reduced the ability of the state to control or influence social actors. Traditional mechanisms of domination, such as state-directed clientelism, became less sustainable. Moreover, the economic crisis contributed to inefficiencies in the state. The reduction in personnel often drove well-trained professionals away from state administration, and conflicts among state elites as a result of both the economic crisis and political violence, especially in the García period, likewise took a toll on state efficacy.

Although there are separate arenas in which state power is exercised (among other states and supranational organizations in the international arena, among groups and organizations in the societal arena, and within the state's own internal bureaucratic structures), shifts in power relations in one arena are likely to influence relations in the others (Mauceri 1996; Evans, Rueschemeyer, and Skocpol 1985; Skocpol 1979). As was mentioned earlier, neoliberalism is not necessarily any more hostile to a "strong" state than was developmentalism. Different policy goals require the use of different state capacities, and in turn they have both direct and indirect consequences on state power capabilities.

For example, in the Latin American experience, neoliberalism's emphasis on fiscal discipline has meant that the social-control functions of the state, including the repressive apparatus, have taken on greater importance in order to counteract the social frustrations caused during the initial implementation of such policies. Which social-control mechanisms are used and how they are used, of course, depends upon the historical context of each nation-state.

In Mexico, the shift toward neoliberalism during the Salinas de Gortari presidency was accompanied by a surprising and unexpected renewal in mechanisms of corporatist control (Bruhn 1996; Camp 1996). By contrast, the Chilean experience represents the most extreme example of the use of repressive force to control the social frustrations produced by radical neoliberal policies. Peru under Fujimori offers a far more mixed scenario, with the use of the military and police for social control common during the first four years of the 1990s, but with President Fujimori turning toward clientelist-based personalism immediately before the 1995 reelection campaign.

Changes in state capacities can often have unintended consequences in society. In Peru, divisions in the state apparatus and the collapse of traditional mechanisms of domination were important factors during the 1970s and 1980s behind the emergence of new social movements and political actors. Weakening state influence increased the political space for social groups to devise new modes of political organization and activities. Several chapters underline how state policies and inefficiencies often have the unintended consequence of increasing opportunities for such groups as business, labor unions, and peasant organizations.

Nonetheless, the greater organization and influence of societal groups vis-à-vis the state is not solely a function of declining state capacities. A vast array of social and economic changes since the 1970s—from the emergence of liberation theology and *clasismo* to the informalization of the economy—paved the way for a dramatic increase in social organization in Peru.

The strengthening of social organization during the 1980s was not accompanied, however, by a reduction in Peru's historic state-society gap. Only a few political parties had national organizations and thus could claim to be effective intermediaries. The institutional disintegration that affected both political and civil-society institutions only worsened this fundamental problem. Moreover, although Peru underwent a transition to democracy in the early 1980s, democratization had a limited impact on the top-down, centralized, and authoritarian state structures in society. Reforms promised in the 1979 constitution regarding regionalization and decentralization, for example, were never fully implemented.

As party and state elites continued to recruit their members from among Lima's middle and upper-class white society, the state-society gap could only persist, if not increase. Fujimori used ethnic, class and, regional divisions in a personalist non-ideological way to guarantee broad-based political support for his candidacy. Yet the failure of the Fujimori administration to democratize state institutions and its disdain for political society and municipal administration have left the problem of a state-society gap largely unresolved.

The gap between state and society in Peru is severe, even by comparison with other Latin American nations in which civil society is less well organized. The unresolved problem of national integration (Cotler 1978) has deep roots in Peru's history. The divisions between Indian, mestizo, and criollo societies contributed to the inability and unwillingness of state managers to penetrate the society beyond Lima and stunted the growth of a nationally integrative political community.

The impact of this historical pattern has been important, as Degregori notes in his chapter, to the emergence and growth of Sendero Luminoso. The "cosmocratic" figure of President Gonzalo had a special appeal among the provincial elite, which had limited access to the distant political and civil society of Lima. Outside of Central America, no other country that underwent a transition to democracy during the 1980s had to contend with such severe problems of national integration as well.

Democracy or Dictatorship?

Transitions and Reversals

Massive human-rights violations in Peru during the 1980s were, in retrospect, indicative of a much more profound problem in Peru's newly installed democracy. The democratic transition did not occur as a result of a mass movement favoring a return to civilian rule and it did not inaugurate a dramatic change in economic or social policies by the new civilian regime.

Rather, the transition was an extrication of the military from direct rule accompanied by a continuity in socioeconomic policies. Beyond a commitment to civilian rule, there was little consensus on the meaning of democracy, let alone on how to expand democratic rights and institutions. The pattern of the early transition and consolidation is thus not significantly different from that found in other Latin American cases (O'Donnell, Schmitter, and Whitehead 1986).

In a seminal article, O'Donnell (1994) has used the term "delegative democracy" to refer to the type of democracy now prevalent in much of Latin America. Such systems, characterized by strong executives and low levels of accountability outside of regularly scheduled elections, meet the minimal criteria of democracies but little more. A significant constraint on the consolidation of many new democracies in the region is the persistence of "tutelary powers" and "reserved domains" (Valenzuela 1992), in which privileged actors retain for themselves special powers and exclusive rights to determine policy in certain issue areas.

In most consolidating democracies, the armed forces have emerged as the major actor claiming reserved domains, primarily involving defense and security issues. These claims of special prerogatives beyond the reach of democratic accountability have been a major source of political conflict between civilian leaders and the military institution during the early consolidation period. While some conflicts have involved increased tensions and even threats, as in Chile, in a number of cases conflicts have resulted in open confrontations, such as the rebellions of the *carapintadas* in Argentina or the rebellion of General Frank Vargas during 1986–87 in Ecuador.

The chapters by Mauceri, Cameron, and Roberts and Peceny all highlight the continued high-profile political role of the military in Peru during the 1980s and 1990s. As a result of the insurgency of Sendero Luminoso, the military increasingly acquired greater powers, reserving the self-defined domain of national security for itself. As Mauceri has argued elsewhere (1991), this was made possible to a large extent by civilian acquiescence. Except for the first two years of the García administration, there were few efforts to assert civilian control over the military during the decade of the 1980s. By contrast, the 1990s offer a far more complex civilmilitary relationship.

The institution most closely identified with President Fujimori has been the armed forces, which made possible the autogolpe of 1992. As Cameron notes in Chapter 2, Fujimori's relationship with the military dates to shortly after the 1990 election. Since that time, there has been a high level of cooperation between the executive and the high command of the armed forces, creating a relationship of mutual dependence. Fujimori redesigned the rules governing the military institution to increase executive control, however he did so in cooperation with a small group of military and intelligence advisers. The result has been a close personal relationship between the president and the armed forces. The military high command is responsible to the person of the president, but it maintains its autonomy from other democratic institutions, including the Congress and the judicial system. The prohibition on civilian courts from reviewing the sentences of military tribunals prosecuting terrorist suspects has illustrated the persistence of reserved domains in Fujimori's Peru.

As has already been noted, both the institutional arrangements and the pattern of state-society relations during the 1980s and early 1990s provided an unfavorable climate for the development of democracy. If this is so, than the breakdown of democracy in the autogolpe of 1992 is less remarkable than the fact that Peruvian democracy persisted as long as it did. Yet the question remains, how can we explain the persistence of democracy between 1980 and the autogolpe of 1992?

McClintock (1989) has convincingly argued that Peru's democracy persisted in this period as a result of the elite's beliefs that all alternatives to the existing system were worse. Thus support for Peru's democracy was largely contingent on the fear of the social conflict and international isolation that an authoritarian regime might provoke. As Peru's crisis worsened in the early 1990s, that support vanished. The benefits of a clean break with the 1979 constitution were calculated as less uncertain than the existing system. It was a risk that business and the military in particular were willing to take. There was nothing inevitable in the autogolpe. Rather, it represented a specific policy choice by both the government and its supporters in response to a severe structural crisis (Mauceri 1995). The experiences of Eastern European and other Latin American countries clearly demonstrate that other policy choices were available.

Although the Fujimori administration, largely under international pressure, was forced to return the country to a version of constitutional democracy soon after the autogolpe, it is clear that the new institutional structure adopted was even less democratic than the previous one. By further centralizing decision making in the executive and limiting legislative and judicial powers, the constitution of 1993 institutionalized a semi-authoritarian political system that went well beyond O'Donnell's concept of "delegative democracy." Fujimori's Peru might be considered a degenerated delegative democracy.

The link between the autogolpe and market reform is a complex one. We are skeptical of the view that there was a necessary relationship between the two. Unilinear and deterministic explanations are more likely to be an obstacle than a source of useful hypotheses in understanding the complexities of the relationship between politics and economics. Moreover, the international system has become more hostile to authoritarianism than it was two decades ago during the period of bureaucratic authoritarianism.

In previous work, Cameron (1994) examined three factors contributing to the Peruvian autogolpe: opposition to neoliberal reforms, institutional gridlock, and the ambitions of the president. His chapter in this volume extends and develops his earlier hypotheses. Based on interviews with key participants in the autogolpe, Cameron finds that tensions between the legislative and executive branches came to a head prior to the autogolpe, but there were also initiatives to reach agreement that were frustrated by the events of 5 April 1992. There seems little question that Fujimori's goal was to create a political system in which power is dangerously centralized in the office of the president.

The perception of a security threat created support for authoritarian measures within the armed forces that was exploited by the president and his allies within the intelligence service, as well as by key officers, all of whom sought to extend their tenure in power. Opposition to neoliberal reforms, by contrast, was not a decisive factor in causing the autogolpe, but it did play a secondary role: concern about the ability of former president García to obstruct the government's economic program reinforced the cohesion of the coup coalition, especially among neoliberal technocrats. The international reaction to the Fuji-coup provides a dramatic illustration of the constraints on presidents who seek to depart, however temporarily, from democratic rule in the post–Cold War era.

Conclusion

Dramatic mood swings appear to be endemic among observers of Latin America's recent economic performance and political evolution. The Mexican peso devaluation provided an example of the collapse of a country's image, as well as its currency, following widespread acceptance of its approach to reform. After implementing policies promoted by international financial institutions and creditor governments, Mexico had ostensibly been poised to "join the First World." It is not our purpose to contribute to optimistic speculations with feeble foundations, nor to pessimistic resignation in the face of overwhelming obstacles, but rather to provide the basis for a more sober and realistic assessment of the achievements and challenges facing one of the region's most complex and fascinating countries. To that end we have focused on enduring underlying problems and trends, as well as on novel features of the emerging regime in Peru.

The chapters in this volume exemplify research on Latin America's development and political economy, as they build on and incorporate insights from previous work on Peru and other countries in the region. However, these chapters also address new trends and problems as the region reaches the end of the millennium: the challenges for democratic institutions and practices, the declining power of organized labor and the rise of the informal economy, the failure of the agrarian reform and the growth of the parcelero movement, the assertiveness of business as a political force, the emergence of a wide range of new social and political movements, and the restructuring of the state and liberalization of the economy.

Naturally, we can only provide a partial guide through the Peruvian labyrinth, but we hope that the chapters in this volume are sufficiently enticing to encourage further research and reflection on Peru and on Latin America as a whole. The outlines of future research programs can be traced according to the questions posed but left unanswered, as well as those not posed in this volume. For example, future research needs to focus more sharply on the mechanisms of international influence and conditionality on Latin America's policy choices and options (how, for example, will the evolving international trading system affect Peru's relations within the hemisphere and globally); still ahead as well lies the task of assessing the new constitution and the Congress. The growing political power of the military will require specialists on Peru to return to that neglected yet crucial subject. Violence in the shantytowns and the highlands has interrupted research on popular-sector lives, organizations, gender relations, and social practices. Above all, the new economic model will have to be carefully examined to determine whether it provides a basis for sustainable and equitable long-term development.

BIBLIOGRAPHY

Abad Yupanqui, S. B., and C. Garcés Peralta. (1993). "El gobierno de Fujimori: Antes y después del golpe." In E. Bernales et al. *Del Golpe de Estado a la Nueva Constitución.* Lima: Comisión Andina de Juristas.

Abramo, L. (1989). "Nuevas tecnologías, mercado de trabajo y acción sindical en Brasil." *Proposiciones* (Chile: Ediciónes Sur), no. 17.

Abuguttas, J. (1991). "The Social Emergency Program." In C. Paredes and J. Sachs, eds. *Peru's Path to Recovery: A Plan for Economic Stabilization and Growth.* Washington, D.C.: Brookings Institution.

Adrianzén, A. (1992a). "Las dificultades del emperador." *Quehacer* 75 (January–February): 4–8.

———. (1992b). "Partidocracia, ajuste y democracia." *Quehacer* 77 (May–June): 24–27.

Adrianzén, A., ed. (1990). *Pensamiento político peruano: 1930–1968.* Lima: DESCO.

———. (1987). *Pensamiento político peruano.* Lima: DESCO.

Alvarez, A. (1991). *Empresas estatales y privatización: Como reformar la actividad empresarial del estado en el Perú.* Lima: Editorial Apoyo.

Amat y León, C. (1978). *La economía de la crisis peruana.* Lima: Fundación Friedrich Ebert.

Americas Watch. (1992). *Peru Under Fire: Human Rights Since the Return to Democracy.* New Haven: Yale University Press.

———. (1988). *Tolerating Abuses: Violations of Human Rights in Peru.* New York: Human Rights Watch.

———. (1984). *Abdicating Democratic Authority: Human Rights in Peru.* New York: Human Rights Watch.

Amnesty International. (1991). *Peru: Human Rights in a Climate of Terror.* New York.

———. (1989). *Peru: Human Rights in a State of Emergency.* London.

———. (1985). *Peru Briefing.* January.

Annis, S., and J. Franks. (1989). "The Idea, Ideology, and Economics of the Informal Sector: The Case of Peru." *Grassroots Development* 13, no. 1.

Arnson, C. (1989). *Crossroads.* New York: Pantheon.

Arroyo, H. (1988). "Experiencias de trabajo en una organización campesina y asociativa-individual." *Alternativa* 9: 77–92.

Astiz, C. (1969). *Pressure Groups and Power Elites in Peruvian Politics.* Ithaca: Cornell University Press.

Atkinson, J. (1986). "Flexibilidad en los mercados laborales." *Zona Abierta* (Spain) 41, 42 (October, March).

Balbi, C. R. (1993). "El desaparecido poder del sindicalismo." In A. Alvarez Rodrich, ed. *El Poder en el Perú.* Lima: APOYO.

———. (1989). *El sindicalismo clasista: Su impacto en las fábricas.* Lima: DESCO.

Balbi, C. R., and J. Gamero. (1990). "Los trabajadores en los 80: Entre las formalidad y la informalidad." In E. Ballón, ed. *Movimientos sociales: Elementos para una relectura.* Lima: DESCO.

Ballón, E. (1990). "Los movimientos sociales en el Perú de los 80." In E. Ballón, ed. *Movimientos sociales: Elementos para una relectura.* Lima: DESCO.

Ballón, E., ed. (1986). *Movimientos sociales y crisis: El caso peruano.* Lima: DESCO.

Ballón Aguirre, F. (1987). "Política de la supervivencia: Las organizaciones de los pueblos indígenas de la Amazonía peruana." *Apuntes* 20, no. 1.

Beltrán, P. (1994). *Pensamiento y acción.* Lima: Instituto de Libre Economía de Mercado.

———. (1974). *La verdadera realidad peruana.* Madrid: Editorial San Martín.

Beltrán Barco, A. (1987). "El gobierno de Velasco. Inversión pública y toma de decisiones: El Caso de Majes." *Apuntes* 20, no. 1.

Bergquist, C. (1986). *Labor in Latin America.* Stanford: Stanford University Press.

Bernales, E. (1980). *¿Crisis política, solución electoral?* Lima: DESCO.

Blacker Miller, A. (1993). *La propuesta inconclusa.* Lima: La Moneda.

Boloña Behr, B. (1993). *Cambio de rumbo.* Lima: Instituto de Economía de Libre Mercado.

Borón, A. (1990). "The Right and the Struggle for Democracy in Latin America." Columbia University, Center for Latin American and Caribbean Studies, Conference Paper No. 35.

Bosworth, B., R. Dornbusch, and R. Laban, eds. (1994). *The Chilean Economy: Policy Lessons and Challenges.* Washington, D.C.: Brookings Institution.

Bourque, S. C., and K. B. Warren (1989). "Democracy Without Peace: The Cultural Politics of Terror in Peru." *Latin American Research Review* 24, no. 1.

Bourricaud, F. (1970). *Power and Society in Contemporary Peru.* New York: Praeger.

Bourricaud, F., et al. (1971). *La oligarquía en el Perú.* Lima: Instituto de Estudios Peruanos.

Bromley, R. (1990). "A New Path to Development? The Significance and Impact of Hernando de Soto's Ideas on Underdevelopment, Production, and Reproduction." *Economic Geography* 66 (October): 328–48.

Bruhn, K. (1996). "Social Spending and Political Support: The 'Lessons' of the National Solidarity Program in Mexico." *Comparative Politics* 28 (January): 151–78.

Burt, J. (1992). "Facade of Democracy Crumbles in Peru." *NACLA: Report on the Americas* 24, no. 1: 3–6.

Caballero, J. M., and E. Alvarez (1980). *Aspectos cuantitativos de la reforma agraria (1969–1979).* Lima: Instituto de Estudios Peruanos.

Caballero, M. V. (1990). "El modelo en Junín y Pasco: Balance y perspectivas del problema de la tierra." In A. Fernández de la Gala and A. Gonzáles Zuñiga, eds. *La reforma agraria peruana, 20 años después.* Chiclayo: Centro de Estudios Sociales Solidaridad.

Calderón, J., and L. Olivera. (1979). *Manual del poblador de pueblos jóvenes.* Lima: DESCO.

Cameron, M. A. (1994). *Democracy and Authoritarianism in Peru: Political Coalitions and Social Change.* New York: St. Martin's Press.

———. (1991a). "Political Parties and the Worker-Employer Cleavage: The Impact of the Informal Sector on Voting in Lima, Peru." *Bulletin of Latin American Research* 10, no. 3: 293–13.

———. (1991b). "The Politics of the Urban Informal Sector in Peru: Populism, Class, and 'Redistributive Combines.'" *Canadian Journal of Latin American and Caribbean Studies* 16, no. 31: 79–104.

———. (1986). "Workers and the State: Protest and Incorporation Under Military Rule in Peru, 1968–1975." Unpublished paper, Department of Political Science, University of California at Berkeley.

Cameron, M., and L. North. (1996) "Las sendas del desarollo en una encrucijada: La agricultura del Perú a la luz de la experiencia del este de Asia." *Socialismo y Participación* 73 (March): 127–40.

Camp, R. (1996). *Politics in Mexico,* 2d ed. New York: Oxford University Press.

Carbonetto, D., et al. (1988). *Lima: Sector Informal.* Lima: CEDEP.

Cardoso, F. H., and E. Faletto. (1979). *Dependency and Development in Latin America.* Berkeley and Los Angeles: University of California Press.

Carter, M. R. (1990). "Una crónica microeconómica de la evolución de la reforma agraria en el Perú." In A. Fernández de la Gala and A. Gonzáles Zuñiga, eds. *La reforma agraria peruana, 20 años después.* Chiclayo: Centro de Estudios Sociales Solidaridad.

———. (1984). "Resource Allocation and Use Under Collective Rights and Labor Management in Peruvian Coastal Agriculture." *Economic Journal* 94: 826–46.

CEPAL. (1991). *Balance preliminar de la economía de América Latina y el Caribe, 1991.* Santiago: United Nations.

Chalmers, D., et al. (1992). *The Right and Democracy in Latin America.* New York: Praeger.

Chávez O'Brien, E. (1990). "La dinámica del empleo y el rol del SIU en un período de inestabilidad económica: 1985–1989." *Socialismo y Participación* (March): 47–61.

Chávez O'Brien, E., and J. Bernedo. (1983). "Los rasgos esenciales de la problemática de los estratos no organizados de la economía." *Serie: Apuntes.* Publication of the Ministry of Labor, No. 8.

Collier, D. (1976). *Squatters and Oligarchs: Authoritarian Rule and Policy Change in Peru.* Baltimore: Johns Hopkins University Press.

Collier, D., ed. (1979). *The New Authoritarianism in Latin America.* Princeton: Princeton University Press.

Collier, R., and D. Collier. (1991). *Shaping the Political Arena.* Princeton: Princeton University Press.

Comisión Especial del Senado Sobre las Causas de la Violencia y Alternativas de Pacificación en el Perú. (1989). *Violencia y pacificación.* Lima: DESCO and the Comisión Andina de Juristas.

Conaghan, C. M. (1995). "Polls, Political Discourse, and the Public Sphere: The Spin on Peru's Fuji-golpe." In Smith, ed. *Latin America in Comparative Perspective: New Approaches to Methods and Analysis.* Boulder, Colo.: Westview Press.

———. (1992). "Capitalists, Technocrats, and Politicians: Economic Policy Making and Democracy in the Central Andes." In S. Mainwaring, G. O'Donnell, and J. S. Valenzuela, eds. *Issues in Democratic Consolidation: The New South*

American Democracies in Comparative Perspective. Notre Dame: University of Notre Dame Press.

Coppedge, M. (1994). *Strong Parties and Lame Ducks: Presidential Partyarchy and Factionalism in Venezuela.* Stanford: Stanford University Press.

Cornell, A., and K. Roberts. (1990). "Democracy, Counterinsurgency, and Human Rights: The Case of Peru." *Human Rights Quarterly* 12, no. 4 (November): 529–53.

Cortéz, J. C. (1991). "Nuevo modelo laboral: El trabajador desprotegido." *Quehacer* 70 (March–April).

Cotler, J. (1995). "Political Parties and the Problems of Democratic Consolidation in Peru." In S. Mainwaring and T. Scully, eds. *Building Democratic Institutions: Party Systems in Latin America.* Stanford: Stanford University Press.

———. (1988). "Los partidos políticos en la democracia peruana." In J. Parodi and L. Pásara, eds. *Democracia, Sociedad y Gobierno en el Perú.* Lima: CEDYS.

———. (1986). "Military Interventions and 'Transfer of Power to Civilians' in Peru." In G. O'Donnell, P. Schmitter, and L. Whitehead, eds. *Transitions from Authoritarian Rule: Latin America.* Baltimore: Johns Hopkins University Press.

———. (1978). *Clases, estado y nación en el Perú.* Lima: Instituto de Estudios Peruanos.

Coward, B. (1991). *Cromwell.* London: Longman.

Crabtree, J. (1994). "The Crisis of the Peruvian Party System (1985–1995)." St. Antony's College, Oxford University.

Crawford, A. (1980). *Thunder on the Right.* New York: Pantheon.

Crouch, C. (1985). "Conditions for Trade Union Wage Restraint." In Lindberg and Maier, eds. *The Politics of Inflation and Economic Stagnation.* Washington, D.C.: Brookings Institution.

Cueva, A., et al. (1987). *Tiempos conservadores.* Quito: Editorial El Conejo.

Daeschner, J. (1993). *The War of the End of Democracy: Mario Vargas Llosa vs. Alberto Fujimori.* Lima: Peru Reporting.

Debray, R. (1967). *Revolution in the Revolution?* Middlesex, England: Penguin.

Degregori, C. I. (1994). "Shining Path and Counterinsurgency Strategy Since the Arrest of Abimael Guzmán." In J. Tulchin and G. Bland, eds. *Peru in Crisis: Dictatorship or Democracy?* Boulder, Colo.: Lynne Rienner.

———. (1990). *Ayacucho 1969–1979: El surgimiento de Sendero Luminoso.* Lima: Instituto de Estudios Peruanos.

Degregori, C. I., and R. Grompone (1991). *Elecciones 1990, demonios y redentores: Una tragedia en dos vueltas.* Lima: Instituto de Estudios Peruanos.

Democracia y Socialismo. (1990). *Perú 1990 encrucijada.* Lima: Democracia y Socialismo.

Department of State. (1994). *Country Reports on Human Rights Practices for 1993.* Washington, D.C.

———. (1992). *Country Reports on Human Rights Practices for 1991.* Washington, D.C.

———. (1991). "An Agreement Between the United States of America and Peru on Drug Control and Alternative Development Policy: May 14, 1991." Office of Andean Affairs, Washington, D.C.

———. (1990). *Country Reports on Human Right Practices for 1989.* Washington, D.C.

De Soto, H. (1989). *The Other Path: The Invisible Revolution in the Third World.* New York: Harper and Row.

Devlin, R. (1985). *Transnational Banks and the External Finance of Latin America: The Experience of Peru.* Santiago: United Nations.

De Wit, T. (1990). "La reforma agraria en Cajamarca: Lo que no se estudió." In A. Fernández de la Gala and A. Gonzáles Zuñiga, eds. *La reforma agraria peruana, 20 años después.* Chiclayo: Centro de Estudios Sociales Solidaridad.

Diamond, L., et al., eds. (1989). *Democracy in Developing Countries.* Boulder, Colo.: Lynne Reinner.

Diario de los Debates de la Asamblea Constituyente Plenario General. (1978–79). Vols 1–8. Lima: República Peruana.

Dietz, H. A. (1992). "Elites in an Unconsolidated Democracy: Peru During the 1980s." In J. Higley and R. Gunther, eds. *Elites and Democratic Consolidation in Latin America and Southern Europe.* Cambridge: Cambridge University Press.

———. (1986–87). "Aspects of Peruvian Politics: Electoral Politics in Peru, 1978–1986." *Journal of Interamerican Studies and World Affairs* 28, no. 4.

———. (1985). "Political Participation in the Barriadas: An Extension and Reexamination." *Comparative Political Studies* 18, no. 3.

Dornbusch, R., and S. Edwards, eds. (1991). *The Macroeconomics of Populism in Latin America.* Chicago: University of Chicago Press.

Downs, A. (1957). *An Economic Theory of Democracy.* New York: Harper and Row.

Durand, F. (1994). *Business and Politics in Peru: The State and the National Bourgeoisie.* Boulder, Colo.: Westview Press.

———. (1992). "The New Right and Political Change in Peru." In Chalmers et al., eds. *The Right and Democracy in Latin America.* New York: Praeger.

———. (1990). "La nueva derecha peruana: Orígenes y dilemas." *Estudios Sociológicos* 8, no. 23: 351–74.

Durand Florez, R. (1985). *Observaciones a la teología de la liberación.* Lima: Obispado del Callao.

Eguren López, F. (1989). "Los nuevos grupos dominantes en la agricultura peruana." *Debate Agrario* 7: 11–32.

Enelow, J. M., and M. J. Hinich, eds. (1990). *Advances in the Spatial Theory of Voting.* Cambridge: Cambridge University Press.

Ermida, O. (1991). "Algunas reacciones de la legislación laboral Latinoamericana ante las políticas de ajuste economico." Unpublished paper, Lima.

Evans, P. (1992). "The State as Problem and Solution: Predation, Embedded Autonomy and Structural Change." In S. Haggard and R. Kaufman, eds. *The Politics of Economic Adjustment.* Princeton: Princeton University Press.

———. (1989). "Predatory, Developmental, and Other Apparatuses: A Comparative Political Economy Perspective on the Third World State." *Sociological Forum* 4: 561–87.

Evans, P., D. Rueschemeyer, and T. Skocpol, eds. (1985). *Bringing the State Back In.* Cambridge: Cambridge University Press.

Fernández de la Gala, A., and A. Gonzáles Zuñiga, eds. (1990). *La reforma agraria peruana, 20 años después.* Chiclayo: Centro de Estudios Sociales Solidaridad.

Figallo, F. (1990). "Parceleros: Tierras, trabajo e ingresos." In A. Fernández de la Gala and A. Gonzáles Zuñiga, eds. *La reforma agraria peruana, 20 años después.* Chiclayo: Centro de Estudios Sociales Solidaridad.

————. (1988). *La parcelación de las cooperativas en debate.* Lima: OXFAM.

Figueroa, A. (1995). "Peru: Social Policies and Economic Adjustment in the 1980s." In N. Lustig, ed. *Coping with Austerity: Poverty and Inequality in Latin America.* Washington, D.C.: Brookings Institution.

————. (1981). *La economía campesina de la sierra del Perú.* Lima: Pontificia Universidad Católica del Perú.

Figueroa, A., and J. Portocarrero, eds. (1986). *Priorización y desarrollo del sector agrícola en el Perú.* Lima: Pontificia Universidad Católica del Perú and Fundación Friedrich Ebert.

Fitzgerald, E. V. K. (1979). *The Political Economy of Peru, 1956–1978: Economic Development and the Restructuring of Capital.* Cambridge: Cambridge University Press.

Fukuyama, F. (1992). *The End of History and the Last Man.* New York: Free Press.

García, A. (1994). *El mundo de Maquiavelo.* Lima: Mosca Azul.

García, I. (1990). "Poder y violencia en el agro hoy." In A. Fernández de la Gala and A. Gonzáles Zuñiga, eds. *La reforma agraria peruana, 20 años después.* Chiclayo: Centro de Estudios Sociales Solidaridad.

García-Sayán, D. (1987a). "Perú: Estados de excepción y régimen jurídico." In García-Sayán, ed. *Estados de emergencia en la región Andina.* Lima: Comisión Andina de Juristas.

————. (1987b). Presentation in "Para asegurar la vigencia de los derechos humanos." In J. Cotler, ed. *Para afirmar la democracia.* Lima: Instituto de Estudios Peruanos.

————. (1982). *Tomas de tierras en el Perú.* Lima: DESCO.

Garland, A. (1905). *Reseña industrial del Perú.* Lima: Imprenta La Industrial.

————. (1896). *Las industrias en el Perú.* Lima: Imprenta del Estado.

Geddes, B. (1994). *Politician's Dilemma: Reforming the State in Latin America.* Berkeley and Los Angeles: University of California Press.

Gereffi, G., and D. Wyman, eds. (1990). *Manufacturing Miracles.* Princeton: Princeton University Press.

Gerschenkron, A. (1962). *Economic Backwardness in Historical Perspective.* Cambridge: Belknap Press.

Ghio, J. M. (1992). "The Latin American Church and the Papacy of Wojtyla." In Chalmers et al., eds. *The Right and Democracy in Latin America.* New York: Praeger.

Gibson, E. L. (1990). "From 'Uncertain Transitions' to Conservative Consolidations: Notes on the Comparative Study of Conservative Electoral Movements in Latin America." Latin American and Caribbean Studies, Columbia University, Conference Paper No. 31.

Giesecke, A., ed. (1985). *Reporte de investigación: La organización del sector público peruano.* Lima: Proyecto de Gestión Publica, ESAN.

Glade, W., ed. (1986). *State Shrinking: A Comparative Inquiry into Privatization.* Austin: University of Texas, Institute of Latin American Studies, Office of Public Sector Studies.

Golte, J. (1980). *La racionalidad de la organización andina.* Lima: Instituto de Estudios Peruanos.

Gómez, V., et al., eds. (1986). *Perú: el problema agrario en debate.* Lima: Seminario Permanente de Investigación Agraria.

Gonzáles, J. (1992). "Guerrillas and Coca in the Upper Huallaga Valley." In Palmer, ed. *Shining Path of Peru.* New York: St. Martin's Press.

Gonzáles, R. (1991). "El Huallaga: Todos los conflictos," *Quehacer* 71 (May–June): 46–52.

———. (1986). "¿Qué pasa en Puno? El PUM, el PAP, Sendero y Alan García." *Quehacer* 43 (October–November): 41–51.

Gonzáles de Olarte, E. (1993). "Peru's Economic Program Under Fujimori." *Journal of Interamerican Studies and World Affairs* 2: 51–80.

———. (1992). *Reforma del estado y políticas de estabilización económica 1979–1992: El Perú, un caso especial.* Lima: Instituto de Estudios Peruanos, documento de trabajo no. 4.

———. (1987). *La lenta modernización de la economía campesina.* Lima: Instituto de Estudios Peruanos.

———. (1984). *Economía de la comunidad campesina.* Lima: Instituto de Estudios Peruanos.

Gonzáles de Olarte, E., and L. Samamé (1991). *El péndulo peruano: Políticas económicas, gobernabilidad y subdesarrollo, 1963–1990.* Lima: Instituto de Estudios Peruanos.

Gonzáles Zuñiga, A., and G. Torre, eds. (1985). *Las parcelaciones de las cooperativas agrarias del Perú.* Chiclayo: Centro de Estudios Sociales Solidaridad.

Gootenberg, P. (1988). "Beleaguered Liberals: The Failed First Generation of Free Traders in Peru." In J. L. Love and N. Jacobsen, eds. *Guiding the Invisible Hand.* New York: Praeger.

Gorman, S., ed. (1982). *Post-Revolutionary Peru: The Politics of Transformation.* Boulder, Colo.: Westview Press.

Gorriti, G. (1994). "Fujimori's Svengali." *Covert Action* 49 (Summer): 4–59.

———. (1990). *Sendero: Historia de la guerra milenaria en el Perú.* Lima: Editorial Apoyo.

Graham, C. (1994). *Safety Nets, Politics and the Poor: Transitions to Market Economies.* Washington, D.C.: Brookings Institution.

———. (1993). "Economic Austerity and the Peruvian Crisis: The Social Costs of Autocracy." *SAIS Review* 1: 45–60.

Gregg, P. (1988). *Oliver Cromwell.* London: J. M. Dent and Sons.

Guadalupe Mendízabal, C. (1992). "De Leviatán a remora: Algunas hipótesis de trabajo sobre el sistema político peruano." *Debates en Sociología,* no. 16: 171–93.

Guillermoprieto, A. (1994). *The Heart That Bleeds: Latin America Now.* New York: Knopf.

Gutiérrez, M. (1988). *La generación del 50: Un mundo dividido.* Lima: privately printed.

Haggard, S. (1990). *Pathways from the Periphery.* Ithaca: Cornell University Press.

Hamill, H. (1992). *Caudillos: Dictators in Spanish America.* Norman, Okla.: University of Oklahoma Press.

Hinkelanmert, F. (1989). "Democracia y nueva derecha en América Latina." La Paz, CEDOIN, Informe "R" 164 (Enero): 4–5, 9–10.

Hirschman, A. O. (1958). *The Strategy of Economic Development.* New Haven: Yale University Press.

Hojman, D. E. (1994). "The Political Economy of Recent Conversions to Market

Economics in Latin America." *Journal of Latin American Studies* 26, no. 1: 191–219.

Human Rights Watch. (1992). *Human Rights Watch World Report.* New York.

Husain, S., et al. (1992). "Crítica al consenso de Washington." Lima, DESCO-CEPES, Foro sobre Deuda y Desarrollo, FONAD, documento de trabajo no. 1.

Instituto de Defensa Legal. (1990). *Perú 1989: En la espiral de la violencia.* Lima: Instituto de Defensa Legal.

International Commission of Jurists. (1983). *States of Emergency: Their Impact on Human Rights.* Geneva.

Jaquette, J. (1971). "The Politics of Development in Peru." Dissertation Series, Latin American Studies Program, Cornell University.

Jaquette, J., and A. F. Lowenthal (1987). "The Peruvian Experiment in Retrospect." *World Politics* 39, no. 2 (January).

Jochamovitz, L. (1994). *Cuidadano Fujimori: La construcción de un político.* Lima: PEISA.

Kahler, M. (1990). "Orthodoxy and Its Alternatives." In J. Nelson, ed. Economic Crisis and Policy Choices. Princeton: Princeton University Press.

Kenney, C. (1996). "¿Por qué el autogolpe? Fujimori y el congreso, 1990–1992." In F. Tuesta, ed. *La Política bajo Fujimori: Partidos políticos y opinión pública.* Lima: Fundación Friedrich Ebert.

———. (1995). "The Politics of Fujimori's Self-Coup and Implications for Democracy in Peru." Paper presented at the Latin American Studies Association meeting, 28–30 September.

King, D. S. (1993). *The New Right.* Chicago: Dorsey Press.

Kirk, R. (1992). "Los desplazados del Perú." *Quehacer* 75 (January–February): 78–87.

———. (1991). *The Decade of Chaqwa: Peru's Internal Refugees.* American Council for Nationalities Service: U.S. Committee for Refugees.

Kisic, D. (1987). *De la corresponsibilidad a la moratoria: El caso de la deuda externa peruana 1970–1986.* Lima: Fundación Friedrich Ebert and Centro Peruano de Estudios Internacionales.

Klaiber, J. (1990). "Fujimori: Race and Religion in Peru." *America* (September): 133–35.

———. (1977). *Religion and Revolution in Peru, 1824–1976.* Notre Dame: University of Notre Dame Press.

Kritz, E. (1988). "Estructura productiva y mercado de trabajo en América Latina después de los años 80." *Desarrollo Económico* (Buenos Aires) 28, no. 109.

Laos, C. (1929). *Lima, la ciudad de los virreyes.* Lima: Editorial Perú.

Lago, R. (1992). "The Illusion of Pursuing Redistribution Through Macropolicy: Peru's Heterodox Experience, 1985–1990." In R. Dornbusch and S. Edwards, eds. *The Macroeconomics of Populism in Latin America.* Chicago: University of Chicago Press.

Leff, N. (1986). "Trust, Envy and the Political Economy of Industrial Development: Economic Groups in Developing Countries." Cornell University, First Boston Paper Series FB- 86–38.

Letts, R. (1990). "Comentarios a los artículos de Fernando Eguren y Alberto Gonzáles." In A. Fernández de la Gala and A. Gonzáles Zuñiga, eds. *La*

reforma agraria peruana, 20 años después. Chiclayo: Centro de Estudios Sociales Solidaridad.

Linz, J. (1978). *The Breakdown of Democratic Regimes.* Baltimore: Johns Hopkins University Press.

López J. S. (1993). "De la dictablanda a la democradura." *Quehacer* 82 (March–
April): 35–8.

Loveman, B. (1993). *The Constitution of Tyranny: Regimes of Exception in Spanish
America.* Pittsburgh: Pittsburgh University Press.

Lowenthal, A. F., ed. (1975). *The Peruvian Experiment: Continuity and Change Under
Military Rule.* Princeton: Princeton University Press.

Lynch, N. (1992). *La transición conservadora.* Lima: El Zorro de Abajo.

Malpica, C. (1990). *El poder económico en el Perú: Los bancos y sus filiales.* Lima: Mosca
Azul Editores.

———. (1968). *Los dueños del Perú.* 3d ed. Lima: Colección Ensayos Sociales.

Manrique, N. (1989). "Sierra Central: La guerra decisiva." *Quehacer* 60 (August–
September): 63–71.

Marka (1975). "La derecha en la iglesia," 13 November, 11–13.

Marx, K. (1963 [1869]). *The Eighteenth Brumaire of Louis Bonaparte.* New York: International Publishers.

Matos Mar, J. (1985). *Desborde popular y crisis del estado.* Lima: Instituto de Estudios
Peruanos.

Mauceri, P. (1996). *State Under Siege: Development and Policy Making in Peru.* Boulder,
Colo.: Westview Press.

———. (1995). "State Reform, Coalitions, and the Neoliberal Autogolpe in Peru."
Latin American Research Review 30, no. 1: 7–37.

———. (1991). "Military Politics and Counter-Insurgency in Peru." *Journal of Inter-
American and World Affairs* 33 (Winter): 83–109.

———. (1989). *Militares: Insurgencia y democratización en el Perú, 1980–1988.* Lima:
Instituto de Estudios Peruanos.

Mayer, E. (1991). "Peru in Deep Trouble: Mario Vargas Llosa's 'Inquest in the
Andes' Reexamined." *Cultural Anthropology* 6, no. 4: 466–504.

McClintock, C. (1994a). "Classifying the Regime Types of El Salvador and Peru in
the 1980s and 1990s." Paper presented at the American Political Science
Association meeting, New York, 1–4 September.

———. (1994b). "Presidents, Messiahs, and Constitutional Breakdowns in Peru."
In J. Linz and A. Valenzuela, eds. *The Failure of Presidential Democracy.* Baltimore: Johns Hopkins University Press.

———. (1993). "Peru's Fujimori: A Caudillo Derails Democracy." *Current History*
(March): 112–19.

———. (1989). "The Prospects for Democratic Consolidation in a 'Least Likely'
Case: Peru." *Comparative Politics* 21, no. 2: 127–48.

———. (1981). *Peasant Cooperatives and Political Change in Peru.* New Jersey: Princeton University Press.

McClintock, C., and A. F. Lowenthal, eds. (1983). *The Peruvian Experiment Reconsidered.* Princeton: Princeton University Press.

Mejía, J. M. (1990). *La neoreforma agraria: Cambios en la propiedad de la tierra 1980–
1990.* Lima: Cambio y Desarrollo.

Meller, P. (1992). "Review of the Chilean Trade Liberalization and Export Expansion Process (1974–1990)." *Bangladesh Development Studies* 20: 155–84.

Mercado Jarrín, E. (1993–94). "Fuerzas armadas: Constitución y reconversión." *Debate* 16, no. 75: 31–34.

Migdal, J., A. Kohli, and V. Shue. (1994). *State Power and Social Forces: Domination and Transformation in the Third World.* Cambridge: Cambridge University Press.

Miliband, R. (1991). "Bonapartism" in T. Bottomore, ed. *A Dictionary of Marxist Thought.* 2d ed. Cambridge, Mass.: Blackwell, 55–56.

Miró Quesada Laos, C. (1961). *Autopsia de los partidos políticos.* Lima: Ediciones Páginas Peruanas.

Mitchell, W. P. (1991). *Peasants on the Edge: Crop, Cult, and Crisis in the Andes.* Austin: University of Texas Press.

Moncloa, F. (1980). "La constitución y el nuevo modelo de dependencia." *Cuadernos Socialistas,* no. 3.

Montero, C. (1989). "Límites y alcances del cambio tecnológico en América Latina y Chile." *Proposiciones* (Chile, Ediciones Sur), no. 17.

Moses, J. W. (1994). "The *Eighteenth Brumaire* of Boris Yeltsin." *Security Dialogue* 25, no. 3: 335–47.

Movimiento Libertad (1988). *Libertad. Primer ciclo de conferencias,* 2 vols. Lima: Movimiento Libertad.

Naím, M. (1993). "Latin America: Post-Adjustment Blues." *Foreign Policy* 92: 133–50.

Nelson, J., ed. (1990). *Economic Crisis and Policy Choice: The Politics of Adjustment in the Third World.* Princeton: Princeton University Press.

Nieto, J. (1983). *Izquierda y democracia en el Perú: 1975–1980.* Lima: DESCO.

North, D. C. (1990). *Institutions, Institutional Change, and Economic Performance.* Cambridge: Cambridge University Press.

Novoa, G., and J. Morelli (1990). "Estado contra cooperativa: El caso de Paramonga." In A. Fernández de la Gala and A. Gonzáles Zuñiga, eds. *La reforma agraria peruana, 20 años después.* Chiclayo: Centro de Estudios Sociales Solidaridad.

Obando, E. (1994). "The Power of Peru's Armed Forces." In J. Tulchin and G. Bland, eds. *Peru in Crisis: Dictatorship or Democracy?* Boulder, Colo.: Lynne Rienner.

———. (1991). "La burocracia antisubversiva." *Quehacer* 71 (May–June): 54–57.

O'Donnell, G. (1994). "Delegative Democracy." *Journal of Democracy* 5 (January): 55–69.

———. (1992a). "Subtantive or Procedural Consensus? Notes on the Latin American Bourgeoisie." In Chalmers et al., eds. *The Right and Democracy in Latin America.* New York: Praeger.

———. (1992b). "Transitions, Continuities, and Paradoxes." In S. Mainwaring, G. O'Donnell, and J. S. Valenzuela, eds. *Issues in Democratic Consolidation: The New South American Democracies in Comparative Perspective.* Notre Dame: University of Notre Dame Press.

———. (1973). *Modernization and Bureaucratic-Authoritarianism: Studies in South American Politics.* Berkeley: Institute of International Studies.

O'Donnell, G., and P. Schmitter (1986). *Transitions from Authoritarian Rule: Tentative Conclusions About Uncertain Outcomes.* Baltimore: Johns Hopkins University Press.

Ordeshook, P. C. (1992). *A Political Theory Primer.* New York: Routledge.

Oroza, J. (1990). "Los problemas de gestión de las cooperativas azucareras y sus planteamientos de solución." In A. Fernández de la Gala and A. Gonzáles Zuñiga, eds. *La reforma agraria peruana, 20 años después.* Chiclayo: Centro de Estudios Sociales Solidaridad.

Ortiz de Zevallos, F. (1992). "Solving the Peruvian Puzzle." In *The Shadow of the Debt.* New York: Twentieth Century Fund Press.

Paerregaard, K. (1987). *Nuevas organizaciones en comunidades campesinas.* Lima: Pontificia Universidad Católica del Perú.

Palmer, D. S. (1996). "'Fujipopulism' and Peru's Progress." *Current History* 95, no. 598: 70–75.

———. (1995). "Peru's 1995 Elections: A Second Look." *LASA Forum* 26, no. 2: 17–20.

———. (1992a). "Peru, the Drug Business and Shining Path: Between Scylla and Charybdis?" *Journal of Interamerican Studies and World Affairs* 34, no. 3: 65–88.

———. (1992b). "United States-Peru Relations in the 1990s: Asymmetry and Its Consequences." In E. Gamarra and J. Malloy, eds. *Latin America and Caribbean Contemporary Record, 1989–1990.* New York: Holmes and Meier.

Palmer, D. S., ed. (1992c). *The Shining Path of Peru.* New York: St. Martin's Press.

Panfichi, A. (1994). "La alternativa autoritaria 'anti-política' en sectores populares de Lima." Paper presented at conference, "Inequality and New Forms of Popular Representation in Latin America," held at Columbia University, New York, 3–5 March.

Paredes, C. (1991). "Epilogue: In the Aftermath of Hyperinflation." In C. Paredes and J. Sachs, eds. *Peru's Path to Recovery: A Plan for Economic Stabilization and Growth.* Washington, D.C.: Brookings Institution.

Paredes, C., and A. Pasco-Font (1990). "El comportamiento del sector público en el Perú, 1970–1985: Un enfoque macroeconómico." In Larraín and Selowsky, eds. *El sector público y la crisis de la América Latina.* Mexico: Fondo de Cultura Económica.

Paredes, C., and J. Sachs, eds. (1991). *Peru's Path to Recovery: A Plan for Economic Stabilization and Growth.* Washington D.C.: Brookings Institution.

Paredes, P. (1988). *Las estrategias de contratación laboral: La experiencia del PROEM y sus alternativas.* Lima: Fundación Friedrich Ebert.

Parodi, J. (1986). *La desmovilización del sindicalismo industrial Peruano en el segundo Belaúndismo.* Lima: Instituto de Estudios Peruanos, documento de trabajo no. 3.

Pásara, L. (1992). "Sin brújula." *Caretas,* 20 April, 53.

———. (1991). *La otra cara de la luna. Nuevos actores sociales en el Perú.* Buenos Aires and Lima: CEDYS.

Pastor, Jr., M. (1992, March). "Democracy, Distribution, and Economic Performance in Peru." Paper presented at conference, "Economy, Society, and Democracy in Developing Countries," part of a Hoover Institution Project supported by the U.S. Agency for International Development, Washington, D.C.

Pastor, Jr., M., and C. Wise (1994a). "The Origins and Sustainability of Mexico's Free Trade Policy." *International Organization* 48, no. 3.

―――. (1994b). "*After NAFTA: Changing U.S. Foreign Policy Concerns in Latin America.*" Unpublished paper, Washington, D.C.: Carnegie Endowment for International Peace.

―――. (1992). "Peruvian Economic Policy in the 1980s: From Orthodoxy to Heterodoxy and Back." *Latin American Research Review* 27, no. 1: 83–117.

Pease G., H. (1994). *Los años de la langosta: La escena política del Fujimorismo.* Lima: La Voz.

―――. (1981). *Los caminos del poder.* Lima: DESCO.

―――. (1977). *El ocaso del poder oligárquico.* Lima: DESCO.

Planas, P. (1994). La república autocrática. Lima; Fundación Friedrich Ebert.

Poole, D., and G. Rénique. (1992). *Peru: Time of Fear.* London: Latin American Bureau.

Portes, A. (1985). "Latin American Class Structures: Their Composition and Change During the Last Decades." *Latin American Research Review* 20, no. 3: 7–39.

Portes, A., and M. Johns. (1989). "The Polarization of Class and Space in the Contemporary Latin American City." In L. Canak, ed. *Lost Promises.* Boulder, Colo.: Westview Press.

Portocarrero, F. (1980). *Crisis y recuperación.* Lima: Mosca Azul.

Portocarrero, G., and R. Tapia. (1992). *Trabajadores, sindicalismo y política en el Perú de hoy.* Lima: ADEC/ATC.

Portocarrero, M. J. (1987). "Haciendas, cooperativas y parcelas en la costa peruana, 1968–1986: el estado de la cuestión." *Apuntes* 20, no. 1: 73–84.

Poulantzas, N. (1974). *Fascism and Dictatorship.* London: New Left Books.

Powell, S. (1976). "Political Participation in the Barriadas: A Case Study." in D. Chaplin, ed. *Peruvian Nationalism: A Corporatist Revolution.* New Brunswick, N.J.: Transaction Books.

Programa Regional de America Latina y el Caribe (PREALC). (1981). *El sector informal: Funcionamiento y políticas.* Santiago: Oficina Internacional de Trabajo.

Przeworski, A. (1991). *Democracy and the Market: Political and Economic Reforms in Eastern Europe and Latin America.* Cambridge: Cambridge University Press.

Przeworski, A., and J. Sprague. (1986). *Paper Stones: A History of Electoral Socialism.* Chicago: University of Chicago Press.

Quijano, A. (n.d.). *Movimiento de pobladores.* Lima: Voz Rebelde.

Quintanilla, E. (1991). "Tendencias recientes de la localización en la industria maquiladora." *Comercio Exterior* 41, no. 9.

Quispe, S., and R. Araca (1990). "Puno: Reestructuración agraria y opciones de desarrollo rural." In A. Fernández de la Gala and A. Gonzáles Zuñiga, eds. *La reforma agraria peruana, 20 años después.* Chiclayo: Centro de Estudios Sociales Solidaridad.

Rakowski, C. A. (1994). *Contrapunto: The Informal Sector Debate in Latin America.* Albany: State University of New York.

Reaño, G., and Vásquez, E. (1988). *El grupo Romero: Del algodón a la banca.* Lima: CIPCA-CIUP.

Remmer, K. (1990). "Democracy and Economic Crisis: The Latin American Experience." *World Politics* 42, no. 3: 315–35.

Revesz, B. (1986). "Necesidad de una nueva interpretación de la reforma agraria y sus efectos." In Gómez et al., eds. *Perú: El problema agrario en debate.* Lima: Seminario Permanente de Investigación Agraria.

Revilla, J. (1981). "Industrialización temprana y lucha ideológica en el Peru: 1890–1910." *Estudios Andinos* 9, nos. 17, 18: 3–40.

Riva Agüero D., J. (1991). "Testimonio personal sobre mi país." *Oiga,* 30 July, 6–7.

Roberts, K. M. (1996). "Economic Crisis and the Demise of the Legal Left in Peru." *Comparative Politics* 29, no. 1: 69–92.

———. (1995). "Neoliberalism and the Transformation of Populism in Latin America: The Peruvian Case." *World Politics* 48: 82–116.

Rochabrún Silva, G. (1988). "Crisis, Democracy, and the Left in Peru." *Latin American Perspectives* 15, no. 3.

Rogger, H., and E. Weber (1965). *The European Right.* Berkeley and Los Angeles: University of California Press.

Roncagliolo, R. (1989–90). "Elecciones en Lima: Cifras testarudas." *Quehacer* 62 (December–January): 16.

———. (1980). *¿Quién ganó? Elecciones 1931–1980.* Lima: DESCO.

Rospigliosi, F. (1994). "Democracy's Bleak Prospects." In J. Tulchin and G. Bland, eds. *Peru in Crisis: Dictatorship or Democracy?* Boulder, Colo.: Lynne Rienner.

———. (1996). "Las fuerzas armadas y el 5 de abril: La percepción de la amenaza subversiva como una motivación golpista." Lima: Instituto de Estudios Peruanos, documento de trabajo no. 73.

Rothrock, V. (1969). "The Autonomous Entities of the Peruvian Government in Perspective." Doctoral dissertation, University of Indiana.

Rudolph, J. D. (1992). *Peru: The Evolution of a Crisis.* Westport, Conn.: Praeger.

Rueschemeyer, D., E. H. Stephens, and J. D. Stephens. (1992). *Capitalist Development and Democracy.* Chicago: University of Chicago Press.

Salazar, P. (1988). "Algodoneros piuranos derrotan a Dionisio Romero." *Quehacer* 55 (October–November): 72–77.

Salcedo, J. M. (1990). *Tsunami presidente.* Lima: Editorial Venus.

———. (1989). "El laberinto de la coca," informe especial. *Quehacer* 59 (June–July): 37–50.

Sanborn, C. (1991). "The Democratic Left and the Persistence of Populism in Peru: 1975–1990." Doctoral dissertation, Harvard University.

Saulniers, A. (1988). *Public Enterprises in Peru: Public Sector Growth and Reform.* Boulder, Col.: Westview Press.

Schamis, H. E. (1992). "Conservative Political Economy in Latin America and Western Europe: The Political Sources of Privatization." In Chalmers et al., eds. *The Right and Democracy in Latin America.* New York: Praeger.

Schlydowsky, D., and J. Wicht (1979). *Anatomía de un fracaso económico: Peru 1968–1978.* Lima: CIUP.

Schmidt, G. D. (1996). "Fujimori's 1990 Upset Victory in Peru: Electoral Rules, Contingencies, and Adaptive Strategies." *Comparative Politics* 28, no. 3, 321–54.

————. (1991). "Electoral Earthquake in Peru: Understanding the Fujimori Phenomenon." Paper presented at the annual meeting of the Illinois Conference for Latin American Studies, Loyola University of Chicago, 1–2 November.

Schoultz, L. (1987). *National Security and U.S. Foreign Policy Toward Latin America.* Princeton: Princeton University Press.

Scully, T. R. (1992). *Rethinking the Center: Party Politics in Nineteenth- and Twentieth-Century Chile.* Stanford: Stanford University Press.

Scurrah, M. ed. (1987). *Empresas asociativas y comunidades campesinas. Puno después de la reforma agraria.* Lima: GREDES.

Seminario Duany, A. (1990). *Inversiones estratégicas del sector público para el desarrollo del agro.* Publicación del Instituto Interamericano de Cooperación para la Agricultura (IICA).

Sheahan, J. (1992). "Peru's Return to an Open Economy: Macroeconomic Complications and Structural Questions." Paper presented at the Latin American Studies Association meetings, Los Angeles, September.

————. (1987). *Patterns of Economic Development in Latin America: Poverty, Repression, and Economic Strategy.* Princeton: Princeton University Press.

Shepsle, K. A., and R. N. Cohen. (1990). "Multiparty Competition, Entry, and Entry Deterrence in Spatial Models of Elections." In J. M. Enelow and M. J. Hinich, eds. *Advances in the Spatial Theory of Voting.* Cambridge: Cambridge University Press.

Shifter, M. (1990). "Derechos humanos: Un nuevo enfoque." *Debate* 12, no. 59: 43–49.

Sikkink, K. (1991). *Ideas and Institutions: Developmentalism in Brazil and Argentina.* Ithaca: Cornell University Press.

Skocpol, T. (1979). *Estates and Social Revolutions.* New York: Cambridge University Press.

Smith, P. H. (1991). "Crisis and Democracy in Latin America." *World Politics* 43 (July): 608–34.

Smith, P. H., ed. (1995). *Latin America in Comparative Perspective: New Approaches to Methods and Analysis.* Boulder, Colo.: Westview Press.

Smith, W. C., et al., eds. (1994). *Latin American Political Economy in the Age of Neo-Liberal Reform.* New Brunswick, N.J.: Transaction Press.

Soberón, R. (1992). "The War on Cocaine in Peru: From Cartagena to San Antonio." Washington Office on Latin America, *WOLA Issue Brief* No. 6 (7 August).

Starn, O. (1992). "New Literature on Peru's Sendero Luminoso." *Latin American Research Review* 27, no. 2: 212–26.

————. (1991a). "Missing the Revolution: Anthropologists and the War in Peru." *Cultural Anthropology* 6, no. 1: 63–91.

————. (1991b). "Noches de ronda por las serranías del norte, con las auténticas rondas campesinas." *Quehacer* 69 (February–March): 76–92.

————. (1991c). "Sendero, soldados y ronderos en el Mantaro." *Quehacer* 74 (November–December: 60–68.

Stein, S., and C. Monge. (1988). *La crisis del estado patrimonial en el Perú.* Lima: Instituto de Estudios Peruanos and the University of Miami.

Stepan, A. (1988). *Rethinking Military Politics.* Princeton: Princeton University Press.

————. (1978). *State and Society: Peru in Comparative Perspective*. Princeton: Princeton University Press.

Stephens, E. H. (1983). "The Peruvian Military Government, Labor Mobilization, and the Political Strength of the Left." *Latin American Research Review* 18, no. 2.

Stokes, S. C. (1996). "Economic Reforms and Public Opinion in Peru, 1990–1995." *Comparative Political Studies* 29, no. 5, 544–65.

————. (1995). *Cultures in Conflict: Social Movements and the State in Peru*. Berkeley and Los Angeles: University of California Press.

————. (1991). "Politics and Latin America's Urban Poor: Reflections from a Lima Shantytown." *Latin American Research Review* 26, no. 2: 75–101.

Strange, S. (1974). "Monetary Managers." In Cox and Jacobson, eds. *The Anatomy of Influence*. New Haven: Yale University Press.

Sulmont, D. (1991). *El camino de la educación tecnica: Los otros profesionales*. Lima: Pontificia Universidad Católica del Perú.

————. (1985). *El movimiento obrero Peruano (1890–1980)*. Lima: Tarea.

————. (1977). *Historia del movimiento obrero en el Perú, de 1890 a 1977*. Lima: Tarea.

Tapia, R. (1992). "Nuevas actitudes en la empresa peruana: El caso INCOTEX." Unpublished manuscript, Lima: Pontificia Universidad Católica del Perú.

Taylor, L. (1990). "One Step Forward, Two Steps Back: The Peruvian *Izquierda Unida* 1980–1990." *Journal of Communist Studies* 6, no. 3: 108–19.

"Testimonios de la guerra." (1991). *Quehacer* 72 (July–August): 52–53.

Thorp, R., and G. Bertram (1978). *Peru, 1890–1977: Growth and Policy in an Open Economy*. New York: Columbia University Press.

Toranzo Roca, C. F., and M. Arrieta Abdala. (1989). *Nueva derecha y desproletarización en Bolivia*. La Paz: UNITAS-ILDIS.

Torre, G. (1990). "Impacto del proceso de parcelaciones: El caso de Lambayeque." In A. Fernández de la Gala and A. Gonzáles Zuñiga, eds. *La reforma agraria peruana, 20 años después*. Chiclayo: Centro de Estudios Sociales Solidaridad.

Torres y Torres Lara, C. (1992a). *Los nudos del poder*. Lima: Desarrollo y Paz.

————. (1992b). "Perú 5 de abril, 1992: Antecedentes y perspectivas." *La democracia en cuestión*. Lima: Centro Norte Sur, University of Miami, CEPES, Instituto de Estudios Peruanos.

Touraine, A. (1987). *Actores sociales y sistemas políticos en América Latina*. Santiago: PREALC.

Tovar, T. (1992). "La política en cielo o la oreja en el suelo: Golpe, democracia y mentalidad popular." *Páginas* 116 (July): 7–26.

————. (1982). *Movimiento popular y paros nacionales*. Lima: DESCO.

Tueros, M. (1984). "Los trabajadores informales de Lima: ¿Qué piensan de la política?" *Socialismo y Participación* 28 (December).

Tuesta, F. (1989). *Pobreza urbana y cambios electorales en Lima*. Lima: DESCO.

————. (1987 and 1994). *Perú político en cifras: Elite política y elecciones*, 1st and 2d eds. Lima: Fundación Friedrich Ebert.

————. (1985). *El nuevo rostro electoral: Las municipales del 83*. Lima: DESCO.

————. (1979). "Análisis del proceso electoral a la Asamblea Constituyente." Unpublished manuscript. Pontificia Universidad Católica del Perú.

Tulchin, J. S., ed. (1995). *Venezuela in Crisis*. Washington, D.C.: Woodrow Wilson Center.

Tulchin, J. S., and G. Bland, eds. (1994). *Peru in Crisis: Dictatorship or Democracy?* Boulder, Colo.: Lynne Rienner.

Uceda Pérez, R. (1987). "Puno entre la violencia y la paz." *AGRO*. Lima: Banco Agrario del Perú.

U.S. Congress. House. (1992). "The Situation in Peru and the Future of the War on Drugs." *Joint Hearing Before the Subcommittee on Western Hemisphere Affairs and the Task Force on International Narcotics Control of the House Committee on Foreign Affairs*, 7 May.

————. (1991a). *Hearings Before the House Select Committee on Narcotics Abuse and Control*, 11 June.

————. (1991b). "Review of the Presidential Determination on Narcotics Control and Human Rights in Peru." *Hearing Before the Committee on Foreign Affairs*, 12 September.

U.S. Department of State. (1995). *Country Reports on Human Rights Practices for 1994*. Washington, D.C.: U.S. Government Printing Office.

Valderrama, M., and P. Ludmann. (1979). *La oligarquía terrateniente ayer y hoy*. Lima: Pontificia Universidad Católica del Perú.

Valderrama, M., et al. (1980). *El APRA: Un camino de esperanza y frustraciónes*. Lima: El Gallo Rojo.

Valdivia H., M. (1987). "Las alternativas de reestructuración empresarial en la agricultura de la costa peruana." *Apuntes* 21: 53–67.

Valentín, I. (1991). "Tsunami Fujimori: Una propuesta de interpretación." Unpublished manuscript, Lima: Pontificia Universidad Católica del Perú.

Valenzuela, J. S. (1992). "Democratic Consolidation in Post- Transitional Settings: Notion, Process and Facilitating Conditions." In S. Mainwaring, G. O'Donnell, and J. S. Valenzuela, eds. *Issues in Democratic Consolidation: The New South American Democracies in Comparative Perspective*. Notre Dame: University of Notre Dame Press.

Vargas Llosa, A. (1991). *El diablo en campaña*. Madrid: El País and Aguilar.

Vargas Llosa, M. (1993). *Pez en el agua*. Barcelona: Seix Barral.

————. (1991). "A Fish Out of Water." *Granta* 36 (Summer): 15–75.

Velasco Alvarado, J. (1972). *La voz de la revolución*, vol. 2. Lima: Oficina Nacional de Informaciones.

Vergara, R. (1986). *Estudio de cooperativas agrarias en el valle de Chincha*. Lima: DESCO.

Vidal, A. M. (1985). "La legalización de la parcelación en las CAP." In A. Gonzáles Zuñiga and G. Torres, eds. *Las parcelaciones de las cooperativas agrarias del Perú*. Chiclayo: Centro de Estudios Sociales Solidaridad.

Warnock, John W. (1988.) *Free Trade and the New Right Agenda*. Vancouver: New Star Books.

Washington Office on Latin America. (1994). *After the Autogolpe: Human Rights in Peru and the U.S. Response*. Washington, D.C.

————. (1992). *Peru Under Scrutiny: Human Rights and U.S. Drug Policy*. Washington, D.C.

————. (1991). *Clear and Present Dangers: The U.S. Military and the War on Drugs in the Andes*. Washington, D.C.

———. (1987). *Peru in Peril: The Economy and Human Rights, 1985–1987.* Washington, D.C.

Webb, R. (1991). Prologue in C. Paredes and J. Sachs, eds. *Peru's Path to Recovery: A Plan for Economic Stabilization and Growth.* Washington, D.C.: Brookings Institution.

Webb, R., and G. Fernández Baca (1993). *Perú en números 1993. Anuario estadístico.* Lima: Cuánto.

———. (1991). *Perú en números 1991. Anuario estadístico.* Lima: Cuánto.

Weber, M. (1968). *Economy and Society.* New York: Dedminster Press.

Wiarda, H., ed. (1982). *Politics and Social Change in Latin America: The Distinct Tradition.* Amherst: University of Massachusetts Press.

Williamson, J. (1983). *IMF Conditionality.* Washington D.C.: Institute for International Studies.

Wise, C. (1993). *In Search of Markets: Latin America's State-Led Dilemma.* New York: Columbia University Institute for Latin American and Iberian Studies, papers on Latin America no. 33.

———. (1990). "Peru Post-1968: The Political Limits to State-Led Economic Development." Doctoral dissertation, Columbia University.

———. (1989). "Democratization, Crisis, and the APRA's Modernization Project in Peru." In B. Stallings and R. Kaufman, eds. *Debt and Democracy in Latin America.* Boulder, Col.: Westview Press.

Wittman, D. (1990). "Spatial Strategies When Candidates Have Policy Preferences." In J. M. Enelow and M. J. Hinich, eds. *Advances in the Spatial Theory of Voting.* Cambridge: Cambridge University Press.

World Bank. (1995). *Trends in Developing Economies, 1995.* Washington, D.C.: International Bank for Reconstruction and Development.

Yañez, A. M. (1992). "Un nuevo reto para los trabajadores: Sindicalizar a los precarios." *Cuadernos Laborales* 61.

Youngers, C. (1994). "Washington Office on Latin America Policy Brief on Human Rights and U.S. Policy Toward Peru." Unpublished manuscript, Washington Office on Latin America.

———. (1992). "E.E.U.U.: Contradictoria y confusa política." *Quehacer* 77 (May–June): 28–31.

Youngers, C., and C. Call. (1991). "Doctrina Fujimori o doctrina Bush?" *Quehacer* 71 (May–June): 32–36.

Zapata, F. (1988). *Trabajadores y sindicatos en América Latina.* Mexico: Secretaria de Educación Política.

CONTRIBUTORS

Carmen Rosa Balbi (M.S., Catholic University of Peru, 1986) is professor of social science and director of the graduate program in sociology at the Catholic University of Peru. In 1995 she was a visiting professor at L'Ecole de Hautes Etudes in Paris. Her publications include *El APRA y el Partido Comunista en los años 30* (1982) and *Sindicalismo y clasismo en el Perú: Su impacto en las fábricas* (Lima: DESCO: 1989). Her current research focuses on political violence and urban poverty during the Fujimori administration.

Maxwell A. Cameron (Ph.D., Berkeley, 1989) is associate professor of political science at the Norman Paterson School of International Affairs, Carleton University in Ottawa, Canada. In 1996 he was a visiting fellow at the Kellogg Institute for International Studies at the University of Notre Dame. His works include *Democracy and Authoritarianism in Peru: Political Coalitions and Social Change* (N.Y.: St. Martins Press, 1994), *Democracy and Foreign Policy: Canada Among Nations,* with Maureen Appel Molot (Ottawa: Carleton University Press, 1995), and with Ricardo Grinspun, *The Political Economy of North American Free Trade* (N.Y.: St. Martins Press, 1993). His current research projects include a study of NAFTA negotiations and a comparative analysis of "autogolpes" in Guatemala, Peru, and Russia.

Carlos Iván Degregori (M.S., Universidad San Cristóbal de Huamanga, Ayacucho) is professor of anthropology at the Universidad Nacional de San Marcos in Lima and a senior researcher at the Instituto de Estudios Peruanos. In 1996 he was a visiting scholar at the Inter-American Dialogue in Washington, D.C. His works include *El Surgimiento de Sendero Luminoso* (Lima: IEP, 1990), *The Peru Reader,* edited with Orin Starn and Robin Kirk (Durham: Duke University Press, 1995), and with José Coronel and Ponciano del Pino, *Las Rondas Campesinas y la derrota de Sendero Luminoso* (Lima: IEP, 1996). His current research focuses on the links between ethnicity, violence, and democracy.

Francisco Durand (Ph.D, Berkeley, 1991) is assistant professor of political science at the University of Texas in San Antonio and has been a consultant with the Inter-American Development Bank. His works include *Business and Politics in Peru* (Boulder: Westview Press, 1994) and *Los Grupos de Poder Económico en América Latina,* forthcoming (Lima: Friedrich Ebert). His research interests include business association involvement in politics, conservative political movements, and tax administration.

Christine Hunefeldt (Ph.D., University of Bonn, 1982) is associate professor of history at the University of California at San Diego. Her publications include *Paying the Price of Freedom* (Berkeley and Los Angeles: University of California Press, 1994) and numerous articles. Her research interests include the social and economic history of the andean region.

Philip Mauceri (Ph.D., Columbia University, 1991) is assistant professor of political science at the University of Northern Iowa and has been a visiting scholar at the Instituto de Estudios Peruanos in Lima. Among his publications are *State Under Siege: Development and Policy Making in Peru* (Boulder: Westview Press, 1996) and *Militares, Insurgencia y Democratización en el Perú* (Lima: IEP, 1989). His research interests include state reforms, civil-military relations, and democratization in Latin America.

Mark Peceny (Ph.D., Stanford University, 1993) is assistant professor of political science at the University of New Mexico. He is the author of various articles and at present is completing a book on the promotion of democracy during U.S. military interventions entitled *Democracy at the Point of Bayonets*. His areas of research interest include U.S. foreign policy, inter-American relations, and democracy in the international system.

Kenneth M. Roberts (Ph.D., Stanford University, 1992) is assistant professor of political science at the University of New Mexico. His research is focused on political parties and social movements in Latin America and he has published numerous articles.

Carol Wise (Ph.D., Columbia University, 1991) is assistant professor at the School of Advanced International Studies of Johns Hopkins University. She has most recently been a Resident Associate at the Carnegie Endowment for International Peace and a Research Associate at the Inter-American Dialogue, as well as a research consultant for Salomon Brothers. In addition to numerous articles, she is writing a book entitled *Streamlining the State: The Politics of Peruvian Economic Reforms* and is editing the forthcoming *The Post-NAFTA Political Economy: Mexico and the Western Hemisphere.*

INDEX

Page references in italics refer to tables or charts.